MAMAJI

Mamaji, Proposal Portrait, 1925

VED MEHTA

M A M A J I

Oxford University Press

NEW YORK 1979 OXFORD

Library of Congress Cataloging in Publication Data
Mehta, Ved Parkash.
Mamaji.
1. Mehta, Shanti Devi. 2. India—Biography.
3. Mothers—India—Biography. 4. Mehta, Ved Parkash. I. Title.
CT1508.M347M43 954'.5 [B] 79-15065 ISBN 0-19-502640-3

The contents of this book originated in The New Yorker

Printed in the United States of America

IN 1972, I PUBLISHED A BIOGRAPHICAL PORTRAIT OF MY father, "Daddyji"; set in the nineteenth and twentieth centuries, it was, by extension, the story of a representative ancient Hindu family from an Indian village, aspiring to enter the modern world. "Mamaji," a biographical portrait of my mother, is a companion book to "Daddyji"; again set in the nineteenth and twentieth centuries, it, too, is, by extension, the story of a representative ancient Hindu family, but this time from an Indian city, and this time not so much aspiring to enter the modern world as trying to consolidate its place in that world. Many of the themes in "Mamaji" enlarge upon themes introduced in "Daddyji." This is because the two books are intended as a cornerstone of an autobiographical work that I hope to be writing, off and on, whenever time permits, for the next twenty or thirty years. I should add that I have already written an autobiography, "Face to Face," but it was written mostly when I was twenty, and was published, in 1957, as my first book. For many years now, it has seemed to me to be a bare outline of the story I really want to write, for now I know in part what then I didn't know at all: how little I saw through the glass— even darkly.

I wish to acknowledge with thanks the help of the John Simon Guggenheim Memorial Foundation, which awarded me a second Guggenheim Fellowship (1977– 78) while I was working on "Mamaji." But there is no way I know to publicly acknowledge another sort of help I received during the years I spent writing this book. When Eleanor Gould Packard was helping me revise the proofs of "Mamaji," she said she felt like a member of my family. This family also included—besides Amolak Ram and Shanti Devi Mehta—Lisa Sloan, Naomi Grob, Harriet Walden and the members of her typing pool, and William Shawn. In fact, there is hardly a sentence in "Mamaji" that I can read without remembering the help of this family.

V.M.

New York
July 1979

CONTENTS

PHOTOGRAPHS

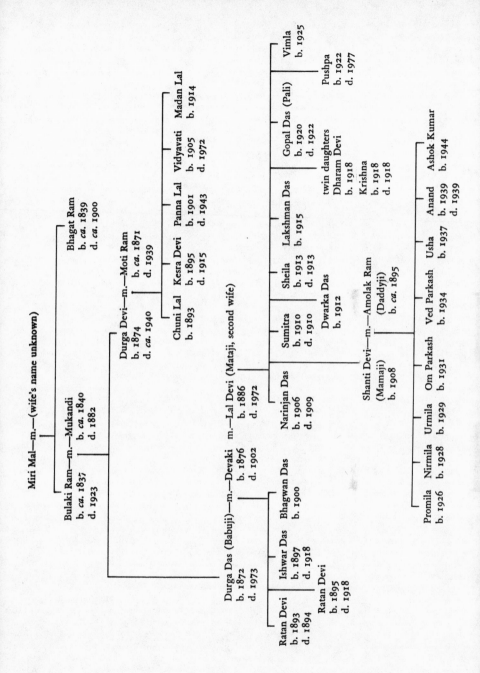

I

GODDESS DURGA

D EEP IN THE CITY OF LAHORE, SOMETHING OVER A
hundred years ago, there lived a moody young
woman known throughout the neighboring
gullis as the Mother. Sometimes she would take
it into her head to appear in a *gulli* with a
young male attendant, who would call out in a
singsong, to the haunting thud of a drum, "You are our
great mother, our supernatural mother! You are the
blessed one! You are the Durga Mata!" (Durga, one of
the consorts of the god Shiva, is the goddess of destruc-
tion, and *mata* means "mother.") The *gullis* would
resound with the thud of the attendant's drum, and
crowds from the surrounding *gullis* would converge on
the pair. Each of those who came would bear an offering: a handful of cardamoms or anise seeds, a bowl
of raisins and peeled almonds, a basket of fruit—whatever he or she could afford. The people would sit everywhere on the dirt, watching expectantly. The thud of
the drum would quicken, growing rhythmic and hypnotic. The woman, sitting languidly on the ground,
would start to roll her head to the beat of the drum,
as if possessed, but her body would remain inert. The
people would edge forward, each hoping to be allowed
to petition the goddess Durga through the Mother.
Sometimes people would go to the Mother's spiritual
sessions for months or years without being called upon
and allowed to petition. "The spirit of Durga Mata has
entered your head!" the young attendant would shout
in ecstasy to the woman. "Speak, speak, Mother!

Speak!" The people would watch tensely, afraid that, with no warning, the Mother would come out of her trance and get up and leave without hearing their petitions.

One evening, during the full moon, people in the *gullis* heard the familiar thud of the drum. They had been waiting for its sound for almost a year, and everyone ran out to see the Mother. One of those who ran out was Leela; her daughter was already over eighteen and no one would marry her. Another was Ram Lal; his shop had burned down, leaving him without a livelihood, and with nineteen mouths to feed. Another was Ram Das; his bride was dying of a mysterious disease, and he wanted the Mother to intercede for her life. And there were Bulaki Ram and Mukandi.

It was the season of the *loo* (hot wind), which stirred up the dust in the *gullis*. The air in the narrow, grimy, cavernous *gulli* in which the Mother sat was heavy and suffocating. The people pressed around her as if they were all trapped in the bottom of a pit and only she could lead them out.

The Mother stared directly at Bulaki Ram and then—her head rolling from side to side to the beat of the drum—called in an unearthly, echoing voice, "You, the man with the white starched turban, what brings you to Goddess Durga?"

"All my ten children have died," Bulaki Ram cried out. "Every child that comes from my Mukandi's stomach dies. The evil eye has cast its spell on me. I don't know what to do."

"You and yours are all accursed," the unearthly voice said, and then it fell silent. As Bulaki Ram and

Mukandi watched, the Mother's head started to roll faster and faster, until it seemed like a top out of control.

"Speak on, Mother, speak on!" the attendant shouted vehemently.

Bulaki Ram was fixed to the spot, afraid to take a breath lest the Mother come out of her trance without telling him how to lift the curse. He had attended her sessions many times before and had all but given up hope that she would call on him.

"Your house is under the evil influence," the woman resumed, haltingly. "And it is because . . . you have neglected . . . to pay homage to . . . the universal mother . . . Durga. In the dark underground room of your house, there is a small altar to Durga Mata in an alcove, but it is overlaid with dust and cobwebs. Go to the dark underground room of your house, dust the altar and sweep away the cobwebs, baste the altar with the holy cow dung, and light there the biggest mud lamp, with the richest ghi, to Durga Mata. Keep the mud lamp burning night and day for six months and pray at the altar daily. Tell your wife to keep all of Durga Mata's fasts. She will be with child. She will be delivered of a son. And if you take care of him he will bring the blessings of Durga Mata on your head."

Bulaki Ram and Mukandi were dazed, and hardly heard the crowd's murmurs of congratulations. They hurried back to their house, in Kucha Kaghzian (Paper Merchants' Lane), and went down into the dark underground room. They found the small altar in the alcove, dusty and covered with cobwebs, just as the Mother had said. They did exactly as the Mother had directed them, and their hope, so long extinguished, began to burn again.

When the six months were over, Mukandi, it seemed, was still not with child, but Bulaki Ram's faith in the Mother was unshaken. "Let's go to Peshawar and make a new beginning," he said to Mukandi. "We've had nothing but misfortunes in Lahore." He had heard Peshawar spoken of by travelling merchants as a thriving cantonment, or permanent military station, in India's mountainous Northwest Frontier Province. He had seen two or three tall and fierce-looking Pathans from the Frontier Province working as watchmen in the houses of the rich outside the old city of Lahore. He had heard that the Pathans were the first cousins of the Afghans, in faraway Afghanistan, and that they spoke a strange-sounding tongue called Pushtu. When people in the *gulli* didn't understand something, they said, "It's all Pushtu to me."

Bulaki Ram rented out his house. He collected his few worldly possessions—bedding, clothes, pots, pans, and wooden kitchen tools—and packed a wicker basket of chapattis, stalks of sugar cane, and chick-peas for the journey. Finally, he set off with Mukandi and his aunt Ganesh Devi on the North Western Railway. This railway was a much-touted amenity of the British raj, although it had originally been built so that the government could move troops quickly to distant cantonments. None of the three had ever been on a train before. They looked ahead at the engine puffing smoke and behind at the guard puffing a cheroot, and wondered whether the engine was going to pull the train or the guard was going to push it. Then, miraculously, as if Durga Mata herself had begun to move the train, it thundered out of the station. They held on to their seats until the steady rocking motion calmed them. The train took them as far as the town of Rawalpindi, and they proceeded from there in a hired bullock cart along the seemingly interminable Grand Trunk Road, now and again exchanging greetings with wayfarers who rested in the shade of tall, leafy shisham trees that lined it.

When they reached Peshawar, after several days on the road, they felt sure that Mukandi was with child. About eight months later, on the twenty-fifth of November, 1872, Mukandi was delivered of a son. They named him Durga Das (Servant of Durga). This was my maternal grandfather, Babuji.

II

DIARY

B ABUJI KEPT A DIARY FOR MOST OF HIS LONG LIFE. It was in a notebook of the kind that schoolchildren used to have. Taller than it was wide, the notebook opened from the bottom. The binding was of sturdy black cloth and the pages were thick and unlined; once white, they grew yellow with age. Like an old-fashioned book, it had a thin, worn tape for a marker. Babuji (Respected Elder, or Hindu Gentleman), as just about everyone called him—his full name was Durga Das Mehra— must have got the diary as a child, in the eighteen-seventies, but in the nineteen-seventies it was still in good condition, and this was a credit to its Victorian manufacturer. Few articles could have survived so well the ravages of the Indian heat, dust, and termites. Most of the pages were covered with a thin, spidery script, written with a nibbed pen, mostly in blue or black ink but sometimes in purple. Babuji had begun by listing, in English, year by year, the major events of his life, but the order was more apparent than real, since some of the pages were blank and, besides, he had written in the diary from both ends. The front pages were mainly straightforward records of births, marriages, and deaths—with a curiously impersonal fatalistic or invocational comment or two appended—and the back pages were given over to random entries of accounts, in English, in Urdu, and in Landay (a special Indian language for keeping accounts), interspersed with home remedies, home truths, and maxims, in Urdu and in Punjabi, that Babuji must have noted down as he came across them. An eventful year might be given a whole page to itself, and several uneventful years grouped together on a page. In either case, an event was never described in more than a few sentences. The diary, in fact, read like a simple chronicle, and yet I found it affecting. Reading it, I felt I was opening a window on an extraordinary life—perhaps even on an extraordinary period. But part of that feeling was no doubt due to the fact that the diary had been inscribed to me, and handed over to me as a keepsake, in Babuji's ninety-ninth year, two years before his death. He lived until I was thirty-nine, and had been almost as familiar to me as my mother, yet the diary made me feel that he had also been a stranger. The inscription was on the flyleaf in a very shaky hand indeed, the last in a progression of hands—at first tight and neat, then increasingly hasty and careless, then merely perfunctory—themselves charting in their way his life's journey. The inscription read:

I have great pleasure & Setisfection [the spelling and punctuation are his] in handing over this my life diary to dear Ved, who is my distinguished grand child. I feel proud of him. God bless him.

DURGA DAS
23/7/71

Babuji's diary begins:

My birthday:—Monday i.e. 25th November, 1872
= Magher Sadi Dashmi st. 1929
= 12th Magher Samwat 1929.

[The second date refers to the phase of the moon, and the third date refers to the Vikrami era of the Hindu calendar, which is based on the solar year but is calculated differently from the Christian calendar—the Hindu year 1929 corresponding roughly to the Christian year 1872. Most of the dates in the diary, however, are given in Christian years.]

Important Memoranda

Dear Ratan Devi (my first-born) died on the night of 8th May 1894, at about 10 P.M. Aged 9 months 6 days. Grief immense. Was very pretty and amiable. Trust in God and resign fate to Him, who does everything for good. Was born on Monday morning the 2nd August, 1893, at 2.50 A.M. [The date of Babuji's first marriage is not recorded in the diary.]

2. Suffered from jaundice for full three months and a half. A sad sequence to the death of my daughter. Sad & miserable. His Will be done.

17th Dec. 94—Grief immense. Did all the papers well in the Inter. Exam. ["Inter." was the Intermediate Exam for a B.A.] Failed in oral. A dire misfortune. The crowning calamity. [He was planning to study law, and it must have seemed to him that his failure had put his very livelihood in jeopardy; fear of poverty could never have been far from his mind. He did, however, pass on his second try.]

Born a daughter on Wednesday the 24th July, 1895, at 1.20 p.m. Named Ratan Devi. [It was typical of him to give the newborn daughter the same name as the daughter who had died. Devi, which means "goddess," is a common invocational name for Hindu girls—a corresponding invocational name for Hindu boys being Das, which means "servant of god."]

1897

Born a son at 2.55 P.M. on Monday 20th, December. Named Ishwar Das.

1900

Born a son on 2nd Oct., 1900, named Bhagwan Das.

1902

Death of my beloved & model wife St. ["St." must here be an abbreviation for "Shrimati," the equivalent of "Miss" or "Mrs."] Devakiji ["-ji" is a suffix denoting affection and respect] after prolonged illness—Misfortune unbearable—God's will be done.

1903

Married on 21st July at Kasur [a town about thirty-five miles east of Lahore] to Lal Devi, daughter of Lala ["Lala" is an honorific of the Kshatriya caste, to which we belong] Bagu Ram Khanna.

1905

Rebuilt house in Kucha Kaghzian From Feb. to Oct.

1906

Born a son on 18th September at 4.20 P.M.—Received news at Quetta. [Quetta is a city up in the mountains, in Baluchistan, where many well-to-do people from Lahore used to go for vacations.] Named Narinjan Das.

1908

1. Purchased a site last year & built my new house outside Shahalmi Gate. Jath took place on Dusehra Day. [Jath
is a housewarming ceremony, and Dusehra is a ten-day-
long autumn festival centering on the Ramayana, which
describes the epic victory of the god Rama over the demon
Ravana. In orthodox Hindu homes, the entire Ramayana
is recited, and on the evening of the last day—Dusehra Day
—elaborate paper-and-bamboo effigies portraying Ravana
with ten heads are burned in public.]

2. Born a daughter on 16th August at 7 A.M. Named
Shanti Devi. [This is Babuji's record of the birth of my
mother, Mamaji.]

1909

1. Died Lala Duni Chand father of my first wife
Devaki on Saturday, 27th Feb. at 8 A.M. at Rawalpindi.
Much grieved.

2. Died my little dear son Narinjan Das of diphtheria,
on Wednesday, 11th Aug. at 4.45 P.M. miserable. Child
bright, intelligent & lovely. His will be done . . . this the
3rd catastrophe of my life. [It is hard to be sure which two
earlier catastrophes he had in mind—probably the deaths of
his daughter and his wife.]

1910

Betrothal of Ratan Devi my daughter with Bishan Das
Overseer North Western Railway, Lahore, grandson of late
Lala Thulla Mal Banker of Lahore.

4th Feby 1910. May Glad bless the engagement.
["Glad" is a slip. Although I have made the spellings of
proper names in the diary uniform, I have preserved
Babuji's other spellings.]

Elected Fellow of Punjab University Votes 183—First. [He had studied law at Punjab University, and he must have got a hundred and eighty-three votes and stood first among the elected fellows.]

Elected on 1st January. Gazetted on 4th March. [The *Gazette* was a government-subsidized publication, and important appointments were not considered official until they were announced in it.]

Born a daughter on 13th Octr. at 10 P.M. Named: Sumitra.

1911

Married Ratan Devi to Lala Bishan Das Overseer of Lahore on 4th Feb.—Basant Day. [Basant is a festival marking the arrival of spring. The Punjabis say *"Aya Basant pala udant,"* which means "Basant came, cold fled."] May God bless the couple & grant them happiness, peace & prosperity.

11th April Ishwar Das, my boy, bitten by Puppy (subsequently proved to be rabies). Left for treatment at Central Institute at Kasauli 13th night. [This was India's only institution for the treatment of rabies.] Most miserable time. One of the bitterest moments of my life. Most anxious. Depends upon His Mercy.

August. Indescribable pain—mental shock. His will be done.

Sept. My little daughter Sumitra aged one died in my absence at Lahore. Returned from Bombay on 22nd. [Babuji had been practicing law for years now. He must have been away in Bombay on legal business.] Disease— Diphtheria which proved fatal in case of my son Narinjan Das. Must submit to His Supreme Will.

1912

Born a son on 16th August at Kasur Named Dwarka Das.

1913

"Firefly" my favorite horse died on 14th Dec. after good service.

A beautifull & serviceable animal. [Firefly was his carriage horse.]

Born a daughter at Lahore on ———— named Sheila.

Died above girl on ———— of high fever & breathing trouble.

His will be done. [It's not clear why he left out the dates of her birth and death.]

1915

Reelected Fellow of the Punjab University standing first—27th Feby.

Born a son on 17-7 at 9.40 P.M. named Lakshman Das.

1916

Had a severe indigestion & nervous attack on night of 23rd Jany which proved very obstinate.

Ishwar Das & Bhagwan Das passed their Inter- & Entrance Exams respectively in Second Division.

Spent Sept. at Kasauli & recruited my health. Change proved usefull.

1917

Purchased Kothi "North View" at Kasauli in partnership with L. Tirath Ram, Pleader. Registered on 17 1. [Kasauli, in the Punjab, is one of many hill stations that the British built for themselves in order to escape from the summer heat of the plains; a *kothi* is a bungalow built in colonial style, also by the British.]

Born a son to Ratan Devi at Mach on ———— named, ————. [Mach was an old-fashioned railway town in the Northwest Frontier Province.]

May he live long.

Passed a bad Sept. in Lahore on account of illness of Lakshman Das, Dwarka & Bhagwan Das. Lakshman Das was bitten by suspicious dog of my syce [groom] on 24th July and had to go to Kasauli with wife [that is, Babuji's wife] & Ishwar Das.

1918

Born twin daughters on 23rd April at 9.30 & 9.40 P.M. Senior named Dharam Devi.

Died Junior of the twin babies on 5th July at 12.15 A.M. after great suffering for these days.

Dear Ishwar Das died on 27-10 at 4.15 A.M. of Pneumonia Influenza after 14 days illness. Pleasure & pride of my life taken away. His will is supreme.

Most miserable. Born 20-12-97. Lost his mother [Babuji's first wife] in Nov. 1902. Passed his Matric from Model School in 1914. His inter. from D.A.V. College in 1916 & his B.A. Exam with Honours from Govt. College in April 18. A good boy with noble instincts of self sacrifice & service to others. Died nobly like a true believer in God reciting Om & Ved mantras. A life full of hope & promise for the country & the community taken away so abruptly. Affliction overwhelming, grief intense. Ostensible causes of his death were his own stubbornness, doctors' blunderings & my inexperience. Death an enigma & mystery. Where does the man go? Is human age fixed or not? Could dear boy have been saved by any human effort? Who knew that death of my dear boy Ishwar Das will be followed by the unexpected demise of his elder sister dear Ratan Devi. She with her husband, Bishan Das, & three children came here to mourn the loss of her brother. They all left for Mach on 9th Nov. On 18th night received a telegram informing that they all had Influenza. Bishan Das's brother & my servant went to see them by morning mail on 19th. At night came the news that Ratan Devi's infant son was dead and she was down with the Pneumonia. Munshie [clerk] Gujarmal & Malan Devi [Babuji's mother-in-law] were sent by next morn. train but on 20th night came the painfull news that Ratan Devi was no more. She expired at 2 P.M. on that day before the party from Lahore could reach. Her younger girl Kunti died on 27th morning and poor miserable Bishan Das came back to Lahore on 28th night with one surviving girl Kaushalya. May she long live & prosper as the remnant of her departed mother & brother & sister. This has filled the cup of my misery and has marked me out as a sinner deserving of all this punishment. Two of my eldest & pure souled children taken away within a month!!! This has made me despondent & lose all confidence in future. Life has become so uncertain & precarious.

May God Almighty grant peace to departed souls & give us all strength to bear it. The Influenza epidemic has worked havoc and the toll taken by it is most heavy. Thank God it has not been worse & I humbly pray that rest of my life be saved from such or other similar mishaps. *His Will is supreme & must be done.*

1919

1. The year passed in sorrow and in daily brooding over the loss of my dear ones who tragically departed this

world one after the other at the end of last year. No light, no consolation. None has solved the mystery of Life and Death.

Growing scepticism of the last year wore off gradually & faith in the Supreme Power of creation restored. Real interest in the worldly side of life reduced to a vanishing point. The whole thing is really a farce & not worth the trouble & worry why men & women foolishly undergo & suffer.

2. Dear Lakshman Das had a very bad attack of typhoid in June which lasted till September off & on. God in his mercy spared him.

3. The Tribune [the Punjab's main English-language newspaper] started an agitation against me about my letter to the University opposing student strikes against the government. This step was taken bonafide & in the best interests of the Students but was misunderstood & misrepresented in some quarters.

The year was memorable for agitation against Rowlatt Act suspending constitutional guarantees and rights and introduction & enforcement of Martial Law in Lahore, Amritsar, Gujranwalla & Lyallpur.

Jallianwalla Bagh tragedy of Amritsar, the British Massacre of Indian protesters, was really scandalous & indefensible. Martial Law administration aimed at showing the inferiority of Indians. It shocked the sense of [British] justice entertained by educated Indians. It was an exhibition of racial superiority & as such seriously injured the good name & reputation of the British Govt. [Babuji was protesting against British atrocities and becoming involved, in spite of himself, in India's struggle for home rule.]

Amritsar Congress a grand popular success owing to Martial Law atrocities.

Bhagwan Das' health broke down in March just before his Inter. Exam.

Very anxious. His will be done.

Went to Kasauli for 10 days in Sept. Bhagwan Das went to Bombay in June & then to Dharamsala [a town in the Punjab]. Regained his health partially in winter & rejoined the College.

1921

Bhagwan Das' health again broke down in Feb. and he had to give up his studies.

Nervous dyspepsia. Went to Kashmir in July.

We all joined him at Srinagar in August & spent about 6 weeks there going about. Dear Ishwar Das' memory was more than once revived specially at Verinag where he had crossed swimming in 1916. [Ishwar Das was probably the only member of the family who knew how to swim. The town of Verinag was known for its ice-cold water.]

At Chashma Shahi, father suddenly remembered him & tears came out of his eyes. I too wept.

Returned to Lahore on 3 Oct.

1922

Bhagwan Das's health much improved. Proposed to go to England for studying Elec. Enging considered & given up. He had mild attack of Typhoid in August.

Born a daughter on 4th Septr at 1.20 A.M. named Pushpa. Went to Solon for 2 weeks & returned on 26.9. Stayed with P. Madhoram, Vakil [pleader].

Another affliction! Dear Gopal died of accident under tragic circumstances when I was out for a walk on the evening of 10th Oct. [Babuji does not record the birth of

Gopal. He was two years old when he died.] Simply be-
wildered & stunned by this sudden blow of Fate!!! Losing
faith in everything.

1923

Spent Vacations at Mussurie [a hill station in the
United Provinces] with family.

Dear old father passed away at 2. A.M. on 23rd Dec.
after 2 weeks' illness. He got fever on Sunday, 9th Decr &
subsequently Pneumonia. Heart became weak & brain
was affected. He was almost delerious throughout due to
poisoning of the system. Throat, mouth & tongue became
inflamed. His will be done, aged over 86.

1924

Bhagwan Das passed his F.E.L. [The initials stand for
First Examination in Law.]

Plague affected the city & had to shift to No. 22 Davis
Road for a month in May. [Davis Road was in the civil
station, some distance from the old, walled city of Lahore,
the center of the epidemic.]

Lakshman Das and Dwarka had bad attacks of fever
in June.

All went to Dalhousie on 16th August & returned on
30.9. Lived in Afzal Villa (middle Bakrota) and enjoyed
the trip. Paid a visit to Khajiar & Chamba. [Bakrota is a
few miles below Dalhousie, a hill station in the Punjab.
Afzal Villa probably belonged to one Afzal Hussein, a
Muslim lawyer of Babuji's acquaintance.]

On return all family down with fever & cough for a
week. Thank God the year passed safely & peacefully.

His blessings invoked for the new year.

Reading these first pages of my grandfather's diary made me curious about everything connected with him, with Mamaji, with that whole side of my family, and I felt the need to look further than the diary and its terse entries, to other clues—to other diaries, to school copybooks, to letters, to family gossip and remembrances, and to land deeds and other public records—in order to gain a better understanding of my antecedents.

III

FOREBEARS

A ROUND 1849, OR ABOUT TWENTY-THREE YEARS
before Babuji was born to Bulaki Ram and
Mukandi, Bulaki Ram had to put the torch to
the funeral pyre of his father, Miri Mal, beside
the River Ravi near Lahore. Bulaki Ram, who
was twelve at the time, and had earlier lost his
mother, was the eldest son, and it was his duty to send
his father's soul to rest. He stood, dazed, at the head
of a long, shallow brick tub, in which his father was
laid out on a neatly stacked bed of dry logs, with more
logs stacked on top of him. Ganesh Devi, the sister of
Miri Mal, told the boy that without the weight of the
second stack his father would sit bolt upright as soon
as the fire was lit under him, and Bulaki Ram would
have to hit his father over the head to get him to lie
back down, for unless his father was cremated in a
restful pose his ghost would wander the *gullis* of Lahore in the night, wailing. The fire started up in such
a rush that the boy was thrown back several feet. He
watched the fire go higher and higher as Ganesh Devi
fed it with ladles of ghi and handfuls of *smugary*
(frankincense and myrrh).

Within two weeks of setting fire to his father,
Bulaki Ram had to tear down Miri Mal's little house
in Kucha Kaghzian—the house in which Bulaki Ram
was born and raised. He then had to divide the small
plot of land, fifty or sixty square yards, with his
younger brother, Bhagat Ram, and start building a
new house, half the size of his father's. Bulaki Ram

27

and Bhagat Ram were the only surviving children of
Miri Mal, and, according to the Hindu law of inheritance, property was divided equally among all male
issue—the result being, of course, that the inheritance
tended to become smaller with each generation. (The
European law of primogeniture, which prevented such
fragmentation of property, was unknown.)

It appears from the narration of itinerant Hindu
bards who regularly visited the family and recited its
genealogical tables that the family was Lahori through
and through (with distant roots in the rural western-
Punjab area of Jhang), and had lived for generations
there in Kucha Kaghzian, in the heart of the city,
except during the nineteenth-century Sikh Wars, when
for a time the family might have fled the old city and
hidden outside its walls. Kucha Kaghzian was a choked
cul-de-sac about six feet wide, which lay over the im-
pacted ancient ruins of vanished cities, each more mean,
congested, and corrupt than its predecessor. The house
that Bulaki Ram built was, like many of the other
houses in the lane, a two-story *pukka* (lasting) structure, of baked bricks and mortar. Three sides were
windowless, but in the front two narrow windows
directly overlooked the big open drain, about a foot
wide, that ran along the middle of the lane and carried
its effluent to the city sewers. A couple of makeshift
partitions and an earthenware jar were set up on one
end of the roof as the lavatory for the house. The upper
floor and the roof could be reached only by a small
outer staircase, hardly wide enough for one person.
Morning and evening, one or another member of an

Untouchable family of sweepers, who claimed service of Bulaki Ram's Kshatriya family as a hereditary right, would come up the stairs, empty the contents of the earthenware jar into a bucket, and carry the bucket to a nearby street and dump it into a communal cart. Periodically, a bullock was hitched to the cart, and the cart was pulled along to the city refuse dump, some of its contents spilling through an old, tattered gunny cloth that covered it.

Bulaki Ram and Bhagat Ram also inherited several stalls in the Fish Market, a *gulli* that got its name from the fact that it was shaped like a fish. (As it happened, the sale of fish there was banned, because the shopkeepers in the *gulli* were all Hindus who considered the eating of fish to be spiritually polluting.) Bulaki Ram and Bhagat Ram, being Kshatriyas, and so belonging to the governing or military caste, did not themselves sit in the market stalls but rented them out, for about twelve annas a month (an anna, one-sixteenth of a rupee, was equivalent to about a cent and a half), to shopkeepers who sold everything from soap, combs, and bangles to cooking oil and lentils.

It seemed that Bulaki Ram did not have a head for business, and anyone could take advantage of him. But Bhagat Ram soon became known for clever dealings. He would buy a dozen mangoes cheap from one vender and sell them to a vender in the next *gulli* for a pice or so more. (A pice was one sixty-fourth of a rupee.) The mangoes were bought on a few hours' credit, so he was able to turn a profit without investing a pice of his own. He was on the move much of the time, and was so fleet-footed that few could catch up with him as he dashed from *gulli* to *gulli,* buying, selling, haggling, dealing.

Bhagat Ram eventually let his house in Kucha Kaghzian and went to Kasur in search of better prospects. (According to legend, the Hindu god and epic hero Ram sired two sons, Lav and Kush; Lav founded Lahore, and Kush founded Kasur.) Bhagat Ram died around 1900, and was survived by three sons and a daughter. One of the sons was named Krishan Dayal, another Har Dayal, but no one could later recall the names of the two other children.

IN 1852, WHEN BULAKI RAM was fifteen years old, Ganesh Devi—who lived with him, because he was her eldest surviving close relative and therefore had the duty of supporting her—presented him with a twelve-year-old bride named Mukandi and with a new turban, to signalize his responsibilities as head of the household. Ganesh Devi, who had been widowed in childhood, was Miri Mal's eldest surviving relative, and it was therefore her duty to see that her nephews were married and the family perpetuated. Mukandi was a thin, fair-skinned girl, five feet tall; she came just up to Bulaki Ram's chin. Bulaki Ram's new turban was of white muslin so fine that it could be drawn through Mukandi's wedding ring.

Bulaki Ram had not been seen in public without a turban since an incident in his tenth year. At the time, he had been sitting in his father's house in Kucha

Kaghzian on a day when the air was stagnant—there wasn't so much as a stirring of wind to cool his neck. Feeling hot and uncomfortable, he had taken off his turban. Suddenly, someone had come up behind him and cuffed him on the head, taking away his breath. "Sitting with a naked head?" his father had cried. "You dishonor your family!" Bulaki Ram, humbled, had brought his palms together, touched his forehead to his father's feet, and begged forgiveness. The cuff on his head was Bulaki Ram's initiation into the importance of the turban to the males of the exclusive Kshatriya subcaste of Dha-ee-ghar ("Two and a Half Houses") Lahoris, to which he belonged. Among the Dha-ee-ghar Lahoris, for a man to walk the *gullis* without a turban was considered disreputable, and no insult was greater than pulling off someone's turban. In fact, in those days the only time a Dha-ee-ghar Lahori voluntarily removed his turban in public was when he placed it at the feet of someone whom he had injured and from whom he sought forgiveness. (The custom of going about with the head exposed became accepted only gradually, with the experience of seeing hatless British masters.) After that early transgression, Bulaki Ram would keep his turban tied next to his pillow when he was asleep, in case he might have to get up unexpectedly in the night. Often, he would draw the sheet over his head in his sleep.

IN PESHAWAR, Bulaki Ram and Mukandi continued to pray to the goddess Durga, in thanks for their baby son, Babuji. They, along with Ganesh Devi, lived in a small rented room in the native city, three miles from the British cantonment. Like many *shehris* (city dwellers), Bulaki Ram believed that sunlight spread consumption, so he kept both the door and the wooden shutter of the single window of their room closed against the sunlight practically all the time, and the family was forced to struggle along in the dark, close room by the flickering light of the cooking fire and of a few kerosene mud lamps. There was only a little chimney to draw out the smoke. Mukandi and Ganesh Devi went daily to a nearby stream to wash the clothes. They sewed and they cooked, and they were careful to keep the fire going.

In Peshawar, Bulaki Ram became an itinerant cloth vender. He would buy cheap, rejected cloth—seconds—at a discount from Kirpa Ram & Brother, well-known cloth merchants in the cantonment, and would skillfully cut it into lengths suitable for shirts and pajama trousers, without wasting any of the cloth. Then he would bundle the lengths in a sheet, and, with the bundle on his back, go from door to door peddling the cloth at the homes of the British officials and soldiers in the cantonment. Partly because few other venders seemed to know about the seconds, and partly because the cantonment was growing, he was able to make a good living. He became known as the *gathri-wallah* (bundleman) from Lahore.

Bulaki Ram couldn't get over the abundance of Peshawar. "Why, I can buy two sparrows for one anna here," he would say to Mukandi, bringing home some ready-cooked birds from the bazaar for supper. (Mukandi was a vegetarian and did not cook meat in the house.) "In Lahore, I couldn't get even one sparrow for one anna. And what fat sparrows they are, too! And they come ready-cooked from the bazaar, so that you don't have to go near the meat. I'll feed them to Durga Das with my own hands, and he'll grow up to be healthy and strong, like a Pathan."

At least once a day, Babuji was given a fried sparrow, two glasses of boiled milk with its skin on it, and plenty of vegetables. He was also fed peeled and soaked almonds and *suji halwah* (*suji* is a form of wheat flour that is a little grittier than white flour), and his chapattis were laced with lots of ghi. Bulaki Ram was so solicitous of the health of his son and heir that the child was always made to sleep with woollen socks on and was never allowed to put his bare feet on the naked floor. If Babuji was ever seen barefoot, Bulaki Ram would rush to his side with wooden clogs. But, no matter what Bulaki Ram did for him, Babuji remained small of stature. Bulaki Ram believed that this was because the child used to slip out of the room to sit in the open air.

Every Saturday, Bulaki Ram would arrange on a brass platter a bowl of melted ghi, a ball of wheat dough, and a couple of spoonfuls of rice and *dal* (lentils). He would show Babuji his reflection in the ghi—to ward off evil spirits—and then give the bowl of ghi to a Brahman, who had come for it, and who would bless the whole platter of food. The family would eventually eat the food. On that day, Bulaki Ram would not eat meat or eggs, and Mukandi would observe a fast, eating only when the sun had gone

down. During the annual Durga festival, Bulaki Ram
would give thank offerings of food to eleven poor
families and veils to eleven poor girls.

Bulaki Ram and Mukandi celebrated Babuji's first
birthday and then his second birthday—he was their
first child to reach this age. Soon afterward, Mukandi
gave birth to another child—a daughter. They named
her Durga Devi, after the goddess Durga. No special
attention was lavished on Durga Devi; she was left to
grow up as she would. At the time, not even sons were
given much education, because, as their fathers never
tired of saying, "in the end, son, you're going to sit in
the shop." But Bulaki Ram, though himself unlettered,
looked to education as a means of freeing Babuji from
the fate of a bundleman. And so every morning Bulaki
Ram would walk with Babuji about half a mile to
school, and every afternoon he would walk to the
school to fetch him back.

The school, Edwardes Memorial Mission High
School, was named after Sir Herbert Edwardes, who
had been the chief commissioner of the Northwest
Frontier Province at the time of the Indian Mutiny of
1857 and had earned government acclaim by rushing
the Army contingent under his control to Delhi to help
quell the Mutiny. After the Mutiny had been sup-
pressed, the Church Missionary Society of England
commemorated his deed by sending missionaries to
Peshawar to start one of the first schools in the province.
The missionaries constructed the school, living quarters
for themselves, and the All Saints Church. In time,
these buildings, along with a few small British-type
shops, became the nucleus of the British community,

which was set apart from the godowns and *mandis* (Indian-type open markets) of the native city. Bulaki Ram could scarcely pronounce the name of the school, but as he walked back and forth with Babuji he would speak of the place as another Durga temple, with mysterious benevolent powers.

❦

WHEN BABUJI WAS SEVEN, he caught a mysterious fever and started turning yellow. Bulaki Ram first treated the child himself with ancient remedies he knew, and then, when Babuji didn't respond, took him to an English doctor in the cantonment. "The boy has jaundice," the doctor said, in a mixture of Hindi and English. "Take him to Murree Hill. Its foggy mountain air will do him good." Bulaki Ram wrapped Babuji up in blankets, and, with Mukandi, Ganesh Devi, Durga Devi, and their few household goods, they set off in a bullock cart for Murree, a hill station near Rawalpindi. The family camped there for many days, until Babuji's fever went down and he regained his normal color. Bulaki Ram felt that the child's fever had been a sign from the goddess Durga for him to leave Peshawar, and that the child's recovery was a sign that he could safely live once again among his own people in Lahore. So instead of returning to Peshawar he went home to Lahore.

The family passed three comfortable years in Lahore. Bulaki Ram still owned a couple of stalls in the Fish Market, from which he received—for those times —a good rent. And he now formed an advantageous connection with some Pathan traders, from whom he bought cloth at a favorable price. From sunrise to sunset, he was out climbing the staircases of tenements with shops below, calling at the doors, and showing his wares to whomever he found at home. He soon made a name for himself as a *gathriwallah* with an inexhaustible store of durable cloth and a sweet tongue. He started doing so well that he was able to hire a boy servant to carry his bundle for him. Babuji was entered in the Rang Mahal Mission School, which accepted boys from devout homes, whether Hindu, Muslim, or Christian. Because the school was in the heart of the city, it did not have playing fields, such as the government's Central Model School, outside the city, had, and so wrestling was one of its main sports. Babuji, it turned out, showed more interest in wrestling than in his studies. Though he was small and frail, he aspired to be a wrestler, because he had seen that wrestlers walked boldly around the mean *gullis* through which his father cautiously wound his way. Previously a solitary child, he now began to form friendships and adjust to his new surroundings.

Bulaki Ram returned home one evening in the monsoon season—the year was 1882—and found Mukandi sitting on a little benchlike stool with her head bowed over a twig of green chick-peas, which she was peeling into a cloth on her lap. "There is no way to lift the evil eye," she groaned, pressing her hand to her stomach. "I didn't want to tell you, but I am burdened with child again."

Bulaki Ram was about forty-five; Mukandi was forty-two. They were both healthy, yet they were frightened, because they could never forget that it was in Lahore that they had consigned to fire or water, as Hindu law commanded, the bodies of ten infant children. Bulaki Ram squatted down at her side. "We should never have come back to Lahore," he moaned.

The next day, Bulaki Ram and his family waded for a mile and a half through *gullis* and streets to the railway station. It had rained the night before, so that the open drains overflowed and flooded the *gullis* with disease-carrying sludge. For the second time, they boarded the North Western Railway. At Rawalpindi, they again hired a bullock cart for the slow, arduous journey to Peshawar. As their bullock cart lurched along the Grand Trunk Road—past the familiar shisham trees—its wooden wheels bumping and echoing, Bulaki Ram felt they had left Lahore behind once and for all. But they had scarcely passed the third milestone on the road when Mukandi started crying quietly, "Ram, Ram, I am dying. O God Ram." Clutching Bulaki Ram's hand, she writhed under a coarse mud-brown blanket. Bulaki Ram shouted to the driver to stop the cart. He jumped down and, with the help of the driver, gathered some sticks and made a fire on the shoulder of the road. He began praying to the goddess Durga. Ganesh Devi, kneeling over Mukandi on the floor of the bullock cart in order to screen her from the children, started calling out instructions—for the driver to get some water, for Bulaki Ram to heat a brick and wrap it in a cloth. Bulaki Ram rushed to Mukandi's side with the hot brick, and he heard her whisper haltingly as she struggled to catch her breath, "Promise me you won't get married. Be mother and father to Durga Das and—" She screamed and then was silent. Bulaki Ram heard the cooing of doves overhead. The children began to wail, and Ganesh Devi beat her breast. Bulaki Ram looked into the bullock cart. Mukandi's face was unnaturally relaxed, and next to her a baby girl lay motionless.

Bulaki Ram cremated his wife and stillborn daughter—their thirteenth child—in the unfamiliar town of Rawalpindi, and, blaming Lahore for his new misfortune, continued his journey to Peshawar with a howling child under either arm and Ganesh Devi wailing by his side. He resolved as he made his way along the Grand Trunk Road to honor his wife's last wish, and, although he lived nearly forty years longer, he never remarried. In all those years, he scarcely mentioned his wife's name—it was as if he couldn't bear to revisit his grief—and his children and grandchildren grew up without knowing her name. (One day some years before Bulaki Ram's death, when, as an old, wizened man, he was once again living in Lahore, he took his grandchildren to a festival celebrating Lord Krishna's birth. They were all sitting on the ground waiting for a folk play about Krishna to begin. A bearded man who, if anything, looked even older than Bulaki Ram came up from behind and said, "Brother, the grandchildren of cursed Mukandi are not allowed on this holy ground." Bulaki Ram recognized him as a former neighbor. Mamaji's younger brother Dwarka, who was three at the time and was sitting in her lap, started chanting, "Brother, Mukandi's grandchildren are not allowed here. Brother, Mukandi's grandchildren are not allowed here." Bulaki Ram covered the child's mouth with his hand and said, "You idiot! Mukandi was the noblest woman on earth. She was your grandmother." He had tears in his eyes. That was how Mamaji learned her grandmother's name.)

❦

WHEN THE BEREAVED FAMILY reached Peshawar, Bulaki Ram found another dark little room and set up his household. Ganesh Devi took over the wifely duties. The room was often filled with the sharp, smoky smell of frying sparrows; unlike Mukandi, Ganesh Devi ate meat, and liked to cook the sparrows at home.

Durga Devi spent her days at her great-aunt's side, watching and learning, and Babuji, who was now ten, was readmitted to his old school, which in the interval had grown to include college-preparatory classes. Indeed, it was now called Edwardes Collegiate Mission School.

Bulaki Ram had become so adept at cutting the seconds into lengths for pajamas and shirts that he could now undersell the craftiest of venders. He did so well that he was soon able to open his own cloth shop on the edge of the cantonment. Ever since his childhood, when he had been given concoctions of roots and herbs to cure him of stomach aches, he had been interested in the Ayur-Vedic system of medicine. (The Ayur-Vedic system, which is based on the Hindu Scripture, the Ayur-Veda, and relies on herbal compounds—together with the Unani system, which is based on ancient Greek medicine and relies on metallic compounds—is more commonly used in India than the

39

Western system of medicine.) The concoctions had invariably been administered to Bulaki Ram with recitations of mantras, as the Ayur-Veda prescribed, the remedies having been passed from generation to generation, along with religious laws and caste taboos. Bulaki Ram had used these remedies with good results on his children and on his neighbors and their children, and had gradually earned the reputation of having a special touch with medicines and people; it was thought that his suffering had aroused the compassion of the gods above and they had bestowed the touch upon him. Now, in his shop, he daily encountered poor people in rags who complained of colds and stomach aches, of coughs and blood discharges. He would minister to them, sending each one home with a concoction and a prayer, a comforting word, and, often, a small purchase of cloth. His grateful patrons would return with their wives and children and aunts and grandmothers in tow, all needing a cure and, of course, a length of cloth.

BULAKI RAM, who had all along been yearning to go home to Lahore, but had not dared to go, for fear of what the evil eye might wreak upon him next, now somehow persuaded himself that the evil eye must have been placated by the death of his wife and by his long exile. He was tired of living in Peshawar. He had never learned to feel at ease with the Pathans. Instead of spending time in their homes with their women and

children, the men were apt to carouse around the
bazaars late into the night, singing songs to each other
and breaking out into fits of laughter. Bulaki Ram
had never managed to learn their intractable tongue,
Pushtu, so he didn't know what the songs meant, but
he could tell that they were lascivious from the way
the men hallooed and hooted. He longed to hear familiar Punjabi voices, to be among his own kind. Besides, Durga Devi was already thirteen years old, and
in order to be married she had to be seen and evaluated
by people of her own subcaste, Dha-ee-ghar Lahoris.
Above all, Babuji had just passed his Middle School
Examination, and Bulaki Ram felt that Lahore, which
he had heard was the supreme educational center of
the world, was where the boy should continue his
studies.

Bulaki Ram closed up his shop, took what savings
he had, and set off with his family for Lahore. He
never returned to Peshawar; in fact, in later years
only one memento remained of the family's life there
—a piece of cream-colored paper set in a black bevelled
frame. (It was the first of several such framed pieces
of paper, which were almost the only ornaments on the
whitewashed walls of Bulaki Ram's dwellings and,
later, of Babuji's houses.) The memento had an impressive picture on it—a lion and a mysterious horse with a
horn on his forehead, both standing on their hind legs
and trying to climb onto a shield and take the crown
above it. To Bulaki Ram, the picture—a reproduction
of the royal coat of arms—looked like the imprint of a
sacred official ring, perhaps from the finger of Queen

Victoria herself. Above and below the picture were words that he could not read but in which he took great pride:

THE UNIVERSITY OF THE PUNJAB
SESSION, 1887

This is to certify that Durga Das, Student of the Edwardes Mission School, Peshawar District, passed the Anglo-Vernacular Middle School Examination, held in January 1887.

REGISTRAR'S OFFICE: Lahore.
The 11th April 1887.

W. BELL, *Registrar,*
PUNJAB UNIVERSITY

DESCRIPTIVE ROLL

Father's Name: Bulaki Mal.
Caste: Hindu.
Residence: Lahore.
Age at year of passing: 14 years.
Remarks: Durgas das is a sharp, quiet and steady lad and very regular in his attendance in school. He now leaves as his father is changing his place of abode. Conduct very good.

PESHAWAR
24 May, 1887
M. GHOSH, *Head Master*
WORTHINGTON JUKES, M. S., *Principal*

Babuji had obtained the certificate by writing this letter to the principal:

42

Peshawar
17-5-87

To
  His honor the Reved.
    W. Jukes
      Peshawar
Hd. Sir

I beg to bring your honour on my miserable state—that I wish to be obliged by your honour, by giving me the certificate of my good conduct, & I am reading & learning in this school. Also your honour can ask about me from Masters. I hope your honor will soon grant me the same.

Yours obedient
Student
DD

As a precaution against the return of the evil eye, Bulaki Ram filled his house in Lahore with freshly painted earthenware idols, mostly of the goddess Durga —flourishing a cobra around her neck, brandishing a trident with each of her ten arms, making a battle charge with her coterie of giants and lions. Each idol, however, portrayed her with the gentle face for which she was known. Morning and evening, the family would sit in front of the idols and sing hymns, beseeching the goddess to spare them from the epidemics of smallpox and plague in her arsenal. Bulaki Ram joined the Sanatan Dharmis, an orthodox religious party, and started taking his children regularly to Hindu temples and also, as an added precaution, to Sikh temples. The better to serve his goddess, he also stopped selling cloth and became a full-time practitioner of Ayur-Vedic medicine, constantly seeking out Brahmans and asking them for new Ayur-Vedic prescriptions.

I V

PARENTS

O NE EARLY-AUTUMN DAY—THE YEAR WAS 1887—
Bulaki Ram took Babuji some distance outside
the old walled city of Lahore to the new, rising
British civil station and there enrolled him in
a school named Dayanand Anglo-Vedic High
School, which was known as the D.A.V. School
and had been founded in memory of Swami Dayanand
Saraswati. (*Swami* means "holy man.") Swami Dayanand had himself founded the Hindu reform movement known as the Arya Samaj (Aryan Society), of
which the D.A.V. School was now a part. The school
was recommended to Bulaki Ram by his neighbors as
a good Hindu secondary school, and Babuji was immediately accepted there, because he had stood first in the
District of Peshawar; in fact, he had won a two-year
government scholarship of four rupees a month—
enough to pay for his tuition and books at the D.A.V.
School.

Around the same time, Ganesh Devi chose a wife
for Babuji. It was felt that he was getting on in years
—he was fifteen—and that, being the elder, he had to
be married before his sister. His bride-to-be was a poor,
weak twelve-year-old girl named Devaki, who had bad
eyesight but who belonged to a Dha-ee-ghar family living in Kucha Kaghzian. She had an adoring, puppylike
nature and had had a devout upbringing. Soon after
Devaki was chosen, Ganesh Devi died in her sleep.
Babuji regarded his marriage to Devaki as the fulfill-
ment of his great-aunt's last wish. Babuji and Devaki

were married quietly one night, without the customary wedding band music, and also without the customary wedding horse, on which the bridegroom rides to the bride's house, because Devaki's parents were afraid that a celebration might attract the attention of some predatory rich Muslim, and that he might abduct her, so that he could boast to his cronies that he had a high-caste Hindu "lily" among his wives.

Two or three years later, Babuji passed his matriculation, or school-leaving, examination. In his schools in Peshawar and Lahore, he had acquired a solid Indian Victorian education, which eventually helped him (as it helped so many of his contemporaries) to become a member of the Indian establishment—a sort of shadow of the British establishment. In truth, the quality of his schooling was as much a tribute to Indian students and teachers as to the British missionaries and rulers who designed it. Yet the rendering of official titles and ranks, the pronunciation and spelling of historic battles and place-names, and even the meaning of mathematical terms and equations were imperfectly grasped and remembered—their character changing in the act of transmission, so that Indian education acquired a distinctive colonial flavor, like Indian English.

To become a good citizen of the Empire, Babuji had to write down and commit to memory lists of the official titles of government posts. (One of his lists read, "Deputy Surgeon General, Lahore; Quarter Master General, Lahore; Deputy Inspector, Punjab; Deputy Commissioner, Ludhiana; District Judge, Peshawar; Divisional Judge, Lahore; Scission Judge, Calcutta; Assistant Commissioner; Royal Kings Rifle Artillery;

Band Master General, Delhi.") To improve his English vocabulary, he had to copy out lists of English words with their definitions. (For instance, "down—soft, fine hairy covering; proboscis—trunk; cartilaginous—grisly; hardly less—almost; visced—sticky; humous—moisture; tendinous—sinewy.") To improve his handwriting, he had to write out exercises that seem to have been intended to help his soul as much as his penmanship. ("Do not laugh if I submitted myself to the sorcery of the world. I am no better than Solomon who had wind as his support.") To train his ear to the sound of English, he had to take down in English dictation whole stories, which at the same time served to increase his familiarity with things Western. ("In the pleasant valley of Ashton, there lived an elderly woman of the name of Preston," one began, and another, "A Russian nobleman was travelling in the early part of the winter over a bleak plain.") To grasp stylistic differences, he had to copy the texts of entire essays and historical narratives in English. ("The beauty of an object is the state of its highest perfection, i.e. which admits of no improvement," he wrote, and "He struggled against the increasing illness with all his might. Day after day, the journal records his taking cold baths, being carried on his couch to take part in the daily sacrifices, and afterwards, conferring with his Generals, and giving orders for the extended expedition, but ever at night the fever returned with increasing violence.") In learning geometry, he had to master, among other things, many definitions. ("A point is that which has no parts or which has no magnitude;" "A line is length without breadth;" "A straight line is that which lies evenly between its extreme points;" "A superficies is that which has only length and breadth.")

Every year, he was required to take government examinations in all his studies: in algebra ("Divide $x^4 - 2nx^3 - [n^4 + n^2 + 3]x^2 - 2n^3x - n^2 + 1$ by $x^2 - [n^2 + n + 1]x - n - 1$"); in mensuration ("Find the value of the interior angle of a regular Duedacagon, and also the value of the exterior angle of a regular Quindacagon"); in history ("What do you know about the following battles—Crecy, Mortimer's Cross, Brunnabourgh, Ethandune, Mesham, Hastings, Stanford Bridge, Bannockbourne and Felkirk?"); in geography ("Draw a map of China, marking everything accurately," "Give the exports of Scandinavia and those of Persia; give also the names of the chief towns," and "Where are the following, and for what are they noted: Cologne, Pisa, Demeraira, Kampore, Golhanda, Kalikat, Nanhin, Cairo, Freetown, Quebec, Ava, Tassisudan, Lisbon, Tabrez, Jaddha & Portsmouth?"); in English ("How would you characterize Scott's genius?" and "Explain the following as fully as you can, give notes where necessary: The war and chase/ give little choice of resting place/ A summer night in Greenwood spent/ were but tomorrow's merriment"); in languages and translation ("It is said that Persian, English, and Sanskrit belong to the same family of language. Give some words of all the three languages that verify the statement," and "Translate into Persian: 'The monarch of Persia has been pronounced one of the most absolute in the world & it has been shown that there is reason to believe his condition has been the same from most early ages. The words of the King of Persia has ever been deemed law and he has probably never had any further restraint imposed upon the free exercise of his authority' ") ; in logic ("Give examples of Disjunctive, Assertary, Problematic, Verbal and real propositions and describe the logical character of the following propositions:—'You must not leave the room till I return.' 'This is the 1st of May 1890' ") ; and in political economy ("What is the proper function of money? Enumerate the qualities which the substance selected as money should possess," and "What is Socialism? Name some of its well known advocates and point out its economic defects").

Although Babuji seldom scored more than fifty per cent on any given examination paper, he often stood first in his class.

After finishing D.A.V. School, Babuji went to D.A.V. College, in Lahore. The college, which was an affiliate of Punjab University, had also been founded in memory of Swami Dayanand and was dedicated to the teaching of "all human knowledge, in Sanskrit and in English." From the first day, Babuji felt at home, and he congratulated himself on not having gone to Government College, though it was an older and more celebrated affiliate. Government College students tended to be a little idle and dilettantish, dressing in starched and ironed clothes and wearing British-type laced shoes, and they cultivated a secular outlook, taking pride in speaking English and in playing British games like cricket and hockey. Babuji preferred to be one of the D.A.V. students, who, in the Arya Samaj manner, were studious, dressed in simple muslin clothes, wore Indian slipperlike shoes, and cultivated a religious outlook, taking pride in their mother tongue, Hindi, and in Hindu culture.

At college, Babuji soon fell under the influence of a leading Arya Samaj teacher named Hans Raj. Every Sunday morning, he accompanied Hans Raj to an Arya Samaj service in a large, bare hall, where the worshippers—many of them prominent Lahoris—sat on a mat on the floor in front of a brazier of burning coals. The service always began with the *havan* (a sacred Vedic fire ceremony), during which the worshippers would toss handfuls of *smugary* and tablespoonfuls of ghi into the fire, and chant Sanskrit mantras. The *havan* was followed by an *updesh* (a short sermon), by some uplifting *bhajans* (hymns), and by an Arya Samaj lecture—on, for instance, the glories of the Hindus' Aryan past. After the clamor of the crowded Kucha Kaghzian and the D.A.V. College classrooms, Babuji found the crackle of the offerings on the fire and the chanting and singing of the worshippers very soothing. He was also thrilled by the self-righteous harangues, and he enjoyed mingling with the prominent Lahoris. But in later years he could remember only one recurring theme of the meetings: the Ghas (Grass) Party of the Arya Samaj is namby-pamby and false; the Mas (Meat) Party of the Arya Samaj is virile and true. Swami Dayanand had died some six years earlier, in 1883, and soon after his death a schism developed between his vegetarian and nonvegetarian disciples.

Some years after entering D.A.V. College, Babuji passed the Intermediate exam, or First Arts, on a second try. This meant that he had completed half the work toward a Bachelor of Arts degree. At the time, that was as far as a student could go at D.A.V. College, so Babuji went on to another affiliate of Punjab University—Forman Christian College, run by the Punjab Mission of the American Presbyterian Church. In due course, he became a Bachelor of Arts. Then he spent three years at the Punjab Law School and qualified for the practice of law, after which he enrolled as a court pleader and started practicing law in the Lahore District Court. In January, 1899—a date that Babuji later remembered clearly—the Chief Justice of the Punjab High Court raised him to the status of a pleader who could appear before the Punjab High Court. Now that Babuji had acquired such status, he started using a surname—Mehra, the name of his family group within his subcaste. This use of a family-group name was becoming a common practice among new Indian servants of the British Empire.

WHEN BABUJI'S SISTER, Durga Devi, was a little over seventeen, the local matchmaker—a buxom fifty-year-old busybody who knew the economic worth and caste status, the scandals and secrets of everyone in every choked byway or blind alley around Kucha Kaghzian and beyond—stopped Bulaki Ram as he was going into his house, and said, "Brother, have you heard of Nedou's Hotel?"

"What would I know about hotels, Sister? I like my lentils and bread as my daughter-in-law, Devaki, cooks them."

"Nedou's is an English-type hotel in the new city,"

the matchmaker informed him self-importantly. "You'd probably have to spend a lot of money to get bread and lentils there."

Bulaki Ram, moving closer to his door, motioned the matchmaker to one side to save her from being spattered by a bucketful of slops that had just been tossed down into the *gulli.*

"At Nedou's, there is a clerk who belongs to the Dha-ee-ghar family of Seths. He has a *ghora-gari* [horse-drawn carriage], and a son called Moti Ram. Moti Ram would make a good husband for Durga Devi."

Durga Devi had grown up into a dyed-in-the-wool *shehran* (city woman)—a good infighter, with rigid notions of caste and class and of family hierarchy. When Babuji brought Devaki to the house, Durga Devi had immediately made it clear to her that she, Durga Devi, was mistress of the house; she had told the new bride that ever since Ganesh Devi's death the ring holding the keys to the family's cupboards, trunks, and tins had hung from where she tied and tucked her sari at the waist, and she meant to keep it there. Devaki hadn't so much as chirped a protest; she was a year or so younger and of compliant disposition. Durga Devi had thereupon set about fortifying and expanding her domain. She ordered Devaki around. She would call for a glass of lemonade, and when Devaki brought it she would send it back: the drink was too sweet; it was too lemony; it wasn't strained, for she thought there was a pip in it. Durga Devi was never satisfied.

Bulaki Ram, who was anxious to see Durga Devi married, betrothed her to Moti Ram on the match-

---

maker's say-so, without inquiring closely into his character. Soon afterward, having loaded Durga Devi down with gold and silver armlets and anklets, combs and earrings, necklaces and nose rings, he gave her in marriage to Moti Ram.

Moti Ram had had an erratic childhood. When he was a boy, his mother would sometimes take him aside as he was setting off for school, and—handing him a few coins to buy potato croquettes with his favorite mint chutney from a vender—ask him to follow his father's carriage and then tell her how his father had spent the day. She suspected her husband of visiting nautch and singing girls in the Tibbi Bazaar, deep in the bowels of the old city, where, she had heard, these girls lured men to their beds. Thus, while Moti Ram's classmates were reciting multiplication tables and taking Urdu dictation, Moti Ram was often running after carriages or hiding in doorways to watch them. He seldom, if ever, saw his father—let alone a nautch and singing girl—for he was unable to distinguish his father's carriage from any other; besides, he was on foot, and the carriages went too fast for him. He would fall asleep in a doorway, only to be startled awake by the sound of a carriage rushing away. In time, his mother realized that she had nurtured what she called a "myopic bungler," but by then it was too late for him to change his ways. He was an only child, his mother was indulgent, his father was prosperous, and Moti Ram grew up to be a spoiled young man who liked to stand around and tell tales to his classmates about his father's exploits with women.

When Moti Ram and Durga Devi had been mar-

ried only a few months, Moti Ram's father died, and
it fell to the young man to support his mother as well
as his wife. His mother pleaded with Nedou's manager
to give Moti Ram his father's job as clerk, and when
the job was offered to Moti Ram she persuaded him to
take it. But Moti Ram was quite unable to sit behind a
desk, keep accounts, and manage the hotel bearers. He
soon lost the job, and settled down into his old life of
a ne'er-do-well. The more furious Durga Devi became
at this, and the more she nagged him about his idleness,
the more he loved her for her fiery nature.

In 1902, when Devaki, Babuji's wife, was barely
twenty-seven, she died, after a long struggle with consumption. In her short life, she had cremated her
mother, then a brother, then a second brother, then a
sister—all, like her, victims of consumption, the scourge
of the cities. (She was survived by one brother, the
only member of her family left to carry on the name.)
She had spent most of her adult life as the wife of a
self-absorbed student, an Arya Samaj zealot, and she
left behind three children: a seven-year-old daughter,
Ratan Devi; a five-year-old son, Ishwar Das; and a two-
year-old son, Bhagwan Das.

So it was that, at the age of thirty, Babuji became
a widower. But the day he completed the prescribed
year of ritual mourning Bulaki Ram was again visited
by the local matchmaker. "Brother, let's marry your
son—what do you say?" she said, sitting down next to

Bulaki Ram on the charpoy. "His three children have been motherless now for a year. It tears at my heart to hear them cry. Surely he doesn't want to stay a widower, like his lonely father. Surely he feels that it is his responsibility to give a good Dha-ee-ghar girl a home."

The Dha-ee-ghar subcaste was a very small one, consisting of only four family groups—the Mehras, the Khannas, the Seths, and the Kapurs. No one could marry within his own family group, and so a Dha-ee-ghar who insisted on marrying within his subcaste was restricted to only three family groups. Moreover, a widow was not permitted to remarry, whereas a Dha-ee-ghar man not only was allowed to remarry but could have several wives, fathering children with each. In fact, a Dha-ee-ghar man, however old or decrepit, was a prize, and Babuji was the best-educated and the most prosperous Dha-ee-ghar man in the Kucha Kaghzian.

"Sister, I've been urging my son to take a wife after the period of mourning," Bulaki Ram said. "But he won't hear of it. And once he makes up his mind he's like the Iron Pillar in Delhi."

"What nonsense, Brother! Your will is his consent."

A couple of days later, the matchmaker arrived at Bulaki Ram's house with a basket of sweetmeats, a coconut, a gold ring, and one silver rupee. It was the *shagan*—the token of betrothal—from the family of one Lal Devi, who was to become my grandmother. Not only had Babuji not been consulted in the matter but the family in whose name the *shagan* was given had not been consulted, either. However, it was traditionally in the domain of the matchmaker to give such pledges in a neighbor's name.

❦

LAL DEVI was the daughter of Baggu Ram and Malan Khanna, who lived next door to Babuji in Kucha Kaghzian. Their branch of the Khanna family was in the grain business in Kasur, and at the time of the *shagan* it happened that Lal Devi and her parents were in Kasur, where Baggu Ram had long been involved in a court case over his father's property. His father had had two wives, of whom the first had given him a son and a daughter, and the second had given him Baggu Ram. After the father's death, some years earlier, Baggu Ram's half brother and the husband of his half sister had conspired to take over Baggu Ram's share of his father's property—something they felt justified in doing because Baggu Ram did not have a male heir. Baggu Ram had taken them to court, even though he felt that his best hope of getting back his share of the property lay not in winning a case in court —for the courts only beggared disputants—but in getting a male heir. Just recently, Malan had been delivered of a son, Shiv Das, and the couple had rushed to Kasur to show him off. And, in fact, as soon as the conspiring relatives were satisfied that Baggu Ram actually had a male heir, they abandoned the court case and divided up the family property with him. Baggu Ram and his family returned to Lahore to find the entire *gulli* waiting to congratulate them. Baggu Ram thought he was being congratulated on having won back his property, and he thanked everyone by saying, "Brothers and Sisters, it was God's will that I should have my rightful property given back to me."

"What does your property amount to when you've found such a paragon of a son-in-law?" someone cried out.

"What son-in-law?" Baggu Ram asked.

"Why, Bulaki Ram's son," a neighbor explained. "The matchmaker has already given a *shagan* for Lal Devi."

"Thank the good Lord!" Malan cried. She liked the thought of her daughter as the wife of a coated and booted Hindu gentleman who carried a walking stick and went to court.

Baggu Ram, however, as soon as he reached home, sat down on the floor and wept. "I don't want to touch foreheads with *shehris!*" he cried—his family had its roots in a small village near Kasur. "I am a simple man. I will marry my daughter only to a *paindu* [villager]."

Malan listened to him for some time and then said cunningly, "Dear, are you a member of the Kshatriya caste or not? Once a *shagan* has been given in a Kshatriya's name, can he ever go back on it? Don't forget we are descended from the same Kshatriya caste as Maharaja Dasharatha, who says in the Ramayana, 'The tradition of the caste is: Your word must not be broken even if you have to die for it.'" Malan went on to console Baggu Ram by saying, "Lal Devi will have lots of money to buy fruits and vegetables. She will wear good clothes and fine jewelry. She will have a very nice bed to sleep in. A servant will wait on her. If she married a *paindu,* she would spend all her time cooking food and preparing buttermilk and carrying them under the hot sun to the fields. Anyway, Lal Devi is almost seventeen years old."

Malan herself had been married when she was only eight years old. In fact, on her wedding day, when she was being prepared for marriage to Baggu Ram, who was fourteen years older than she was, she thought she was being prepared for the ceremonial good-luck swing under the wedding horse of the man she took to be the bridegroom who was coming to fetch her aunt. As the bridegroom arrived, and everyone started laughing and clapping, murmuring about how handsome he was, no one could keep Malan still long enough to henna her hands and feet. During the wedding ceremony, she sat in her mother's lap, wriggling, laughing, and hiccupping, and then she was lifted into the bridal palanquin and told by her mother, "Be a good wife to your lord and master, Baggu Ram. Make sure he always has clean clothes to wear and good food to eat and a nice bed to sleep in." Malan, finally realizing that she was being carried off by a stranger, started wailing. The family covered the palanquin with a heavy woollen shawl to muffle her screams, and she was taken away.

The very first day of Malan's married life, her mother-in-law ordered her to cook a meal for Baggu Ram. She didn't know how to knead the dough, let alone roll it and cook it into a chapatti. And it was months before she realized that she was not only a housewife but also a stepmother: Baggu Ram was a *dohaju* (a widower who had remarried) with a son and a daughter about her age, who were living in the house. Until then, she had regarded them simply as playmates. Within four or five years of her marriage, Malan underwent several pregnancies, but, because of her tender age, they ended either in miscarriages or in stillbirths. By the time she was thirty-three—her age at the time of Lal Devi's *shagan*—she had had nine pregnancies; but only two children, Lal Devi (Bright Goddess) and the long-awaited male heir, Shiv Das (Servant of Lord Shiva), had survived. (In the interval between her marriage and that of Lal Devi, her step-daughter had died in a plague epidemic, and her step-son of consumption.) Still, Malan felt that her married life had been a happy one.

Baggu Ram had a well-paying regular job as a clerk with the North Western Railway. It always thrilled Malan to go to the railway station and see Baggu Ram sitting in a chair behind a desk and writing something in a government file. She felt there was a direct connection between his pen and the train that mysteriously flew out of the station and disappeared into the distance, like a stone flung from a wooden sling. He was the only Indian she knew who daily sat in a chair, and she kept telling everybody in the *gulli* that the government thought so highly of Baggu Ram's work that one day, when he was old, it would pay him for doing nothing. She thought of his pension as a "pen-shunt"—the ultimate reward for his moving "pen" that "shunted" the train.

After the news of Lal Devi's *shagan,* Baggu Ram

remained restless and intransigent for ten or fifteen days. Then he yielded to the inevitable and agreed to the marriage.

🌺

SHORTLY AFTER the *shagan,* Babuji and his family went to Kasur for the wedding. At the ceremony, the officiating Brahman asked Babuji, "What would you like to call your bride?" During a wedding, the husband generally gave his wife a new first name, to signify her birth as a new person. "Dhan Devi," Babuji replied. The name meant Wealth Goddess. Arya Samaj condemnations of idolatry notwithstanding, Babuji thought that every time he called "Dhan Devi" he would be invoking the name of a goddess who could shower blessings upon him and make him prosperous.

It was only after he brought his bride back to Lahore and unveiled her that he saw the face of the woman with whom he was to spend the next sixty-nine years of his life; because boys and girls were so strictly forbidden to have any contact with each other, he had never before caught even a glimpse of her, though she lived next door. She was petite—about four feet nine—and pretty. She had a fair complexion, long black hair, and a small face, with a round chin and a turned-up nose. She was not quite nine years older than Babuji's daughter, Ratan Devi. To Mamaji and to her other children, and to us, she was known simply as Mataji.

Baggu Ram never really recovered from having given his only surviving daughter in marriage to a *shehri.* Soon after the wedding, he was retired from his job with the railway and put on pension. He sold his house in Lahore and went with Malan and Shiv Das to Kasur, where he lived for the next few years. Then he developed a boil under his right jaw. He returned to Lahore for treatment. The boil was excised, but the wound would not heal. He started losing weight rapidly and grew very weak. He and his family took shelter with Babuji. When he was dying, he called Babuji to his bedside. He caught hold of the arms of Malan and Shiv Das—the boy was just five—and had Babuji hold them. "Be their support," Baggu Ram said to his son-in-law. "Don't let go of Shiv Das's arm until he can stand on his feet and look after my wife."

Baggu Ram died that night.

CONVERSATION didn't interest Babuji; it was something that women engaged in to pass the time, and its self-evident frivolity mirrored a woman's nature. Sports generally didn't interest him; they were something that the sons of rich men went in for because they had nothing better to do than to waste their time and their fathers' money. Babuji's main passion as he was settling down into his professional career was Arya Samaj.

Babuji had come to feel embarrassed when he saw his father sitting and chanting every morning before the idol of Goddess Durga and anointing it with ghi. In the evening, while Babuji was massaging his father, kneading and pressing his legs—a Hindu filial ritual— he would tell his father about Arya Samaj, dwelling on points that he thought would appeal to his father's nature: Arya Samaj was a charitable society that did good works; in addition to schools and colleges, it ran orphanages, homes for widows, and ashrams; many Arya Samajists were pure and strong, because they practiced celibacy; Arya Samajists were committed to restoring Hindus to their ancient, martial Aryan values and to promoting Ayur-Vedic medicine; Arya Samajists believed in discipline. Somewhere he would slip in the fact that Arya Samajists were also dedicated to purifying Hinduism of superstition and idolatry. "How often have I heard you say, Baba, that a young man who doesn't cultivate discipline and purity will not amount to much in this world?" Babuji once asked. He would repeat slogans that were current in the city—taking care to make homey comparisons. For instance, he tapped the wall behind Bulaki Ram's head and said, "This wall, Baba, is our defense against the overflowing drains of Kucha Kaghzian. Arya Samaj is the wall against the flood of conversions to Christianity and Islam."

Bulaki Ram listened to his son's Arya Samaj talk, yet always distractedly, with only a part of his mind, as if it were in the nature of things for father and son to drift apart, and live in separate worlds. But he began to look interested when Babuji told him one evening that the real purpose of the movement was to recover the Aryan Hindu heritage of the Vedas. "Our family is here today only because of the Ayur-Veda and Goddess Durga," Bulaki Ram responded enthusiastically. "That is why we have always honored Goddess Durga in our house." He asked Babuji to press down harder on his legs.

"But you are only honoring a clay idol, and Arya Samaj is against all forms of idolatry," Babuji said, thinking that he might succeed in making a convert of his father after all.

Bulaki Ram, however, retorted sharply, "Goddess Durga has watched over you even as I have, and this is how you repay her!"

Babuji felt both ashamed and lonely. He knew that the bazaars and *gullis* he had grown up in were depraved, but he also knew that his father was as pure as any Arya Samajist. After this conversation, Babuji always felt uncomfortable not only when he saw his father praying to the idol but also when he heard Arya Samajists denouncing superstition and idolatry. Perhaps as a consequence, he continued to profess Arya Samaj principles but, when it came to practice, often reverted to his father's ways, thus causing detractors to say that he had "a mouth of elephant's teeth, one set for show, the other for chewing."

The life of Swami Dayanand, who was born in a village near Ahmedabad in 1824, is wrapped in legend. It is said that when he was fifteen and was keeping a night-long vigil in a Shiva temple, he saw a mouse nibbling at an offering before the Shiva lingam. At first, he was aghast at the sacrilege. Then he had a flash of insight: the god Shiva could not be omnipotent, or he would have smitten the abomination. For years, Swami Dayanand was troubled by what he had seen, and when he was twenty-one he went up into the Himalayas on the traditional yogi's search for salvation. Here he met a blind monk, who told him that idol worship was decadent, and had no source or sanction in the original text of the Vedas at all; in fact, idol worship was the most flagrant example of the superstition that had hidden the truth of Hinduism from believers for thousands of years. This truth would be exposed and the ground prepared for complete reformation, he said, only when all superstition was cast out. In the presence of the blind monk, Swami Dayanand vowed that as long as there was breath left in his body he would labor to that end.

In 1875, when Swami Dayanand was fifty-one years old, he founded the Arya Samaj, with the slogan "Back to the Vedas!" and with tenets of faith that were later codified as follows: God, formless and unseeable, is the source of all existence; men and women must wean themselves from superstitious untruth by studying the Vedas, which contain all human knowledge; and Hindus should always follow their dharma (moral duty), practice love, righteousness, and justice, and look for their own good in the furtherance of the good of others. Swami Dayanand and his followers founded branches of the Arya Samaj in many major cities. His greatest success, however, was in the Punjab and in the United Provinces.

When Swami Dayanand died, in 1883, his disciples decided to found an institution of learning in his memory, but they eventually fell out among themselves about the direction that this institution should take. The Grass Party, considering itself true to the tradition of the Vedas, wanted the institution to use Sanskrit and Hindi and to revive the Vedic guru-and-chela system of learning. The Meat Party, considering itself modern, wanted the projected institution to use English

—the nation's official language—and to prepare its students for participation in the civil and military services. The Grass Party established itself in the United Provinces, and the Meat Party in the Punjab. Beginning with the founding of the D.A.V. School in Lahore, the Meat Party gained so much support that in time there was hardly a town of any consequence in the Punjab which did not have its own D.A.V. school, while the D.A.V. College in Lahore, starting with a few dozen students, went on to become the largest college in Punjab University.

Babuji was one of the star alumni of the D.A.V. College, which continued to attract bookish boys who had patriotic, religious fervor. In fact, after he qualified as a lawyer he started playing an increasingly important part in the affairs of the Meat Party. It became for him church, club, professional society—his entrée into social and political life.

V

NEW HOUSE

I RRITATED BY THE OPPRESSIVE HEAT, WHICH SEEMED
never to budge from a hundred and ten de-
grees, and also by the humming and buzzing
of mosquitoes and wasps, and the noise from
Kucha Kaghzian below, Babuji lay on the roof
of his father's house—where the family slept in
summer—and brooded. Babuji was thirty-three, and he
felt that he was spending his life like a drone in the
honeycomb of *gullis* filled with cobblers, coin minters,
grain sellers, colliers, and cloth peddlers. Even such
professional people as lawyers, government servants,
and schoolteachers, who, like him, worked outside the
old city, came home to their dark cells in the evening,
and mostly buzzed back and forth between *gulli* and
gulli.

Babuji remembered walking as a child along the
road outside the wall of the old city of Lahore and
pointing to the birds and insects that nested in the crev-
ices of the ancient wall as high as he could see. He
and his parents were going to Peshawar, and the road
to the railway station seemed endless. He remembered
calling out the names of the gates to his parents as they
passed them. There were Lahori Darvaza, Shahalmi
Darvaza, and Mochi Darvaza—the Gate of Lahore, the
Gate of the Great Emperor Alam, and the Gate of
Cobblers. (The name Mochi Darvaza was actually a
corruption of Moti Darvaza, or Gate of Pearls.) He
remembered thinking how glad he was that his father
was not a *mochi;* the *mochis* he saw working inside

71

Mochi Darvaza were black and hairy, like monkeys.
Bulaki Ram said that Mochi Darvaza was a realm of
ungodly darkness, because Muslims and Untouchables
lived there and they consumed their capital, spending
it all on food, drink, and many wives, while Shahalmi
Darvaza had a godly lustre, because Hindus lived there
and they conserved their capital. Babuji came to think
of each gate as closing off a separate hive of *gullis,* a
different group of workers, another whole city—even
though these gates were only a few hundred feet apart
and consisted of little more than arches, their portals
having long since fallen under the ravages of con-
querors and the siege of weather and time. He felt
glad that he lived near Shahalmi Darvaza.

As he lay on the roof, he could not ignore the
stench of raw sewage from the open drain below, and
he imagined the sewage sluggishly moving through the
network of *gulli* drains, slapping against the doorsteps
of the houses, inundating the footpaths, washing over
the bare feet of children, as the collected filth made its
way to the Ganda Nallah (Dirty Drain), which surrounded the old-city wall, and as it moved on from the
Ganda Nallah to the river in which the ashes of his
ancestors had been scattered and to which the corpses
of his nameless brothers and sisters had been committed. In a sense, he felt trapped in the drain of the
Kucha Kaghzian. He felt trapped in the *gullis* through
which his father as a bundleman had daily wound his
way. He felt trapped on his ancestral plot of land,
where generations of Mehras had died, leaving scarcely
a hand mirror to mark their passage through its various
houses.

A number of bridges over the Ganda Nallah connected the old city to the Circular Road, which, like
the Ganda Nallah, formed a circle around the old city,
separating it from the new. Ever since Bulaki Ram took
Babuji outside the old-city wall, across the Ganda Nallah and the Circular Road, to enter him in the D.A.V.
School, some nineteen years earlier, Babuji had daily
walked the mile or so to his school, college, or court,
and the mile or so back. Sometimes, in the evening, he
would walk, for pleasure, into the new city, pushing
his way through the crowds in the fashionable Anarkali
Bazaar, which lay to the south of the two main gates—
Shahalmi Darvaza and Lahori Darvaza. (The bazaar
was named after a courtesan, Anar Kali—Pomegranate
Blossom—who had supposedly been buried alive on this
spot, by order of the Moghul emperor Akbar the Great,
for her illicit love of his son Selim.) From Anarkali,
Babuji would walk southeast to the upper Mall, around
which stood the beckoning British city, with its impressive monuments and buildings. He would pass the University Hall, the Museum, the General Post Office, the
statue of Lord Lawrence, the statue of Queen Victoria,
Nedou's Hotel, and then Government House (the governor of the Punjab lived there), with Lawrence Gardens opposite. But whether he was attending school,
college, or court, or taking his evening walk, in the
end he would have to retrace his steps to the congested
old city.

Every day—especially after he had become a lawyer
—he would try, as he went past the open British gardens and the imposing British buildings, to devise
some way to uproot his family and set them down in

the new city. But, even as he thought up scheme after scheme, he knew there was only one scheme that would succeed, and this was to exercise enough prudence, diligence, and caution to save up—sometimes no more than a rupee a day—for each brick of a new house in the new city. Every morning, he would dream of the day when he could leave the old city for good, and every evening he would go back to his father's house to sleep. The old city seemed to hold him like a powerful bear, and was as frightening to him.

Beyond the ancient wall and across the Ganda Nallah, a stretch of wasteland lay between the Circular Road and the new city. At one time, it had been used as a rubbish dump, and donkeys and cows had been let loose there to forage, but recently some of this wasteland had been landscaped with grass and tall shade trees, and named the Circular Gardens. As Babuji returned from court now, he saw athletes wrestling there and doing calisthenics or yoga, and sometimes he saw people holding an engagement or a marriage party. To him, the air in the Circular Gardens felt fresh, clean, and lively.

As he remembered it many years later, it was only a few days after his restless, anxious night on the roof that he persuaded Bulaki Ram to rent out the house in Kucha Kaghzian (the house was sold just before the Partition of India, in 1947), and they moved to a *pukka* rented house on the new-city side of the Ganda Nallah and the Circular Road. The house was near Lahori Darvaza, and it overlooked the Circular Gardens. Within a year, Babuji had built his own house, also *pukka,* and also on the new-city side of the Circular Road, but looking out on Shahalmi Darvaza. It almost immediately came to be known as the Shahalmi Gate house. It was one of a long, tight row of identical brick houses, each about three and a half stories high, with the low, cramped doors of houses in the old city (anyone wearing a formal turban, wound over a turban cap, had to stoop to enter)—houses built by recent émigrés from the old city, who had taken little more than their first step outside it.

Babuji was to live in the Shahalmi Gate house for the next eighteen years—until 1926—and it was in this house that Mamaji was born, brought up, and married to Daddyji, my father. A short distance in front of Babuji's house was a mosque with a sort of yard, where Muslim laborers from the old city would gather in the evening to joke, gossip, and pass around a hookah. Just in back of the house was a hay stall, where all day long victorias, gigs, and tongas would draw up and syces and drivers would alight to feed and water their horses. All day long, there were the new-city sounds of the clip-clop, neighing, and snorting of horses, the shouts and imprecations of syces and drivers, and the knocking and grinding of carriages. The Shahalmi Gate house had a little enclosed front courtyard, where the family would hang out its wash to dry, or set up a charpoy for sitting in the evening. Behind the courtyard was a *daori* (entrance hall) a few feet square, which served as Bulaki Ram's headquarters. He would post himself in the *daori* for hours at a time, and, sitting on a small charpoy, would direct the household affairs—bargain with hawkers and venders who came to the house with their wares, chat with neighbors, keep the family's accounts. Beyond the *daori* was a large room containing a big desk and a few chairs with jute sacking for seats. This room served as Babuji's office. Opening off it was a small chamber fitted with two charpoys, where father and son slept. Farther along was a still smaller room—the *munshi khanna* (clerk's room). This was the eye of office and domestic storms, for it was the perch of Babuji's *munshi*, Gujarmal, who served him for thirty years, from 1899 to 1929. He was a sort of factotum: when he was not at court canvassing cases for Babuji, he was in the *munshi khanna,* at Babuji's beck and call, or else he was functioning as the family's major-domo—bringing from the bazaar samples of shoes and clothes on approval for the women, who rarely ventured out of the house.

A narrow staircase led up from Babuji's office to a gallerylike room just under the second floor. Here the family would spread out sheets and take naps in the burning afternoons of the Lahore summer. The staircase continued to the second floor, where there were several small rooms, one of them a kitchen. At mealtime, a servant would dish out the food, and the family, sitting on a cotton mat on the kitchen floor, would eat from brass plates and brass bowls with their fingers. (The family did not use any cutlery even after Babuji introduced into the house, some years later, the new custom of sitting on small wicker stools and eating off small tables.) The meal would begin and end with everyone in turn washing his or her hands with water poured from a jug into a basin. (There was no plumbing in the house, and water had to be carried from a communal tap at the end of the row of houses.)

Around the kitchen were a storeroom, a prayer room, and two other rooms, in which the women laundered and sewed the clothes for the family, talked, and slept. On the third floor were a few more rooms, including the *chaubara,* which was the women's sanctuary. It contained steel trunks to be filled bit by bit with saris and matching blouses, petticoats and shoes, bangles, chains, pendants, earrings, compacts, mirrors, combs, silver kohl flasks, embroidered tablecloths, sheets— everything a girl would need to make herself a desirable bride and to establish herself in a new house. Just the fact that a house was prosperous enough to have a *chaubara* invited perpetual speculation among families in the neighborhood with unmarried sons—speculation about the size and weight of the dowry, about the width of gold borders on saris and the number of silver buttons on blouses. Girls who had grown too old to run about the *gullis* with their brothers and cousins would spend hours with their mothers, grandmothers, and aunts behind the locked door of the *chaubara,* absorbing the ways of the world while they learned to do cross-stitching, make buttonholes, and concoct home remedies for headaches and indigestion, and also learned the knack of making meals without seeming to measure the ingredients.

Above these rooms was the roof of the house. It had a parapet, and the family slept there on charpoys during the hot summer nights. If a sudden summer rainstorm broke, they dragged the charpoys inside the *barsati* (rain shelter), an open shed with three walls and a corrugated-tin roof. (Every summer morning, the bedding was rolled up, the charpoys were stacked, and both bedding and charpoys were stored for the day in the *barsati* to protect them from bird droppings and detritus.) Next to the *barsati* was the lavatory.

ORDINARILY, BAGGU RAM'S WIDOW, Malan, would have turned to her husband's family for support, but she couldn't, because of the residue of bitterness over the old property dispute. She used to say, "Nothing can sweeten bad blood between half brothers. The spectre of their quarrels will walk alongside their children and their grandchildren and their widows." She had no blood relative to turn to except her daughter. And yet, as a good Hindu parent, Malan could at first no more imagine herself accepting a glass of water from her daughter's house than she could imagine herself stealing mangoes from a fruit vender. When she and Baggu Ram gave their daughter to Babuji in marriage, they had completely relinquished all claim on her; after that, she belonged body and soul to Babuji and his family.

Yet when Baggu Ram, on his deathbed, handed over the charge of his wife and son to Babuji, Malan went home, took out her savings of three thousand rupees, removed the gold bangles from her wrists and the gold bracelets from her ankles, undid her gold earrings, chain, and pendant, gathered together her eleven silk saris embroidered with heavy gold thread, rolled up these possessions and everything else she owned in a couple of bed sheets, and, dragging Shiv Das behind her,

Babuji, Lahore, 1914

arrived on Babuji's doorstep. She put her precious bundles—in a sense, her second dowry—at Babuji's feet and said, "Everything I took away with me as an unwilling bride of eight, I willingly give to you as a poor widow. As long as there is life in my hands and feet, I will serve you and your loved ones. In return, all I ask is a home for my son and bread and lentils for myself."

Babuji pulled the small boy to him and pointed to his walking stick in the corner. "Are you a naughty boy?" he asked. "Do you see that stick over there? It always stands in that corner." The child started to howl. Malan pressed him against her to muffle his cries and quickly took him into the house.

Babuji sent his *munshi* to fetch the pawnbroker, and by the end of the day he had pawned most of Malan's possessions, lent out the money they brought, and also her savings, at a high rate of interest, and worked out with pencil and paper the income he would get from the interest and balanced it against the cost of keeping mother and son and educating the son. The projected debits and credits came out even. Moreover, Malan tried to make up for receiving the hospitality of her daughter by ceaselessly working in the kitchen and around the house. (She lived until 1942, when, in her seventies, she suffered a brain hemorrhage.) Naturally intelligent and kind, she didn't begrudge the family anything. After all, she felt, the recipient of her sacrifices was none other than her own daughter, and Shiv Das was blessed in having the watchful and learned eye of Babuji upon him.

But Babuji took no particular interest in Shiv Das's

education. In the morning, Shiv Das would set out for the D.A.V. School. He would circle the row of houses, deposit his schoolbag in a ditch, and spend the day eating *halwah* and playing games with other truants. If Babuji did ask "How was school today?" Shiv Das would regale him with stories, complete with imitations of teachers he'd never met and lessons from books he'd never read. He was a born storyteller, and for years he was able to stay a step ahead of the truth. But when the results of his matriculation examination were published in the papers, the truth caught up with him. He had failed all his subjects and distinguished himself by scoring some of the lowest marks in the examination. "Because of a promise to your dying father, I took hold of your arm!" Babuji said, exploding into a rage. "I've held on to it through thick and thin, and this is how you repay me!" Babuji took hold of Shiv Das's arm again, picked up his walking stick, and swung it, aiming vaguely at the boy's bottom. "Get out!" Babuji yelled. Malan felt that she didn't have the right to utter a word of protest.

Shiv Das was fifteen years old and penniless. He traded the only talents he had—for games and for storytelling—to get himself across India to Calcutta and land himself a job as an assistant clerk: folding letters, sealing and stamping envelopes, tying files with red tape, overseeing the office peons. It was the first of an endless series of jobs. Along the way, he married, and, though he was never quite able to support his wife, fathered three children. Thus he began a long career as one of the family's many poor relations—impecunious but cheerful.

❧

MATAJI PRAYED for a son throughout her first pregnancy. As a widower's second wife, her position in the family was insecure. Moreover, Babuji's first wife had left three children, and Mataji had been brought up hearing stories of the dire misfortunes of women who were cursed with stepchildren. ("Beware of suckling a *dohaju's* children," she remembered hearing one of the *gulli* women say. "They'll gnaw at your breast and then spit at you in the *gulli*.") And, as ill luck would have it, she was expecting her baby in the dreaded month of September—the month following the last rains of the monsoon, when the networks of open drains overflowed and the pools of stagnant water bred mosquitoes and fever everywhere. By September, the so-called month of fever, there was scarcely a *gulli* in the old city or a house in the civil station which hadn't been struck by the fever, and sometimes its victims never got over it, the disease of sudden chills and fever becoming either chronic or fatal. Mataji feared for her September baby. But the baby, when it arrived—on the eighteenth of September, 1906—was a son. He had bright eyes and a full head of golden hair. Babuji named him Narinjan Das.

On the sixteenth of August, 1908, Mataji was delivered of a second child—a daughter, named Shanti Devi. This was Mamaji. When Mamaji was barely a year old, Narinjan Das contracted diphtheria and died within a matter of days. Babuji was away on one of his vacation trips. On his return, he guessed from the frightened silence of the house that there had been a

death in the family, and, from the frightened look on
Mataji's face, that it was a son.

In 1910, Mataji was delivered of a third child. It
was another daughter, who died before she was a year
old.

As an Arya Samajist, Babuji had forsworn superstition, but the old dread of Lahore as a fatal place for
Bulaki Ram's progeny began to stir in him. So in 1912,
when Mataji was well along in her fourth pregnancy,
Babuji, after himself making substantial offerings to
Goddess Durga, sent her off to Kasur in the care of
Malan. On August 16th of that year, Mataji gave birth
to a son. Malan hired a barker to go up and down the
neighboring *gullis* shouting the news of the family's
good fortune: "He's come, he's come! Baggu Ram's
daughter has a healthy boy again!" She also hired a
"loud" two-man band of flute and drum to parade
through the *gullis* playing Punjabi folk tunes. The
barker and the band brought out the neighbors, who
arrived with their congratulations. Each was served a
stick of crude sugar and a cup of tea rich with fresh
milk.

A grain merchant bringing flour from Kasur to
the Shahalmi Gate shouted the news to Bulaki Ram in
his *daori,* and Bulaki Ram and Babuji travelled by train
to Kasur, where, in a cozy domestic ceremony, they
named the child Dwarka Das, invested him with a
gold bracelet on each wrist, and put a new gold neck-
lace around Mataji's neck. The bracelets were so heavy
that they practically pinned Dwarka Das's arms to his
sides, and he bellowed and kicked. Mataji and Malan
revelled in his cries, because they were a sign of health

and also restored the two women's position in the family—a position that had been shaken by Narinjan Das's death. But no sooner had the men turned their backs than Mataji took off the baby's gold bracelets and put him to her breast.

Over the next decade or so, there was hardly a year when Mataji was not suckling a child or mourning the loss of one. She gave birth to eleven children, of whom just six survived to adulthood.

ONE RAINY DAY late in the monsoon, Mataji was in bed. She was completing the rigidly observed forty-day lying-in period after the delivery of her tenth child, Pushpa. She called for some cold water, and Mamaji brought it to her in a clay pitcher. Mamaji was fourteen now and had practically taken charge of the household duties during Mataji's confinement.

"It's so quiet," Mataji said. "Where are the other children?"

"The boys must be up on the roof flying kites."

"And Pali?"

Pali was the nickname of Gopal Das. He was two years old, and was noisier and more active than any of the other children had been at his age. A few days before, however, he had come down with pneumonia. A practitioner of Hindu medicine had directed that he should not be given anything to eat—only a glass of milk each day, with regular doses of Howard's Chocolate-Covered Quinine, to ward off the complication of malaria. Hungry and sick, Pali had become peevish, and when he was not asleep in his crib he cried continuously.

"He must be asleep," Mamaji said.

Mataji lay back on her pillow. "Did you think to take his temperature?" she asked. "When I am in bed, the whole house seems to come to a—"

There was a crash. Mamaji ran to see what had happened.

"Has someone fallen down on the roof?" Mataji cried weakly, raising herself. When she received no answer, she got up. Never a strong woman, she was worn down by frequent deliveries and long months of breast feeding and now by her convalescence, and she felt dazed and unsteady on her feet.

Just as she began struggling up the stairs to the roof, she heard Mamaji shout from the next room, "Get down, Pali! Medicine!"

Mataji rushed into the room. There was Mamaji trying to lift Pali down from a chair and take the bottle of quinine from his left hand, while with his right he clung fast to a shelf scattered with quinine tablets. His mouth was covered with chocolate.

Pali looked sheepishly around at Mataji and brought out, between a cry and a swallow, "Toffee."

Mataji hit him on the back. "You dolt! You fool! It's medicine!"

Pali spat out a couple of half-chewed tablets, and she wiped his tongue with her finger.

It was around six o'clock in the evening. Bulaki Ram had gone with the *munshi* to the bazaar to buy vegetables and milk. Babuji was taking his evening walk.

Mataji called out for a servant to fetch Dr. Salig
Ram, who lived next door. Dr. Salig Ram was not
home, but within a couple of minutes the servant returned with Prakash Mehrotra, a family friend in the
last year of medical college, whom he had happened to
meet in the road. Prakash Mehrotra took one look at
Pali, dissolved some salt in a glass of hot water, and
started spooning the solution into Pali's mouth. Before
he was able to force down two spoonfuls, the boy died,
with both Mataji and Mamaji holding him.

Babuji returned home an hour or so later. He saw
a small, solemn crowd in front of his door, and knew
immediately that there had been another death in the
family.

Babuji stared at the empty crib and lashed out bit-
terly at everyone: Why hadn't Mamaji immediately
stuck her finger down Pali's throat and made him
vomit? What was wrong with her finger—didn't she
have one? And Mataji—if her legs could carry her to
the room, what was wrong with *her* finger? Why
hadn't Prakash taken Pali to the hospital? Why had
Pali been left alone in the first place? And why had
the Howard's Quinine been left out on a shelf? "It's all
your fault," he called out, to the room—to the household—at large.

Mamaji and Mataji, had they dared, could have
explained. In all of Lahore, there was hardly a house
worthy of the name which did not have Howard's
Quinine in the bedrooms. Pali, because of his empty
stomach, had had such a fast reaction to the quinine
that nothing could have saved him. He had died within
minutes of being discovered. But they were women, and

in front of men they were supposed to be silent. They bore Babuji's bitter reproaches without a word.

Babuji was devastated. First he had lost a daughter, Ratan Devi; then a son, Narinjan Das; then another daughter, Sumitra; then another daughter, Sheila; then one of twin daughters, Krishna; then another daughter, a second Ratan Devi; and now Pali. And, worst of all, he had lost his oldest son and support, the keepsake of Devaki, the boy whose gentle face never ceased to remind him of her—his Ishwar Das. The death of Ishwar Das had taken place four years earlier, but to Babuji it might have been yesterday.

THE SHAHALMI GATE barber had run along the spidery *gullis,* striking his scissors against a brass plate and shouting, "Ishwar Das, the eldest son of Durga Das, is dead! He will be cremated at sunrise! All those whom he knew and who knew him, let them gather at the house of his bereft father and beat their breasts!"

When Ishwar Das died—he succumbed to influenza, pandemic in the world in 1918—he was just twenty-one years old. He had looked after his half brothers and half sisters as if he and they had, in Mataji's words, "come out of the same stomach." A serious boy of religious temperament, he had excelled at his studies, first at Central Model School and later at Government College, and he had been active in the Young Men's Arya Samaj Association—patterned after the Y.M.C.A. He had intended to dedicate his life to teaching.

The morning after Ishwar Das died, his body was placed on a narrow plank, which was hoisted up onto the shoulders of Bulaki Ram, Babuji, and two neighbors—Dr. Salig Ram and his brother, Advocate Tirath Ram—and carried along the Circular Road to the cremation ground near the River Ravi. Old men dragging young children, women with their heads covered—weeping and beating their breasts and moaning *"Hai, hai!"*—walked behind the bier, all prodded on by the professional mourners. These were a troupe of deformed gypsies, such grotesque human specimens that Ishwar Das's mourners had only to look at them either to laugh or to cry. Cast out by their families and often unable to have families of their own, such gypsies earned their keep by marching in funerals and crying laments, or by dancing at weddings and giggling as they made bridal-bed suggestions. Curious children came out of the *gullis* and fell in behind the procession to follow it to the cremation ground.

At the cremation ground, a Brahman handed Babuji a burning brand, and he stepped forward and lit the pyre of his son as the Brahman chanted Vedic mantras and the assembled mourners threw *smugary* and ghi to intensify the flame.

Afterward, all the women in Babuji's house huddled together upstairs in the *chaubara*. An ageless woman from the troupe of professional mourners, who had a beard and a deep voice, stationed herself in front of them and began beating her breast, chanting, "Oh, mothers and sisters, he's left you! *Hai, hai!*"

"Hai, hai!" the women cried after her, beating their breasts.

"Oh, Ishwar Das, why have you left your home? *Hai, hai!*"

"*Hai, hai*—our beloved Ishwar Das is gone!"

"You have left your loved ones ever sorrowing. *Hai, hai!*"

"*Hai, hai!*"

Some of the women, the better to beat their breasts, tore off their blouses and threw a bedsheet over their shoulders. The atmosphere in the room was heavy and close, and the women, worn out by their exertions and tears, were dripping with perspiration.

"Oh, Ishwar Das, you have left your father and grandfather bereft!" wailed the bearded woman. "You have left your brothers and sisters bereft!"

"Our beloved Ishwar Das has left us. *Hai, hai!*"

"In the flower of manhood, a god-fearing, god-loving man, cut down in his prime! Oh, mothers and sisters, are your eyes dry so quickly? Are your hands so weak? Hearts so little? Grief so short?"

The bearded woman slapped her thighs and beat her breast faster and faster.

The women repeated her movements as if they were being drilled in grief by a sergeant. With a quick jerk of the hand, a woman wearing a sheet would toss aside her sheet long enough to slap her breast hard and expose the redness to her neighbors, now and again surreptitiously glancing over to size up her neighbors' welts.

Babuji's sister, Durga Devi, stole frequent glances at Mataji's chest to see if the redness revealed true grief or if she was only making a show of grief while secretly feeling relieved that one of her stepchildren had fallen.

Now Mataji, aware of Durga Devi's eyes on her, pounded her breast and secretly prayed to Goddess Durga to make her crimson from top to toe.

The chorus of lamentation for Ishwar Das lasted thirteen days. Less than a month after his death, the family received news that his twenty-three-year-old sister, Ratan Devi, her as yet unnamed infant son, and her daughter, Kunti, were all dead. They, too, had succumbed to influenza. And a new chorus of laments was begun.

A YEAR OR SO after Pali died of quinine poisoning, Bulaki Ram, who was eighty-six, contracted a fever, which was diagnosed as pneumonia. He then developed a lump on his neck, and began to have trouble swallowing, and moving his head. He also had trouble sleeping, because he could find no comfortable position in which to lay his head. Soon he became delirious, and after two weeks he died in his sleep.

In Kucha Kaghzian and the Fish Market, on the Circular Road opposite the Lahori Gate and the Shahalmi Gate, in the streets and bazaars of Lahore, Rawalpindi, Peshawar, Murree, and Kasur, people remembered Bulaki Ram as an enterprising bundleman, as a father with a mother's touch, as the tireless head of his family. Some of them had grown up hearing the warning "Goddess Lakshmi is fickle. She never stops with anyone for long," and as they watched Bulaki Ram's progress in the world they had marvelled at his steady good fortune. Some attributed it to the offerings he used to make to the poor, others to his not succumbing to the temptation to take a second wife.

From the time Babuji began earning his own livelihood, he had always turned all his income over to Bulaki Ram as a matter of course. "I'm the earner, and, Baba, you are the spender," he would say. And, indeed, Bulaki Ram had been free to spend the money any way he liked—to buy fruits and vegetables for the day's meals, to pay the children's school fees, to buy clothes and jewelry for his granddaughters. Babuji had never asked any questions, but whatever was left over at the end of the month he would lend out at a high rate of interest.

As long as Bulaki Ram was alive, no grandchild could step across the *daori* without being greeted, lifted, patted, and hugged by the old man. It was to him that the children always ran with their quarrels and demands; they knew Babuji mostly by his walking stick— the sound of it at the doorstep, the sight of it leaning inside the doorway—and understood that he had no time for them.

The moment a granddaughter was born, Bulaki Ram would start collecting a dowry for her. He would buy a clay coin bank for her and, when she was old enough to know about her dowry, would regularly give her a coin, and watch her dip it in the milk of a holy cow and deposit it in her bank. When the coin bank was full, he would empty it to add to the dowry, sometimes sitting an entire day by a jeweller to make

Bulaki Ram, Lahore, 1915

certain that a given piece was fashioned out of twenty-two-carat gold and that its workmanship was of high quality.

As soon as the neighbors heard that Bulaki Ram had died, they came to Babuji and set up a great clamor. They wanted him to hire a band of horns and drums to accompany his father to the cremation ground —to parade and serenade according to custom. "He lived to be a wise old man," a spokesman for the neighbors said. "He lived to see his grandchildren grow taller than he was. Such venerable men should be sent on their way with happy tunes in their ears."

"What idiocy!" Babuji burst out. "I've lost my father, and you want to sing and dance! They didn't have a band when I got married, and I am supposed to hire a band now!"

"You must get your head shaved as a sign of respect for your old father," the spokesman continued, ignoring Babuji's outburst as that of a grieving man who had temporarily taken leave of his senses. "You must get an impressive bier. The bier of someone like Bulaki Ram should be decorated with flags and coconuts, with many fruits and flowers. We must have some trimmings from the bier to give to our children as good-luck charms for long life."

Babuji declared angrily, in a tone that left no doubt of his meaning, that he would not have any music, would not have his head shaved, would not have an ornate bier, and would not even make any offerings to the gods. He was an Arya Samajist, and would not follow any of the Sanatan Dharmi customs. (Only five years earlier, when Ishwar Das died, the observance of

Sanatan Dharmi customs of professional mourning had been taken for granted in the house. Since then, the Arya Samaj and Babuji had become increasingly stubborn in their opposition to all forms of superstition and to all orthodox customs in both private and public life.)

Babuji and some close friends, accompanied only by a group of Arya Samajists singing hymns, carried Bulaki Ram's body to the cremation ground and placed it on the funeral pyre. Throughout the simple cremation ceremony, Babuji remained dry-eyed.

Back at home, the professional mourners had quietly gathered. Babuji had them chased out, and forbade Durga Devi, Malan, and Mataji to wail or beat their breasts. They could cry all they liked, but they must not mortify themselves in any way.

For days, many of the neighbors talked of nothing but Babuji's heartlessness. No band, not even one professional mourner, and his own wife forbidden to grieve as she liked for her father-in-law! Arya Samaj principles were all well and good, but was respect for a dead father to be sacrificed to them?

Babuji had little idea of the consternation he had caused all around him. Years later, he could remember only two or three disconnected moments: his father's body half sitting up on the pyre, as if to protest the ignominy of death; the mourners involuntarily stepping back, as if the stare of his father, the most loving of men, had already become, in their superstitious minds (Arya Samajists though they were), the evil eye; at home, Durga Devi garlanding the children with strings of cardamoms and almonds. (Cardamoms were used to ward off the evil eye, and almonds were talismans of life.) He remembered retreating to the little room next to his office, where he and his father had slept for fifteen years.

❧

BABUJI'S SISTER, Durga Devi, and her husband, Moti Ram, had three sons, Chuni Lal, Panna Lal, and Madan Lal, and two daughters, Ratan Devi and Vidyavati. By the time the last child, Madan Lal, was born, in 1914, Moti Ram had gone through all his father's savings.

Durga Devi turned for help to Babuji, who bought a little betel-nut-and-*pan* shop and made a gift of it to Moti Ram, took in the eldest son, Chuni Lal, and arranged to pay Durga Devi a monthly allowance in perpetuity. It is said that the shock of having to go every day to the shop and work there—Durga Devi saw to it that he did not squander her brother's bounty as he had squandered his father's—made Moti Ram an invalid. Although Durga Devi was now in and out of Babuji's house every day—she practically lived there—Chuni Lal was so incensed with his mother because of her treatment of his father that he refused to have much to do with her, or, for that matter, with either of his brothers or with his sisters. (Bulaki Ram lived to marry off Chuni Lal and Panna Lal, and when he died Babuji continued his support of Durga Devi, Madan Lal, and Vidyavati; Ratan Devi had died in the interval.)

Chuni Lal grew up to be a self-centered young man. He finished school and became a draftsman in an architect's office, got married, fathered four sons and two daughters, and built himself a house on Beadon Road, in the new city. Constructed on a plot of land only fifteen feet square, it was the smallest *pukka* house in the area, and therefore became something of a landmark.

Panna Lal and his wife, son, and five daughters lived as a "joint family" with Madan Lal and his wife, three sons, and two daughters, and with Durga Devi and Moti Ram, in a four-room house, also on Beadon Road. Panna Lal and Madan Lal, neither of whom had gone beyond the eighth standard in school, borrowed five hundred rupees from Babuji and rented a long room in Anarkali, curtaining off the back part of it for storage and filling the front with dolls, hair oil, socks, bandages, hairpins, soaps, combs, brushes, handker-chiefs, notepaper, and pencils. The two brothers were good businessmen, and the shop was such a success that they were able to pay back Babuji's loan, with interest, in a matter of months; in fact, the shop did so well that eventually they took on as a third partner Ram Chander, a brother of Madan Lal's wife. Ram Chander, who was unemployed, had been agitating for a share in the shop, and now he moved, with his wife and his several children, into the four-room house on Beadon Road.

The moment Ram Chander became a partner in the shop, he began to feel that the shop was only big enough for two, and that he should be one of the two. For years, he schemed how to "deal out" Panna Lal, so that "the two brothers-in-law might do business to-gether." The atmosphere in the shop became bitter.

One morning—the year was 1943—as Panna Lal was busy arranging boxes and unpacking new merchandise in the back of the shop, he called out to Ram Chander, "It's hot back here. Would you please go across to the vender and get me a glass of cold buttermilk?"

"Yes, Brother," Ram Chander answered obligingly. "I'll be back with it before you have to lift another box."

As soon as Panna Lal drank the glass of buttermilk, he collapsed on the floor and died.

Cries went up among some sharp-witted customers standing in front of the shop—cries that were picked up by the crowd in the bazaar:

"He's been poisoned!"

"His brother-in-law has poisoned him!"

"He is dead in his shop—of buttermilk!"

Ram Chander tried to run out of the shop, but the crowd, pressing to see what had happened inside, blocked his way. Many assumed—though there wasn't any definite proof—that Ram Chander had in fact murdered his brother-in-law.

"I've lost my brother," Madan Lal wailed, "and you don't have the pity to leave us alone!"

Eventually, the crowd dispersed.

It was feared that Panna Lal's wife would prosecute Ram Chander and break up the joint family, but when she heard of her husband's death she said nothing. She quietly cremated her husband and quietly mourned him for many days.

In time, she called Madan Lal's wife to her side

and said, "Sister-in-Law, I bear no grudge against you or your loved ones—against your brother, Ram Chander. What has happened has happened. There's no use in taking revenge or having the family broken up with enmity. My wish is that we—all three families—should continue to live together."

"Sister-in-Law," said Madan Lal's wife, "if my brother, Ram Chander, is responsible for Brother-in-Law Panna Lal's death, I want you to prosecute him."

Madan Lal joined them, and said, "Sister-in-Law, prosecute him if you think he's guilty. Take him to the court and let the judge decide. Blood is one thing, crime another."

Panna Lal's wife wouldn't hear of it.

For many years—long after the deaths of Durga Devi and Moti Ram, and even after Partition, when Babuji and all his relatives were uprooted and fled to Delhi—the families of Panna Lal, Madan Lal, and Ram Chander continued to live together. In Delhi, they started a wholesale business, making and selling mirrors, and eventually built a house in Punjabi Bagh, within bicycling distance of the house where Babuji had resettled. (Chuni Lal and his wife and children also migrated to Delhi, but, as before, they stayed apart from the rest of the family, meeting them only on important family occasions.)

Whenever Babuji, toward the end of his life, remembered Durga Devi, he would mention with pride his role in helping her and her family, and he could point with delight to the fact that one of Durga Devi's grandsons was a chartered accountant and two of her granddaughters were university graduates.

As a STUDENT, Babuji had started taking an interest in politics, and in 1893 he attended the annual session of the recently formed Indian National Congress Party. Its annual sessions were essentially debating pageants staged by some Indian lawyers and academicians and a few British reformers, who advocated more rights and freedoms for the few educated Indians. Babuji attended the 1893 session—the first to be held in Lahore—as a volunteer. He did little more than show the Congress dignitaries to their places and try to meet the "grand old man" of Indian politics, Dadabhai Naoroji. All the same, he was fired up by being in the same room as such dignitaries, and the more so when he learned that the liberal goals of the Congress were the same as those of the Arya Samaj.

In 1898, because of his unflagging espousal of Arya Samaj principles, Babuji was elected Secretary of the Meat Arya Samaj, now called the College Party, and in 1900 he was made a member of the Managing Committee of the D.A.V. College Trust Society, which handled requests for financial support from practically every Arya Samaj college and school in the Punjab. To Babuji, Arya Samaj increasingly seemed an island of probity, patriotism, and high-mindedness amid the moral depravity of Indian bazaars and *gullis,* on the one hand, and the pretensions of British cricket fields and churches, on the other. He became known for his attacks on orthodox Hindus, who condemned the Arya Samaj for its rejection of two thousand years of Hindu religious tradition and its acceptance of corrupt, seductive Westernism. He also became known for his attacks on Anglicized Indians, who dismissed Arya Samaj as a childish attempt to update animism with modern rationalism, and as being, in its way, as superstitious and idolatrous as the "decadent" religion it sought to reform.

In 1910, he stood as a candidate for one of the three elected seats in the governing body of Punjab University, known as the Senate. Founded in 1882, Punjab University was the only channel through which a Punjabi could hope to join the civil or military establishment or participate in the political and cultural life of the province. Although Babuji could easily have been appointed to the Senate, he objected to such a perquisite on principle, contending that appointments involved string-pulling and influence-peddling, while election by one's equals conferred respect and honor. As it turned out, he garnered more votes than anyone else, partly because D.A.V. College was the largest constituent of the university, and the votes were cast by "registered graduates," alumni in good standing. Altogether, he served as a Senate Fellow for six successive five-year terms—three of them in the Syndicate, a smaller and more powerful governing body within the Senate. In 1912, he became vice-president of the D.A.V. College Trust Society, under Mahatma Hans Raj, its president. (Hans Raj, his old teacher, had become known as Mahatma, which means "great soul," in part because he had renounced a distinguished, financially secure career in the civil service for the lowly position of a college teacher, which carried only an honorarium, and in part because of his intellectual contribution to

Mamaji churning milk, Lahore, 1931

the college.) In 1918, Babuji succeeded Hans Raj as president of the Trust Society, and paid this tribute to the Mahatma, who had been his mentor since his student days: "Mahatma Hans Raj has tended to the root of all political troubles—want of character in a man. In his opinion, strong, honest, truthful men with character cannot remain political slaves for long. He has believed all along that if Indians were to become physically strong, religiously pure, and socially open-minded, their political emancipation would follow. Thanks to Mahatma Hans Raj—and to Swami Dayanand—every Arya Samajist is an iconoclast, and a religious purist, who stands out in any crowd as a man of consequence. The simple Hindu greeting of '*Namaste*' ["I greet you in the name of God"] opens the door of brotherly love and hospitality among total strangers all over India."

Within the year, the brotherly love that Babuji had spoken of turned to enmity between the followers of the two leading College Party apostles of Swami Dayanand—Mahatma Hans Raj and Lala Lajpat Rai. When Swami Dayanand died, thirty-six years earlier, he had left behind thirteen apostles, chosen for their *tan* (self), their *man* (mind), and their *dhan* (philanthropy). Babuji was not one of these apostles, but he had come to think of himself—in the course of his nearly thirty years' association with Mahatma Hans Raj—as the fourteenth apostle. The enmity between Mahatma Hans Raj and Lala Lajpat Rai was touched off by Mahatma Gandhi's call, in 1919, for a national civil-disobedience campaign to protest the British refusal to grant Indian home rule, and by the repressive measures taken by the British to quell the Indian protest that followed. In response to Gandhi's call, students and teachers at colleges everywhere went out on strike, but Babuji, with the support of Mahatma Hans Raj, would not close down D.A.V. College, on the ground that Arya Samaj was essentially a religious movement, not a political one. Besides, Babuji was concerned about jeopardizing the careers of teachers and students. He felt, too, that Gandhi's campaign of noncoöperation pandered to the anti-social, selfish, anarchic traits in the Indian character—traits that he felt had allowed the British, natural champions of law and order and united effort, to subjugate India in the first place. Babuji therefore saw Gandhi as an antediluvian force, and a pernicious one, and made his stand on twin principles *cum* slogans: "Politics has no place in educational institutions" and "I am a coöperator."

Lala Lajpat Rai, or Sher-e-Punjab (the Lion of the Punjab), as he was popularly called (he was deemed by the Punjabis to have proved his leonine qualities by, among other things, standing simultaneously for two seats in the Punjab Legislative Assembly and winning them both), believed, as Babuji and Mahatma Hans Raj had themselves once believed, that religion embraced everything—politics, social life, economics—and he had a greater following in Lahore and the Punjab than any other leader. In fact, popular feeling in Lahore ran so strongly in favor of Lala Lajpat Rai and Mahatma Gandhi that Babuji, Mahatma Hans Raj, and their associates felt they were under siege.

One hot evening, Babuji was sitting in his office at home correcting a draft of a letter to the *Tribune*—a sort of Bible of the Punjabi establishment—in which he

attacked Lala Lajpat Rai's views. He was distracted by
the approaching sound of a group of men chanting
something. He was surprised; under martial law—imposed in response to Mahatma Gandhi's civil-disobedience campaign—all public gatherings had been
banned. He looked out and saw the silhouettes of men
marching in a group toward his house. They were waving black flags and shouting, "*Hai, hai,* toady *bachcha*
[child]! *Hai, hai!*" Babuji was indignant. It was one of
the mock funeral processions for which Lahore had become notorious before the imposition of martial law,
and the men were marching in *his* "funeral." Babuji
picked up his walking stick and went out. He shook
the stick and shouted, "You fools! You idiots! When
will you ever learn?" Then he marched back into the
house and shut the door against the mob.

Despite the closing of other colleges, Babuji managed to keep D.A.V. College open. Martial law finally
broke the strike at the other colleges, and all the students and teachers at the university returned to their
classes. Babuji and Mahatma Hans Raj were elated at
having struck a blow for Arya Samaj and for the separation of education from politics; they also savored the
defeat of Lala Lajpat Rai on the issue.

In time, even Babuji and Mahatma Hans Raj fell
out. The occasion of their quarrel was a difference of
opinion over the appointment of a Sanskrit professor at
the college, in 1924. Mahatma Hans Raj supported a
relative, on the ground that he was the best-qualified
man for the position, while Babuji favored another
candidate, on the ground that he was better qualified.
Babuji wrote Mahatma Hans Raj a stern letter accusing

him of nepotism. Mahatma Hans Raj's man nevertheless got the appointment. This conflict marked the beginning of Babuji's disillusionment with the Arya Samaj movement. As time went on, he came to feel not only that the movement had fallen into the hands of a self-serving clique but also that its members were hypocrites. (Aside from preaching merit and indulging in nepotism, they preached widow marriage but took care not to marry widows themselves, with the result that the fate of widows remained as bad as ever.)

Around 1930, Babuji withdrew from Arya Samaj— his faith for almost forty years.

❦

AS A MAN OF CONSEQUENCE in Lahore—in university circles and at the High Court bar—Babuji went about in a victoria, a curtained carriage, driven by a syce and drawn by a chestnut-colored horse named Firefly. The horse died in 1916, and thereafter the carriage was drawn by a brown-and-white horse, which Babuji also named Firefly. The victoria was so well known that on seeing it people would step aside to let it pass. Returning home from the court, Babuji would often have the syce pull up by the edge of Anarkali and then have him dash in to pick up a tin of Babuji's favorite glucose biscuits. In the evening, Babuji would go out for long drives through the gardens. He would take deep breaths, as if he couldn't get used to the idea that he was smelling clean, fragrant air. When he wasn't riding in his victoria, it stood conspicuously outside the High Court or the Shahalmi Gate house.

In addition to Firefly and the victoria, Babuji kept a cow, which was tethered in his back courtyard. Each day, the first draught of milk was put aside for him. It was boiled and mixed with Ovaltine and served to him in bed morning and evening, always in the same cup and saucer—a ribbed, pastel-colored English-china teacup with a handle that fitted Babuji's forefinger exactly.

Babuji laid down strict rules for family gatherings —births, engagements, weddings, festivals, funerals. The ceremonies connected with such gatherings all had to be simple. (The women of the house did not abandon the more elaborate Sanatan Dharmi rituals, but they performed them in secret in the *chaubara*.) He was very particular that on every occasion all the "kittens," as he called the girls of the house, and all the "naughty boys," as he called the boys, should be around him, and that every relative from his first or second marriage, close or distant, should be invited. He took pleasure in the continuity represented by such gatherings, which always included, for instance, Devaki's only surviving relative, a brother, and Ratan Devi's husband, Bishan Das, and her only surviving child, a daughter named Kaushalya. Devaki's brother would come with his wife, two daughters, and only son, and Babuji would never fail to remark that the brother of poor Devaki had risen to be manager of the Bombay branch of the Punjab National Bank, or that anyone who saw Kaushalya couldn't help noticing her bright face—how easily and how often she laughed, as though she had never known tears.

From the moment Babuji had his Ovaltine in the morning to the moment he had his Ovaltine at night—winter, spring, summer, monsoon, and autumn—he liked a certain order to his life, for it provided an anchor in the turbulence of calamity and change that threatened to overwhelm him.

❧

BABUJI'S DIARY—his stark record of births and marriages, deaths and calamities, vacations and returns—continues:

1925

12/1. Born a daughter at 3 a.m. named Vimla. (Lohri Day.) [Vimla, Babuji's fifteenth child and Mataji's eleventh, was born in the middle of the winter festival called Lohri, when people can be seen in the courtyards of their houses, on rooftops, on roadsides—in any open place—warming themselves in front of blazing fires, tossing oilseeds into the fires, and munching *raoris,* or crystallized-sugar sweets.]

28/3. Lakshman's tonsils removed. [Lakshman, Babuji's third son by Mataji, was then ten years old.]

Bhagwan Das passed his LL.B. Exam. [Bhagwan Das, Babuji's second son by Devaki, was then twenty-five; he was rather old to be qualifying as a lawyer, but he had taken seven years, instead of the usual four, to get his B.A., in part because of ill health.]

31/10. Shanti betrothed to Dr. Amolak Ram Mehta. [This is my father.]

Shagan given on 1-11-25.

31/10. Bhagwan Das engaged to daughter of L. Ganga Ram Soni.

Shanti married to D. Amolak Ram. May God bless the union.

Milni was 5/12. [Milni is an occasion when each relative of the bridegroom ceremonially meets his counterpart in the bride's family.]

Ghori was 6/12. [Ghori is a ceremony in which the bridegroom, holding a sword, rides to the bride's house on a horse. The sword and the horse suggest a warrior come to take his woman, but they have long been merely symbolic. Since most modern bridegrooms can neither ride a horse nor wield a sword, the horse is usually a tractable mare or a gelding, and the sword is hung on the bridegroom like an ornament.] & marriage on 7th morning.

1926

30 May. Presided over the D.A.V. College Prize Distribution.

Agreed to purchase House at 16 Mozang Road from Seth Ram Parshad for 36250 rupees. [Mozang, a spacious, open road, was in the new city, within walking distance of the Mall Road and Lawrence Gardens. Babuji lived there until Partition.]

Receipt of Indemnity Bond of above house registered after great worry & trouble.

—Shifted to the new house on Mozang Road on Guru Nanak's birthday. His Blessings invoked in all humility. [Guru Nanak was the fifteenth-century founder of the Sikh religion, and so one of the most eminent Punjabis.]

Bhagwan Das's name called for by High Court for consideration for nomination of S. Judge [sub-judge].

18/12. Selected for interview but [ink here is faded and illegible] to be elected. Bhagwan Das disappointed at his result & felt very miserable for sometime. Bhagwan Das took it keenly—His will be done—I am a *confirmed fatalist*.

22/12. Shanti gave birth to a daughter at 4.10 pm— Amolak Ram here—named Promila.

Lakshman got measles & so did Pushpa a week after. [Pushpa, Babuji's fourteenth child, was then a girl of four.] Passed Xmas days in Lahore anxiously & in a dejected mood.

Bhagwan Das's marriage fixed for 23/1 was postponed owing to illness of his fiance in August & Sept.

1927

Improved & added 2 rooms to new Kothi on Mozang Road. Bhagwan Das's marriage passed off very successfully. It took place at Ludhiana [a small city in the Punjab] on 17/4. [Bridegroom's] Party consisting of 70 persons was comfortably lodged & sumptuously feasted by R. B. Lala Ganga Ram. [R. B., or Rai Bahadur, was the highest title that the Viceroy could bestow on distinguished Indians.] Ghori ceremony took place at Lahore on 16th evening & was well attended.

Garden Party held on 26th April was a good success. May God grant the married couple success & prosperity in life.

Bhagwan's mother-in-law Mrs. Ganga Ram died after a fortnight of his marriage & before ladies' Milni could take place. Very sad & serious loss for R. B. Ganga Ram.

Bhagwan Das went to Kashmir & stayed there with his wife in Company of his father in law's family.

I went with family to Kasauli to live in "North-View." Shanti & Amolak Ram were there for a short period.

1928

Received the title of Rai Bahadur on New Years Day.
Friends appreciated it very much & gave Dinners & Parties.
Recommendation of H. Crt [High Court] made 18 months
back was accepted by Govt. this time & to me the news
came most unexpectedly.

Nominated Director of P.N. [Punjab National] Bank
by the G. [Government] Board. Agreed to this at the request of M. [Mahatma] Hans Raj & other friends.

Yaghopavit ceremony of Dwarka & Lakshman performed on 27/1 Basant Day. [Yaghopavit is a rite-of-pas-
sage ceremony for high-caste orthodox Hindus during
which a thread is ceremonially tied around the neck and
the left shoulder—or sometimes only around the wrist—of
a young man, a thread he is supposed to wear for life.
Dwarka and Lakshman—the two surviving sons of Babuji
and Mataji—who were fifteen and twelve, wore the
thread only around their wrists and only for the length of
the ceremony.] Rain came in & interfered with arrangements.

Born a son to Bhagwan Das at 5.17 a.m. on 10.4.
Named Om Parkash.

Made further additions & improvements in the Mozang
House—June-July.

Bhagwan Das went to Dalhousie with his wife. I went
to Dharamsala with Dwarka & Lakshman for 2 weeks.
Stayed with Mr. Mehr Chand & enjoyed my trip. [Mehr
Chand Mahajan was a prominent Arya Samajist, like so
many of Babuji's close friends, and was a judge of the
Punjab High Court.]

1929

Born a daughter to Bhagwan Das's wife 6th April at
——————. [She was named Bawa.]

Bhagwan Das had rheumatic fever of a persistent type for full one month, due to his [illegible word] habits. Passed very anxious times. By Gods' grace he got well under Ayurvedic treatment, which proved very efficacious.

1930

Mundan Ceremony of Bhagwan Das's Children pereformed on Baisakhi Day, 13th April Sunday. [Mundan is a sort of christening ceremony, in which the child's hair is shaved off.]

Dinner to Ladies.

Dear Moti Sagar passed off suddenly on ——— November. He was in Court, attended P.N. Bank meeting where he felt ill. On reaching home he expired. An old lifelong friend of boyhood gone! With all his weaknesses Moti Sagar was Jewel of a man. Good though greedy. Sincere & inoffensive toward all. [Moti Sagar was a judge of the Punjab High Court.]

1931

A son born to Shanti at my house on Mozang Road on 25th April noon at 12.10 pm. Named Om Parkash. [Bhagwan Das's son was also named Om Parkash, but he was known by his nickname, Kuku. In the diary, there is no mention of the earlier births of Mamaji's second and third daughters, Nirmila and Urmila, although Nirmila was also born in Babuji's Mozang Road house.]

Went up to Simla with family. Stayed at Simla for 6 weeks in Dr. Amolak Ram's house "Glenarquhart" on Anandale Road. Enjoyed the trip. [Babuji would go up to Simla with his family every summer and stay with Mamaji and Daddyji for a month or two.]

Another friend gone. R. B. Dhanpat Rai passed away after 3 month's illness—in Sept at Lahore—with all his weaknesses he was a shrewd businessman & an obliging friend. May his soul rest in peace. [Rai Bahadur Dhanpat Rai and Babuji were close, and speculated in land together.]

Munshi Gujarmal, my faithfull servant & friend for thirty years, died in Septr after retiring from my service in Nov 29. Passed his last days in trouble. A good soul.

Nominated a member of the Lahore Municipality by Dr. G. C. Narang. In view of Communalism & inefficiency prevailing in the Municipality I doubt very much if my presence as a member will improve matters. [Sir Gokal Chand Narang was a barrister who, like Babuji, appeared before the Punjab High Court.]

Improved Mozang Road house by adding one bedroom & bath for Bhagwan Das and by sinking a tube well.

1932

Shanti's illness from Bronchitis which she contracted at Delhi continued here throughout winter. She went to Delhi in March & to Simla in April where she improved.

Dwarka failed to pass his B.A. & felt his failure very much. This was unexpected.

Dwarka & Lakshman went to Simla in July & stayed with Shanti.

Built new house as part of 16 Mozang Road. It cost about Rs 6000/ Finished September.

Completed my sixtieth year on 25/11.

Bhagwan Das appointed a Law Reader temporarily. He felt very nervous & funky over it in the beginning. [The Law College, where Bhagwan Das was to be a teacher, consisted of one building, a principal, and a small clerical staff, and the teaching was done entirely by practicing lawyers on a part-time basis.]

Sent a memorandum & appeared as a witness before Punjab University Enquiry Commission on 26.11.

Presided over Brahm Mahavidyala Prize Distribution & made a short speech on the work of the Arya Samaj & its failure on religious & spiritual side. [Brahm Mahavidyala was a branch of the Arya Samaj which trained lecturers to propagate the principles of the movement.]

A bad year financially—though paid highest Income Tax for the last year.

1933

Shanti's health continues indifferent. She spent winter here before going to Simla, where she improved by God's grace.

My sister's daughter Vidyavati married to L. Bishan Das, Clerk in Imp. [Imperial] Bank.

Bhagwan Das re-appointed part-time Reader in Law College for one year.

Children suffered from Chicken-pox & Measles in April & May. I too had a boil trouble.

Last year 32.33 proved poorest from prof. [professional] point of view. Prof. income gone down. His will be done. Having experienced real stringency in early age am Contented & feel gratefull to Him for all I have. [Here follows a proverb written in Devanagari script which means "All days cannot be the same."]

Wife ill of haemorrage for over 2 months recovered under Hakim's treatment. [A Hakim is a Muslim practitioner of the Unani system of medicine.]

Kaushalya passed her Matric this time & Dwarka was successful in his B.A., but Lakshman failed in F.Sc [First Science examination, leading up to Bachelor of Science degree] by 1 mark each in Physics & Chemistry.

Spent Vacations 6 weeks at Pehalgam & Srinagar

(Kashmir) with family. This was my 3rd visit to Kashmir. On the whole the stay & the trip was pleasant & satisfactory.

1934

In Jan. Amolak Ram continued ill at Delhi from Dec. 33 & came here on 2/2—remained in Mayo Hospital for 2 weeks.

Born a son to Shanti here on 21-3 at 10.5 a.m. Amolak Ram here. Named Ved Parkash. [This is Babuji's record of my birth.]

Thank God Amolak Ram recovered & joined duty on 1st April.

Dharam passed Matric by private study. [Dharam, Babuji's eleventh child and Mataji's seventh, was then a girl of sixteen.] Lakshman fell ill before Exam. Appeared & passed in all subjects except English. Joined Hailey College. Passed his F.A. in Supplementary.

Bhagwan's wife & Bhagwan's daughter Bawa got Diphtheria. Thank God it was not worse.

Dwarka went to Delhi & started business with Mr. Gandharva Sen Kashyap. May God bless him.

1935

Addl. rooms begun in [the date is missing] were completed & let in March. Good investment.

Bishan Das [the husband of Babuji's second deceased daughter Ratan Devi] anxious about Kaushalya's engagement. Trying our best to secure a good match.

Reelected a Fellow for 6th time.

19/1. Kaushalya engaged to Mr. Somnath.

28/3. Went to Delhi visiting Kurekshetra on the way. There negotiations with R. S. [Rai Sahib] Soi for engagement of Dharam with his second son Mr. Jagmohan began.

Shagan of Dharam given at Delhi on 15th April by her mother. [Dharam was perhaps the plainest of Babuji's daughters, and the first one to be engaged after Mamaji. There was much jubilation.] May God shower his blessings.

Dharam failed in her Inter Exam.

Marriage of Kaushalya with Somnath s/o [son of] L. Madho Ram Passi of Lahore took place on 6/8. Everything passed off successfully. Thank God Bishan Das & I relieved of this duty. May Almighty Lord bless the Union.

Dharam's marriage fixed for 24.2.37. May God shower his blessings.

Dwarka separated from M.G. [Mr. Gandharva] Sen Kashyap from 1.10.35 & continued his business independently.

On Divali Day Lakshman Das joined Central Life & General Assurance Company Ltd. as Partner. [Divali, the festival of light, is the day that commemorates the restoration of Rama's kingdom to him after his long exile and his victory over the demon Ravana.] May God Bless the Enterprise.

1936

January. Amolak Ram fell ill in Calcutta of typhoid. Passed most anxious time but, God in His mercy restored him to health.

1937

Dharam's marriage took place on —— Feby at night. May God bless the Union.

Barat [bridegroom's party] came from Delhi & were accommodated at late L. Harkishen Lal's house.

Everything passed off successfully & satisfactorily.

Just before Milni time it rained & upset arrangements but it stopped at the Milni hour. Barat & Doli [ceremonial carrying away of the bride] left on ———— evening.

Dr. Amolak Ram left for England on leave. Shanti & her family stayed in our flat up to 8/8. A girl born to Shanti on 5th July at 6.10 a.m. [This was my younger sister Usha.]

A son born to Kaushalya, my granddaughter, at Ferozepore on —— July at 7 p.m.

Lakshman Das passed his B. Com. [Bachelor of Commerce] Exam. He was in Kashmir for a month with Bhagwan Das & his family.

1938

The year opened with serious illness of Ved Parkash younger son of Shanti who was brought here from Gujrat on 21/1 suffering from a bad type of Meningitis. He was seriously ill for 2 months. His life was saved but dear boy lost his eyesight! What a tragedy! Ways of Providence are mysterious & one has to submit.

9 4/38. A son was born to Dharam at 6 a.m. in Lahore. On a/o [account of] delayed delivery she had to be removed to Lady Willingdon Maternity Hospital.

August—Went to Dalhousie for a week & stayed with Bakshi Tek Chandji. [Bakshi Tek Chand was a leading lawyer who became a judge of the Punjab High Court.]

Lakshman Das came back from Delhi & joined P. N. Bank as a paid apprentice in November.

1939

L. Moti Ram Seth my brother in law died on 12 Nov after protracted & painfull illness. Even amputation of his

leg proved useless to check the disease. His will be done.
Shanti's little son aged 2½ months died on —— Dec.
after a short illness. Was congenitally weak & had defective
heart. [The baby was a victim of X-ray treatments that
Mamaji had received during pregnancy for her bronchial
asthma.] Shanti naturally felt the loss keenly after poor
Ved's blindness.

1940

Second son born to Dharam here on 28th June at 6
a.m. Dwarka's marriage proposals fell through as he could
not make up his mind.

Did not want to press him in a matter which was
mainly his own concern.

Dwarka had to sell his Delhi business which was
running at a loss.

Being a fatalist no use blaming him for this result. A
loss of Rs 10,000/ or so.

Rs 101 received for Patri. [A horoscope. Dwarka's first
would-be father-in-law must have had one cast at the time
of his daughter's engagement to Dwarka, and then returned it along with the engagement offering of a hundred
and one rupees.]

War clouds hung over Europe causing anxiety to all.
Purchased a gun after getting a License.

1941

1/2. Basant Day.

Dwarka Das betrothed to Kumari [caste honorific]
Santosh daughter of Lala Pokhar Das. Shagan received 12
noon. May God bless the engagement.

In May Dharam came here on short visit but got ill.

Promila, Urmila, Mamaji, and Nirmila, Simla, 1932

Septic fever for a few days & then Pneumonia kept her in bed for over a month.

Left for Delhi at the end of July but there got renal colic & muscular pains. Continues ill.

Dwarka's marriage fixed for 10/10.

Pushpa engaged to Mr. Payare Lal Tandon, Auditor at Cawnpore, a nephew of Mr. M. L. Tannan, Late Secty P.N. Bank. Well spoken of by all. Shagan given by Dwarka at Cawnpore on 9/41. Rs 500/—cash. May God shower his blessings upon the engagement.

Dwarka's marriage on 15/10 on a/o blackout, Barat token.

Garden party on 17th. Everything passed off successfully. Everyone satisfied. May God bless the Union.

Bhagwan Das had another disappointment due to his being let down by friends who had pledged support to him for post of At. [Assistant] Registrar in the Punjab Uty. I feel disgusted at the duplicity & hypocracy of friends. [The "friends" must have been people whom Babuji had served with in the university Senate, but it is not clear whether they could have done much for Bhagwan Das, given his university record. In any event, it is interesting that, at least in the case of Bhagwan Das, Babuji should have set aside his principle of job-by-merit for the expediency of job-by-paternal-intervention.]

1942

Pushpa married to Mr. Payare Lal Tandon on 4th March. Barat consisted of over 150 guests who were entertained to Dinner after the Milni.

Next day it rained very heavily & Doli left at 9 am when it was drizzling. Ladies lunch & Milni had to take place indoors.

Another bolt from the blue. Dear Kuku son of Bhag-wan Das suffered from fever for 32 days and died on Sunday night at 2 a.m. on 25th October. The boy was not only a pet of the family but a favourite of all who knew him. He made friends all around whether his juniors or seniors in age. I had cremated my three sons but knew not that I shall live to do the same with my oldest grandson. I am as much stupefied today as I was in October 1918 when I had to record the death of Ishwar Das. In spite of study & thinking of the problem of Life & Death I am as ignorant today as I was in 1918.

HERE THERE IS A BREAK in the diary, and what fol-lows is "Investments & Private accounts etc.," but the entire page has a line through it, probably because the accounts were liquidated.

VI

BRIDE

M MAMAJI WAS BORN IN THE SHAHALMI GATE HOUSE, on the sixteenth of August, 1908, at 7 A.M., and was named Shanti Devi (Peace Goddess). The women of the neighborhood beat their breasts and cried, "*Hai, hai!* A daughter has come to Babuji!" That was the way women greeted the birth of a girl in any family. Occasionally, if a girl's birth coincided with a stroke of luck, such as an increase in her father's salary, the women would say, for example, "Look! She came and brought good luck, for his salary has been increased," and for the rest of that girl's life the stroke of luck would be remembered and attributed to her blessing. But, failing any such happy coincidence, it was believed that a girl would cast a shadow on her family all her life.

Mamaji brought no particular stroke of luck, but the women in Babuji's house refrained from showing grief, because they were afraid of Babuji and his Arya Samaj principles. However, when Mamaji was a year old, and her brother, Narinjan Das, died of diphtheria, Babuji's sister, Durga Devi, was heard to mutter, "Look! She came into the world and her brother died." When Mamaji was two and her sister, Sumitra, also died of diphtheria, Mamaji's reputation as a girl who brought bad luck was confirmed. And then, when she was ten, her half brother Ishwar Das, to whom she was deeply attached, died of influenza, and Mamaji grew up thinking that she really did bring bad luck.

Still, Mamaji was pretty from birth and always had

about her an air of health and freshness. From the moment Bulaki Ram first took her in his arms, she was his favorite, and as long as he was alive no one could look askance at her in his presence. Often, when he saw her, he commented on her irresistible smile and her fat cheeks; he nicknamed her Ghuloo (Chubby), and the name stuck to her into adolescence.

When Mamaji was seven or eight, she was entered in Maharani Burdwan School, a quarter of a mile inside the Shahalmi Gate. With two or three other girls, she would skip to school every morning and skip home every afternoon. When she was eleven or twelve and could no longer go about in public with her head uncovered, Babuji's *munshi* would accompany her to school and back. She remembers little about her school. To her it always seemed a foreign place, without purpose, to which she was sent because she was too young to be married and run a house. Indeed, the moment she stepped inside the door of her own house and dropped her books on a chair Mataji would call down to her from the kitchen, "Come here and give me a hand!" Somehow, through the crying of babies, the clatter of feet going up and down the stairs, and the slamming of doors, Mataji would always hear the sounds of Mamaji's return. Mamaji was immediately put to work picking stones out of the rice or lentils, scrubbing the kitchen floor, or feeding babies. She doesn't remember ever once being asked "How was your day at school?" or "What did you do today?" The household tasks pulled and tugged at her.

Mamaji does remember that when she was in fifth

standard she was much excited because she was given a part in a school play. It was actually a pantomime skit, with two characters—a rustic Punjabi girl and the British governor's wife. Mamaji was cast as the rustic girl, and her friend Krishna as the governor's wife. The rustic girl was awkward and self-conscious, the governor's wife relaxed and self-confident. While the rustic girl was being taught ballroom dancing by the governor's wife, she caught her heel in the wide cuff of her pajama trousers, tripped, and fell, spraining her ankle. With characteristic British aplomb, the governor's wife thereupon produced a first-aid kit from under her hoopskirt and bandaged the Punjabi girl's ankle. The skit, which lasted just a few minutes, was a great success, and Mamaji and Krishna were the stars of their class. Mamaji felt she had never before been so happy.

One day not long afterward, as she was standing on the school veranda, she got her first monthly period. She didn't understand what was happening to her. She feared that she was dying. Krishna, noticing the look of terror on Mamaji's face, took her aside. Mamaji went home to Mataji in tears. She was fourteen. Strange as it may seem, although she was in constant contact with her mother and grandmother, and was a constant witness of womanly matters, she was told nothing about them and she asked no questions, with the result that she grew up in complete ignorance of her own body. A few days later, Mamaji failed a test. She thinks that it was a test in geography, since she could never quite get it straight where Peshawar was. Babuji happened to hear of the failure, and he said to Bulaki

Ram, in Mamaji's presence, "I have been thinking for some time now that Ghuloo is too old to be out in the *gullis*. She is educated enough—she can keep household accounts and write a letter. What use is there in filling her head with more studies? In the end, she's only going to get married." Bulaki Ram did not object. He had heard a rumor that a couple of Taxali Gate girls had been converted to Christianity at the school.

The next day, as Mamaji was leaving for school, Babuji stopped her, told her she was not meant for books, and sent her back upstairs. Mamaji felt sad at being taken out of school, because it meant that she would not be able to see many of her school friends, but it never occurred to her to protest the change or to ask why it had been made; she simply assumed that she had been taken out because of her monthly period. When she confided her surmise to Krishna one evening, Krishna laughed. "You silly goose!" she said. "I got my monthly period a year ago, and my father is planning to send me to college."

Babuji did not want his oldest living daughter to forget everything she had learned at school, for he wanted to marry her to a Hindu gentleman, so he engaged an Anglo-Indian woman named Mrs. Humphrey to come once a week, sit with Mamaji in the *chaubara,* and drill her in simple English sentences:

"Would you like a cup of tea?"

"Yes, thank you, I would like a cup of tea."

Years after Mamaji was married to my father—or Daddyji, as we children called him—he asked her, "What school did you go to?"

"I don't remember," she said. "It was called something like Rani School or Bard School."

"Maharani Burdwan School!" he exclaimed. The name no longer meant anything to her, but for him it conjured up a world of trouble and waste. "The school has an interesting history," he began. She listened, because he had a way of making everything into a story. "It was named after a Punjabi girl who married the Maharaja of Burdwan and went to live in his remote princely state near Bengal. They had a daughter, and when the time came for her to marry, the Maharaja gave the princess's hand to Nand Lal Khanna, who was the brother of a friend of mine at Government College. In fact, he was the youngest of the five handsome Khanna brothers of Lahore—they all wanted to marry the princess, but Nand Lal Khanna's horoscope tallied with hers. The Maharaja of Burdwan used his influence to get his son-in-law accepted as an Indian Civil Service Probationer, and no sooner were they married than the government sent him to England for the required I.C.S. examination. There he fell into bad company and learned to drink. He had come from a modest family and wasn't used to riches. He failed his examination and returned to Burdwan in disgrace. His wife didn't like the drink on his breath, and she would see him only infrequently, and then only at fixed times. He complained to her parents, but they told him that she had a delicate constitution and that seeing him was too much of a strain for her. He became demented with misery and drink, and the Maharaja sent him out of his princely state with a little pension." Daddyji concluded with an Urdu saying: "The truth is that neither the friendship nor the enmity of the rich is agreeable."

At the time, Mamaji felt thrilled that he knew so much about her school, but she soon forgot the story. A couple of years after Partition, Daddyji and Mamaji were walking along Connaught Circus in New Delhi when, suddenly, Daddyji said, "Look, there is the Khanna boy, the son-in-law of the Maharaja of Burdwan." Mamaji saw a shrunken man stumbling along the sidewalk, looking neither to right nor to left, oblivious of people, carts, and dustbins. Daddyji had to tell her the Burdwan story all over again.

She said that though she had forgotten the story, she could never forget the moral—that the company of rich people was dangerous—and she reminded Daddyji (as she had at intervals during their married life) that he hadn't always managed to remember it himself.

It was soon after Mamaji was taken out of school that Bulaki Ram died. Without his presence in the house, Mamaji felt frightened and unprotected. While she was growing up, Babuji was so deeply immersed in his law practice and in the Arya Samaj that he did not give her or anyone else much attention. To her he remained a distant, awesome figure. Each day, as soon as she and the other children heard what they called "his stick's tuk-tuk," they would vanish. In regard to him, she developed a *hauwa* (literally, "fear of a demon"). Moreover, Bhagwan Das, Babuji's eldest surviving son, who was now twenty-three, had grown into the proverbial disgruntled stepson. With Bulaki Ram out of the way, he discovered that he had new power over his father's second family—especially his stepmother and his eldest half sister. He had enrolled in Government College, and some mornings, just at the time Babuji was leaving for the court, Bhagwan Das would set out for his classes—with a great show of books and papers—only to return after an hour or two. But more often than not he would say he was ill and would stay at home, demanding attention—calling for Mamaji to bring him now a cup of Ovaltine, now a hot-water bottle. He acted as if he were the only rooster in the chicken coop—and so, in a sense, he was, since Babuji spent so little time in the house. Bhagwan Das would hover around, alternately pulling Mamaji up short and flattering her. He would stand in the kitchen watching her cut up vegetables, and laugh if her knife missed the tip of the carrot or if her eyes smarted from the onions. Sometimes, without provocation, he would glower at Mamaji and Mataji and say, "I'll pull down this house." Both women trembled before his threats. Mataji was keenly aware of being a *dohaju's* wife, and Mamaji of being her mother's daughter. It took Mamaji years to realize that her half brother's outbursts were those of a child who had lost first his mother, then his brother, then his sister, and had grown to manhood feeling that he was a feared stranger in his father's house. His threats were actually a demand for the sympathy of the mother and daughter. Only much later did Mamaji remember how he would say to her, when they happened to be by themselves up on the roof, "I'm all alone, without a real mother, brother, or sister to love me."

Even when Bhagwan Das wasn't in the house, Mamaji had no peace. Mataji would trap her in a doorway or a corner and complain about Durga Devi, who spent almost more of her time at Babuji's house than at her own. "Durga Devi just shouted at me, 'Go drown yourself! The yogurt bowl is dirty,'" Mataji would whisper. "What does she want me to do—serve her yogurt on a mirror?" Nothing that Mataji did seemed to please Durga Devi, who was forever finding fault with her as the second—and therefore especially unworthy—wife of her paragon of a brother. Durga Devi, unhappy in her own married life, was becoming more capricious and demanding every day. Since Mataji had no mother-in-law, Durga Devi arrogated to herself the mother-in-law's traditional coercive role— just as, after the death of Bulaki Ram, Bhagwan Das had, in a sense, arrogated to himself the role of the "man of the house."

❧

MAMAJI had been promised in marriage to a man named Vishnu, who was an officer in the Forestry Service with good prospects for advancement. Like Babuji, Vishnu's father was a lawyer, and although at the time the arrangement was made the boy was in England for further study, his father had promised Babuji that when Vishnu returned he would marry Mamaji. From the roof, one day, Mamaji had caught a glimpse of a young man standing at the door. He was well dressed, handsome, and confident-looking, and she realized that he was Vishnu. He sat with Babuji for a few minutes, and left without committing himself to a date for the *shagan*. The next the family heard of him, he had married a rich heiress.

Valuable time had been lost waiting for Vishnu to return from England, and Mamaji was now over sixteen years old. Most girls in her neighborhood were married at the age of fifteen. The women of the neighborhood began saying "Stain her hands with henna," because at the time of marriage the bride's hands—and often her feet—were stained with henna. Babuji tried to arrange a marriage for her quickly, but it was some time before he found someone—a middle-aged widower with a couple of children. Mamaji was by then approaching seventeen, and the women were saying, "The water has risen up to her neck." But when Mataji's mother, Malan, heard about the widower, she said to Mataji, "I was married into a widower's house and I had no peace of mind. You were married into a widower's house and you've had no peace of mind. How can we marry our Shanti into a widower's house?" and Malan reminded her of Bhagwan Das.

Mataji, however, felt helpless to prevent the marriage; besides, she felt that any marriage was better than no marriage.

A few days later, Dwarka, who was thirteen, ran up to the kitchen shouting, "Sister Shanti has a new proposal!"

Mamaji looked up from the mortar and pestle with which she was crushing some mint for chutney. "Go away," she said. "Go play with your kite."

"I heard Babuji talking about it downstairs with the three women you let into the house," Dwarka said, excitedly jumping up and down. "They are talking about the date of the *shagan*."

The new proposal was from Daddyji, and was a much more enticing one than that of the widower, who was immediately sent a polite message of refusal.

Soon the house was filled with the whirr and clatter of sewing machines as several tailors busied themselves with the clothes for the dowry. Bulaki Ram, before his death, had accumulated and put by much of Mamaji's dowry: a collection of gold jewelry, seven silk-crêpe saris with heavy, intricate gold embroidery, six heavy silk suits (with matching veils) embroidered with heavy gold thread, four silk sleeping suits, twelve tablecloths, a silver tea set, twelve big silver glasses, brass dinnerware, two chairs, a bed, twelve sheets, twelve pillow cases. Her dowry clothes were all sewn with silk thread, and there wasn't so much as a cotton tape in her pajama trousers. But to make her dowry complete she needed a few more petticoats and blouses, tea cozies and kitchen towels.

MAMAJI HEARD the putt-putt of a motorcycle, then footsteps, and the sound of the unbolting of the doors downstairs. She knew that it was he, and that he had come to see Babuji. She stationed herself behind a curtain, listening, her face hot with worry that someone would guess the secret joy she was feeling and make fun of her. (In later years, she used to say to him, "In

my previous life, I made a sacrifice of pearls and diamonds. It was my destiny that I would be paired off
with you.") She heard a deck chair being dragged
across the stone floor of the courtyard. From what
Mataji had told her, she could picture him, if hazily:
he was a tall, thin man, wearing a felt hat, like an
Englishman, and perhaps fingering a walking stick,
and he would be leaning forward attentively to catch
Babuji's words.

"I knew Ishwar Das," she heard him say. "I felt
he was like a brother to me. He was two or three years
younger than I, so I didn't get to know him as well as
I would have liked to. But he was a fine, religious fellow. We used to meet at the Young Men's Arya Samaj
Association and play Ping-Pong."

"As long as I live, I will never get over the death
of Ishwar Das," she heard Babuji say.

After a silence, Babuji asked, "What kind of watch
would you like in the dowry?"

"I already have a watch, thank you," she heard
him say.

She felt weak and frightened. He has everything,
she thought. There is nothing we can give him. He will
withdraw, like the other one. (In later years, he would
often reënact the scene for her—how he had held up
his wrist and proudly shown Babuji his big wristwatch
—and each time she would feel weak and frightened
all over again.)

"She will have plenty of changes of clothes,"
Babuji said. "For winter, for summer, and for monsoon—day wear and evening wear. There are, of course,
the usual ornaments of twenty-two-carat gold. In addi-

tion, I plan to give you two thousand rupees. I would like to give you more, but I have four daughters."

"Babuji, like you, we are Arya Samajists," came the reply. "We don't believe in dowries."

"How would you like the two thousand rupees—in cash? What do you need?" Babuji asked. (Later, Daddyji learned that Babuji had been afraid that yet another son-in-law would slip through his hands, and had therefore been determined to impress him with the lavishness of the dowry.)

"I don't really need anything."

"What about a motorcar?" Babuji asked.

"I have a motorcycle."

"That's dangerous," Babuji said. "A married man should not ride one of those things."

"One day, I hope to buy a motorcar," Daddyji said.

"A motorcar would look impressive in the dowry, and it would be a good talking point for the neighbors," Babuji said. "Many prominent Lahoris are giving motorcars in dowries these days."

Overcome with fear that she might be discovered, Mamaji ran up to the *chaubara*.

That very day, Babuji went in his victoria to see the leading motorcar dealer in Lahore, who was the sole agent for Chevrolet in the Punjab. A rich gentleman from the region of Sind, he received Babuji in a large office, and when Babuji mentioned his interest in buying a motorcar he called his salesman over and told him to give Babuji a ride.

Babuji wasn't satisfied with the ride, because it was too short to convey much of an impression. He walked around the motorcar and pointed at the tires with his walking stick. "They are dirty," he said.

"It's a demonstration model," the salesman said, with a mysterious air, as if demonstration models were special and were to be preferred.

There was some haggling with the Sindhi inside, and Babuji managed to get a good discount on the stated price. Writing out a check for two thousand-odd rupees, he bought the demonstration model.

Babuji had the motorcar driven up to his house and parked outside for the neighbors to see and admire. But as soon as Daddyji saw the motorcar he realized that the dealer had palmed off the previous year's showroom car on Babuji, for it was a 1924 Chevrolet. (Within the year, Daddyji had to get a new battery and a new set of tires for the car.)

THE NIGHT BEFORE THE WEDDING, Babuji sent carriers to Park Lane—not far from the Mall—where Daddyji's family was living in a bungalow that his younger brother Daulat Ram had rented for himself, and where all Daddyji's relatives and connections from around the city and from distant villages had assembled. The carriers brought twenty-one huge platters of coconut meat, almonds, pistachios, raisins, a dozen different kinds of sweetmeats. The most conspicuous offering was a wide-mouthed, big-bellied brass vessel half full of yogurt—twenty pounds of it. Along with these offerings, Babuji sent a message saying that the sweet-

meats and yogurt were in lieu of the usual entertain-
ment and lodging of the *barat* for a couple of days at
the bride's parents' expense. He said that as an Arya
Samajist he didn't believe in the traditional claptrap of
weddings—in elaborate feasts and entertainments, in a
lot of band music and fireworks. Anyway, his Dha-ee-
ghar forebears had long since decided to do away with
noisy wedding celebrations, for fear of Muslim abduc-
tors. He would therefore have to keep the pomp and
circumstance of his daughter's wedding day to a minimum.

Much later, Daddyji told Mamaji that some of his
relatives—especially his maternal uncles, who had come
from some distance—were scandalized. As members of
the *barat,* they had expected at least to be regaled by
music and fireworks, and, if nothing else, to be treated
to a couple of big meals at the bride's house. Daddyji
recalled that his mother—Bhabiji—mollified them as
best she could with food and yogurt until the next
afternoon, when they all assembled for a *havan* to send
the bridegroom on his way to the wedding ceremony.
At first, they sat around the brazier grumbling, but
eventually they were coaxed into praying for the happiness of the bride and bridegroom, and invoking
blessings on them.

Just as the *havan* was ending, Daddyji recounted, a
horse-wallah who had been hired by Babuji arrived
with a docile horse for the *ghori*. He assured the assembled *barat* that the horse was a gelding and would
not kick. Daddyji mounted the horse as the women of
his family sang songs of fertility and joy. He wore a
gold coat with a closed collar, and a starched muslin

turban decorated with three silver panels—they portrayed Brahma, Vishnu, and Shiva, the Hindu trinity—
and overhung with garlands of flowers, which hid his
face; and he carried a sheathed sword. There was a lot
of confusion and laughter among the women as Daddyji's sister, Bibi Parmeshwari Devi, stepped forward
with wet maize on a brass platter for the horse, and
there was some uncertain clapping as the horse started
nibbling at the offering. Then Daddyji's female cousins
stepped forward one by one with more food for the
horse, and after they had fed it Daddyji handed money
to each of the women relatives, the amount depending
on the closeness of her relationship to him.

A wedding band played crackly tunes, exaggerated to give a festive effect, Daddyji said later, but they
couldn't cheer up the men in the *barat,* who, surly and
discontented, pulled in their stomachs and slapped
them—like the hungry Brahmans who regularly call at
houses begging for food. Out of respect for Babuji's
wishes, the band did not accompany Daddyji to the
Shahalmi Gate house but stopped its music as he set
off, in the twilight. Daddyji clip-clopped on his horse
to the house of his bride, accompanied only by the
horse-wallah and by a Brahman sent by Babuji, who
walked ahead tinkling two hand bells, in a feeble imitation of the absent band. The horse-wallah carried
Daddyji's briefcase, which contained a new suit of
clothes for Mamaji—the bridegroom always brought
the bride to her new home in the clothes of her new
family. (Lalaji, Daddyji's father, had had the suit
made when Daddyji was previously betrothed. After
the betrothal fell through, the suit had been packed

away for the day when Daddyji would marry someone
else.) When Daddyji arrived at the Shahalmi Gate
house, he was met by Babuji and surrounded by Babuji's sons and close male relatives.

❦

UPSTAIRS in the *chaubara,* the women of the house
spent the night gathered around Mamaji. They washed,
combed out, and put up Mamaji's long hair, and
dressed her in red pajama trousers, a red shirt, and a
red veil. (The veil was a present from Malan.) They
adorned her with her dowry jewelry—six gold bangles
and one big gold bracelet on either wrist, a heavy gold
choker with a heavy gold charm around her neck, a
gold barrette and a gold ornament in her hair. They
painted her hands and feet with henna, and around
5 A.M. they seated her next to Daddyji (he had spent
the night in the *munshi khanna* and had then shaved
and dressed himself again in the gold coat and the
starched turban) under the *vedi* (wedding canopy),
which had been set up in the courtyard and hung with
flowers, fruits, and tinsel ornaments. It was an excep-
tionally chilly December morning.

Earlier, some of Daddyji's relatives had arrived on
foot and gathered in the courtyard for the wedding
ceremony. Even as the members of his family gar-
landed and embraced the members of hers, they had
muttered under their breath, "What kind of family is
this? What kind of people are they? It's an insult!"

Each family member ceremonially greeted his or
her opposite number, the cramped courtyard echoing

with their names. Many of Daddyji's party held back, standing rigid, as if to underscore the point that they might be going through the motions of the greeting but were not taken in by the stingy in-laws—who, for their part, thought the Mehtas greedy and self-satisfied.

As everyone sat down, there was a jumble of familiar and unfamiliar voices: some soft and sweet, unmistakably from her side of the family, and others bold and resonant, unmistakably from his side.

Mamaji remembers the glow of the sacred fire under the *vedi*. She vaguely remembers being raised to her feet, circling the *vedi* several times with Daddyji leading her, and saying her vows with him, as the Brahman recited the mantras and the relatives flung fistfuls of *smugary* into the fire. At the end of one *lavan* (lap), she touched her head to his; at the end of another, she touched her hand to his; at the end of another, she touched her head to his feet. During another, she put her foot next to his on a slab of stone. (Subsequently, whenever there was some trouble in their marriage he would say, "We put our feet on the stone—there is no going back.")

After the *lavans,* the women took Mamaji indoors and removed the red clothes of her family; they put on her the new suit of clothes of her in-laws. It was made of rich silk and embroidered all over with gold wire —*salma* work. In addition to her dowry jewelry, one more gold bracelet was put on each wrist—a present from her in-laws. Mataji then covered Mamaji's face with a new veil, also from her in-laws.

Shrill pipes in a band that had been hired to serenade the *doli* (the ceremonial taking away of the bride) began a mournful tune, to signify the passing on of the young girl. Mamaji was led out of the house. Babuji and Mataji, Malan and Bhagwan Das, Dwarka and Lakshman, Dharam and Pushpa—all the family—gathered outside with tearful faces as Mamaji, sniffling behind her veil, was ceremonially lifted onto a palanquin and then helped into a victoria with a folding top, which belonged to Daddyji's closest friends, Basheshwar Nath and Sheila Khanna. It was drawn by two chestnut horses. Daddyji stepped into the victoria and closed the door. The syce cracked the whip, and the victoria went off, showered from all directions with flowers.

VII

BRIDEGROOM

A FTER THE WEDDING NIGHT, DADDYJI AND MAMAJI were separated, for custom dictated that the bride return to her mother for a couple of days. During that time, he wrote her a long, admiring letter in English, telling her these things, among others: He was twenty-nine years old and was a medical doctor. Two years before, when he was in New York, his father had died suddenly, and, as the eldest son, he had become the head of the Mehtas —a large and diverse joint family, of which she was now to be the mother. Until lately, he had been for many months in the United States and Europe, where he had been doing postgraduate medical studies, and where he had had to bear alone the grief of his father's death. He had recently become the health officer in the Punjab district of Montgomery and had moved into a house of his own in the town of Montgomery. How he wished that his father were there to take pride in his eldest son's success. He felt he had found in Babuji another father.

Until the letter arrived, Mamaji had known almost nothing about Daddyji's life or his family, and even after struggling through it she did not understand much. Medical doctor, postgraduate studies, United States, Europe, health officer, Montgomery—all these meant little to her. During the following months—from snatches of conversation under ceiling fans in what seemed to her gigantic rooms; from introductions to Mehta after Mehta, until she imagined that the vil-

139

lages of the Punjab were filled with them; from stories he told about this friend or that friend as they were having bed tea in the early morning or driving to a party in the motorcar in the evening—she was able to form her own impression of his life. She always listened carefully to every detail of his past, and in time his past became almost more familiar to her than her own; and that was how she wanted it, because she felt that a good Hindu wife should sacrifice her life to her husband's—merge her life with his, and exist in his reflection.

Like her, Daddyji was one of seven children, but he had five brothers and one sister and they were all from the same mother. Only his sister was older than he was. Unlike Babuji, Daddyji's father, Lalaji, had not risen very high in the world. He must have been more like Bulaki Ram—a good, strong, simple man. He had died at an early age, two or three years before Daddyji's marriage to her.

Although Daddyji and his forebears were from a village, and he had spent his early childhood in a village, he had gone to school in Lahore, like her. Even while she was living in the Shahalmi Gate house, Daddyji had been living next to Phoos Kothi (Hay House), in the civil station. (She was amused to learn that Phoos Kothi had a sloping roof made out of thick hay, to keep the house cool—real hay, no different from the hay that horses ate in the stall behind her house.) But even before she was born Daddyji and his brother Daulat Ram had been entered in Central Model School, where they had not only studied but also played mysterious games called cricket and hockey in big open fields. Lalaji's younger brother, Bhaji Ganga Ram, was the first university graduate in the family's history. He was connected with Government College, and it was thanks to him that the two boys had studied and made something of themselves. Daddyji had become a doctor, like an Englishman, and had gone to England for still more study.

❦

DADDYJI returned from that stay in England in August of 1921, when he was twenty-five years old. During the early months of his marriage, he would entertain Mamaji—and sometimes mystify her—by telling her the story of what happened to him then. He didn't have any money to set himself up in a practice, and had to help with the education of his younger brothers. He rushed to Simla, the summer capital, to look for a job. There he called on some officials, and one of them told him that he should try applying for the post of municipal health officer in Rawalpindi—that the government was having difficulty finding a good man for the post, because plague was endemic in the city.

Daddyji set out for Rawalpindi, stopping on the way in the town of Jullundur to see its district health officer, Dr. G. C. Sehgal, in order to acquaint himself with the duties of a health officer. Dr. Sehgal received him cordially in his office and began by talking enthusiastically about the climate of Rawalpindi, but then he frowned. "I have my public-health qualifications, like you, from Britain—from Edinburgh," he said. "Yet the president and the members of the Municipal Committee, who have qualifications from nowhere, are constantly interfering in my work. And when I ask for money they turn me away as if I were a beggar. I can't even get enough money from the committee to improve the sewage system. If my teachers in Edinburgh knew that we still remove human filth here in broken-down handcarts, they would declare war on Jullundur. Dr. Mehta, tell me this: Do they need an 'England-returned' man for this kind of job? Any coolie would be better."

Dr. Sehgal took Daddyji to his home for tea. It was just the kind of house that Daddyji had pictured himself living in. The drawing room had big armchairs and a sofa, rather than the usual Indian divans; it had drawings rather than the usual family pictures on the walls; and there was even a big piano in one corner. Dr. Sehgal introduced Daddyji to his wife, a delicately pretty woman, with big, dark eyes, who was dressed in a Benares-silk sari, and who spoke to him in chaste, convent-school English. She was just the kind of wife Daddyji had imagined for himself. Mrs. Sehgal served tea English style, pouring a little milk in the cup before she poured the tea. Although it was not the high tea that he might have got in London, with lots of savories and sweets, still, for an Indian house it was elaborate, with two sweets—biscuits and chocolate cake. Chocolate cake was Daddyji's favorite, and he praised the piece he was eating. "It was prepared by my wife's own hands," Dr. Sehgal said.

Daddyji's eyes wandered toward the piano, whereupon (he told this to Mamaji just after she had seen her first piano, in an Englishman's house) Mrs. Sehgal, as if it were the most natural thing in the world, walked over to it with dainty steps and, sitting very erect on the stool, began playing a piece of Western classical music. At the end of the piece, she said, "That was Chopin," as if she took it for granted that Daddyji was familiar with Western composers. Daddyji complimented her on her playing, and added, "When you walked over to the piano, I thought you were going to play a raga. What a pleasant surprise to hear Chopin in Jullundur!" She smiled and looked toward her husband, like a demure Hindu wife.

"All credit goes to her father, Dr. Mehta," Dr. Sehgal said. "He's a great gentleman of the old school. You've no doubt heard of Colonel Ram Nath Chopra. Well, he's my wife's father. He sent her to a convent school and later took her to England so that she could learn the accomplishments and graces of a lady. Colonel Chopra's entire family is Westernized, and the family lives like aristocrats here. And Colonel-Sahib's brother, Uncle Chopra, is a gentleman in his own right."

Daddyji was amused by Dr. Sehgal's tall talk. Though Daddyji, too, had been bitten by England, he was still proud of his upbringing as a simple middle-class Hindu.

A few weeks later, Daddyji took up his duties as municipal health officer in Rawalpindi. (He told Mamaji he would always remember the date of the first day of his first job—October 4, 1921.) This was a gazetted post, and everywhere he went, fellow-officers greeted him as if he had been inducted into a new class of being. Hardly had he got settled in Rawalpindi when he received a letter from Dr. Sehgal: "Remember the uncle I told you about? He has a talented daughter of marriageable age. She looks and acts like my wife, and she, too, was educated in a convent school. Would you be interested?"

Daddyji wrote back that he was financially in no position to consider marriage, because he felt he had to help educate his younger brothers, one of whom, Daulat Ram, was already studying medicine in England. Then he forgot all about Dr. Sehgal's suggestion until one day a month or so later, when he was sitting in his office writing a report on the plague, and a tall, well-dressed gentleman appeared at the door. "I'm Mrs. Sehgal's uncle," the man said. "I've come to see you at her suggestion. We live in Kashmir, and we are on our way to Lahore. We are breaking our journey in Rawalpindi for a couple of days. I am very keen for you to meet my daughter. Could you honor us by having lunch or tea with us at your convenience? No harm could come of it. You would be committing yourself to nothing."

Daddyji had resolved that he would not go to the length of meeting a girl unless he had first settled upon her as the girl he would marry. But he thought of Mrs. Sehgal floating over to the piano and looking at her husband with her big, dark eyes, and he said to himself, "If the daughter is as accomplished as they all say, maybe she'll be a good influence on my growing brothers. Maybe I could even be financially in a position to get married if Daulat Ram gets a good job when he returns from England this summer."

"If you don't feel comfortable about lunch or tea,"

the uncle was saying, "we are going to see a picture this afternoon at the cinema across the road. Perhaps you could stop by there for a few minutes, and then you could see her without her ever suspecting that you were viewing her as a prospective bride."

As it came about, Daddyji arrived at the cinema just as the picture was about to begin, and he barely had time to nod to the girl's father and to notice that there were several women with him before the lights went out. He became so absorbed in the picture that he forgot all about the Chopras, and left without meeting the girl. He did not hear anything more from the uncle. (In later years, Mamaji would often smile and ask Daddyji the name of the picture, but he had forgotten it.)

After a few months, Lalaji wrote that he had received a proposal from a well-placed barrister in Amritsar who had a convent-school-educated, beautiful, talented daughter.

Without much hesitation, Daddyji wrote back that he would marry the girl provided that that was what Lalaji wanted. But then Daddyji was selected as a travelling Rockefeller Fellow. As soon as the girl's father heard about that, he asked for the *shagan* back, saying, "If I let my daughter go across the seas with your son, I am sure I will lose her to the great Britannia."

Daddyji, though he had never so much as seen a picture of his bride, had looked forward to showing her London and New York. However, he now quoted to Lalaji:

The world is a garden, where beautiful girls grow like flowers. A good man may pluck whatever flower he would.

As A YOUNG BRIDE, Mamaji used to say, "London and New York seem to be on the other side of Heaven. What chance does someone like me have of ever getting there?" Daddyji would promise to take her abroad someday, but would tell her that she had to understand that life there was very different and would require a lot of adjusting to—although for one Indian woman he knew, Manika, it had been a breeze. Mamaji was soon engrossed in his story about Manika.

Manika was the wife of Captain Sahib Singh Sokhey, who had gone with Daddyji to America, also on a travelling Rockefeller Fellowship. When Daddyji had been in America scarcely four months, the Rockefeller Foundation ordered him to Europe to work on an antimalaria project. Before he left, Sokhey gave him some presents to take to Manika, who was a professional dancer and was then giving dance performances in Europe. Daddyji caught up with Manika in London, where she was staying at the Savoy. She was tall and young, with a small mouth and large, expressive eyes. She was a Bengali—Daddyji had heard that the most temperamental and exciting women came from Bengal—and had an enticing smile. Daddyji greeted Manika from a distance, Indian-style, bringing the palms of his hands together and bowing slightly. But she came toward him, her long, shapely hand extended in welcome. She shook hands with him. His upbringing had been so chaste that he had never been alone with a strange woman before, let alone touched one. The feel of

Manika's hand made his hand tingle. (In later years, whenever Daddyji told this story, he would laugh at his own innocence about women. For twenty years, he and Mamaji knew Manika and Sokhey intimately as a couple—he had even unwittingly read about Manika in Louis Bromfield's "The Rains Came," one of whose characters was modelled on her—without guessing that Sokhey and Manika had never been legally married.) As if she were in her own house, Manika rang for tea, and he spent the afternoon with her in the hotel, drinking cups of Ceylon tea, eating chocolate cake, and talking about America, Sokhey, and himself.

A couple of days later, on her initiative, he escorted her to a reception at the Ritz Hotel for His Highness the Aga Khan. A direct descendant of the Prophet Muhammad through his daughter Fatima, the Aga Khan was the spiritual leader of the Ismaili sect of Muslims and, as it happened, had served as the first president of the All-India Muslim League, but he was best known for his unimaginable wealth. It was said that on occasion the Aga Khan's followers presented him with his weight in gold as a token of their esteem. His Highness's secretary opened the door of the Aga Khan's suite and greeted Mrs. Sokhey with a peck on the cheek. Daddyji felt he was in high society.

It was general knowledge that the Aga Khan was enamored of horses and horse racing.

"Where does Diophon race next?" Daddyji asked the secretary.

"Oh, you know about the races," the secretary said. "Come meet His Highness."

The secretary took Daddyji by the shoulder and led him to the Aga Khan, a kindly, genial-looking, heavily built man in his forties. His hand alone seemed so heavy that Daddyji thought that if just its weight was presented to him in gold by his poor followers it would eat up the life savings of dozens of them. (Mamaji, listening to this, wondered whether all the gold jewelry in her dowry would be equal to the weight of the Aga Khan's hand.)

"I was glad to see that Diophon won the Two Thousand Guineas," Daddyji said to the Aga Khan. "He is a beautiful horse. How many hands does he stand?"

The Aga Khan looked very much pleased. "You'll be interested to know that I am running Charley's Mount in the Cesarewitch in October," he said. "I'm sure it will be a one-horse race and Bolet Satan will win. Not surprisingly, the bookies are quoting hundred-to-one odds on Charley's Mount!"

Daddyji knew that Charley's Mount was a rank outsider, but he had intended to put two pounds on the horse, because if she won he could live for months on the two hundred pounds he would collect. But here was the Aga Khan, the horse's owner, saying that the Cesarewitch was a one-horse race. Daddyji decided to save his two pounds.

As it happened, Charley's Mount won the race. Daddyji fingered the two pound notes in his pocket and rued the day that Manika had presented him to the Aga Khan. He felt, however, that he had learned the first lesson of gambling: one must have the courage to back one's hunches, or else one must forever stand on the sidelines and look longingly at the winners departing with their pockets full of gold.

Weeks passed. Daddyji and a friend named Musafir were stopping in Deauville for a couple of nights on their way back to London from a short holiday in the South of France. They had heard that Deauville was famous for horse racing and gambling.

On the first evening, they looked into an elegant, brightly lit establishment. They stopped at a green table on which was a wheel with black and red numbers. The table was surrounded by people in evening dress but with the hungry expression of Indian beggars. They were putting stacks of chips on various numbers. The man in charge of the table called out something in French and spun the wheel, and a white ball bounced into a numbered slot. The man called out *"Dix-sept."* Both Daddyji and Musafir took out all their cash—ten pounds each—and bought chips, which they put on the number eleven. In the Hindu numerology of the Punjab, three, seven, and eleven were lucky numbers. Some considered seven the luckiest number, in part because there were seven planets. Daddyji was one of seven children, but he had got his first job on the fourth. Seven and four made eleven.

The man again said something in French. Daddyji looked at him closely for the first time. He was swarthy, short, and tense—rather like a dacoit whose picture Daddyji had once seen in a newspaper after a train robbery in the Punjab, except that this fellow was wearing evening clothes. Suddenly, Daddyji wanted to take his chips back. But before he could make a move the Deauville dacoit had spun the wheel, called out

"Dix-huit," reached over with a long rake, and begun raking all the chips to his end of the table. (As Mamaji listened to this story, the knitting needles dropped from her hands. She felt she had married a man who would mortgage her home and dowry for some foolish game with a dacoit.) Daddyji and Musafir walked out of the casino consoling each other that at least they had had the foresight to pay in advance for their hotel room and their return tickets to London.

Back at their hotel, they heard from the chambermaid that the next day all of Deauville was going to the races.

"How I wish we could stay for the races," Daddyji said after she had left. "If we could get hold of some money, we might be able to recoup our losses."

They tried to cash a check at the desk, but the concierge, without even looking at the check, shook his head sorrowfully and said, *"C'est impossible."*

As they paced up and down in front of the hotel, dispirited and hungry, Daddyji told Musafir how he had lost his chance to make money on Charley's Mount.

"Then you know His Highness the Aga Khan," Musafir said. "I just saw his picture in the newspaper. His horse won the race yesterday. He has a house here." He suggested that Daddyji go and see the Aga Khan and get him to cash the check.

At first, Daddyji wouldn't hear of the idea, but Musafir persisted. Daddyji calculated in his head that so far his handshake with Manika and his handshake and dozen words with the Aga Khan had cost him a hundred and ninety-eight pounds for listening to the

Aga Khan and ten pounds more for his venture into
the town where the Aga Khan was the ruling spirit. It
seemed that the Aga Khan owed him something, and
he decided that he would go to see him after all.

Daddyji arrived at the Aga Khan's house very
early the next morning, so as not to miss him. He saw
the Aga Khan through a low, closed gate, doing some
fashionable Swedish exercises. The Aga Khan looked
up, saw Daddyji, and called to his gateman to let the
fellow in.

"Good morning," Daddyji said when he was a few
feet from the Aga Khan, who didn't let up in his exercises. Daddyji didn't know how to go on.

But the Aga Khan looked at him encouragingly.

"We met in London, at the Ritz," Daddyji said.
"And Charley's Mount won after all."

"But what do you want, and so early in the morning?" His Highness asked, breathing heavily and wip-
ing sweat off his face with a large white towel.

"I want Your Highness's help in cashing a twenty-
pound check," Daddyji said.

"Come back at ten o'clock, when my accountant is
here."

"I'll wait," Daddyji said.

Daddyji watched the Aga Khan do his exercises,
and once or twice, when he tried to do something impossible for a man of his weight, said rather cautiously,
"Sir, if I may say so as a doctor, this movement may
put a strain on your heart," or "Sir, that posture is not
medically advisable."

When the accountant arrived, His Highness instructed him to cash Daddyji's check, and Daddyji went back to Musafir in the hotel room and lent him half the money.

In the afternoon, they went to the races. Musafir didn't bet, but Daddyji returned to the hotel eight pounds lighter. (As Mamaji waited up night after night until eleven or twelve for Daddyji to come home from the club and the card table, she would think of the Deauville dacoit and worry about Daddyji and about local dacoits coming to rob her. Sometimes, if she heard the door rattle without having heard the tires of his car on the gravel, she would sit up in bed and say boldly "Who's there?"—hoping to scare away the intruders. Then she would lie back in her bed and reflect that the man she had married was no less than an Aga Khan, and feel pleased that she was the wife of such a worldly man.) That night, Daddyji and Musafir took the boat train for England.

ONE WINTER MORNING in 1925, after Daddyji had returned to London from Deauville, he was sitting in the Indian Students' Hostel, on Gower Street, going over the notes of some research he had been doing, when the porter brought him a letter. It was from his old friend Basheshwar Nath Khanna, who was in London, at the Tudor Hotel, and who promised a surprise —as if there could be a surprise greater than his being in London. As Daddyji read the letter, he felt as though his friend had just walked into the room with his cricket bat and his perennial deck of cards. Like Daddyji, Basheshwar Nath was an addict of cricket and bridge; in fact, he had been captain of the cricket team in Lahore on which Daddyji was a batsman, and he had been a frequent partner of Daddyji's at the bridge table. Basheshwar Nath had made a lot of money in cotton speculation just after the First World War, and he had bought a house and a couple of acres of land on a fashionable road near Lawrence Gardens, in Lahore. He also had a place in Peshawar and a commodious bungalow up in the hills, in Murree. When Daddyji went to Murree, he would often stay with Basheshwar Nath, and whenever Basheshwar Nath came to Rawalpindi, Daddyji would try to repay Khanna's hospitality in his own small way by entertaining his friend at the Pindi Club, of which Daddyji had become one of the first Indian members. Though Basheshwar Nath was ten years Daddyji's senior and a widower with four small children to raise, the two had become close friends. Daddyji now telephoned his friend and arranged to have lunch with him at the hostel. Entering the lounge punctually at twelve-thirty, he saw Basheshwar Nath just coming through the front door. They embraced in the Indian style—a good strong hug with a lot of back-slapping and inquiries about each other's health and well-being. "Tell, friend, what news?" Daddyji said, gently propelling Basheshwar Nath toward a sofa in one corner.

They must have sat talking for about half an hour before Daddyji remembered what Basheshwar Nath had said in his letter. "What's your surprise?" Daddyji asked. "Let's go in to lunch. You can tell me about it over some mulligatawny soup."

"I'm afraid, old man, I can't stay for lunch."

"Why not?"

"My wife is outside in a taxi," Basheshwar Nath said. "You see, I've remarried—"

"You're a fine fellow!" Daddyji broke in, jumping up and starting toward the door. "She will lunch with us. I'll see to it."

Basheshwar Nath put a restraining hand on his arm.

"Is she a Muslim?" Daddyji asked, taken aback. "Are you keeping her in purdah?"

"No, it's not that," Basheshwar Nath said. "When we left our hotel, we were both coming to lunch with you. I thought I would give you the surprise of your life, but on the way *she* gave *me* a surprise! I was checking your address, and she said to me, 'Is he the same Dr. Mehta who was municipal health officer at Rawalpindi?' I said yes, and she said, 'I don't want to see this friend of yours,' and became very quiet."

"How could someone I've never seen or met take exception to me?"

"She wouldn't explain," Basheshwar Nath said. "She just had a sad look on her face."

"Let me at least try to talk to her," Daddyji said.

A beautiful young Punjabi woman in starched pajama trousers and a loose coat, her head covered by an orange veil, was sitting stiffly in a taxi pulled up in Gower Street. Daddyji walked up to her and folded his hands and bowed respectfully in greeting. "Won't you please join us for a little lunch?" he asked.

"No, thank you," the young woman said curtly. "I'm not well. I've got a headache."

Daddyji felt challenged. "They serve very good

Indian food here, and there are turmeric balls in yogurt on the menu today. I'm sure you can't resist that dish, or you are not a true Punjabi."

She shook her head emphatically.

"I didn't tell you, but she's in the family way," Basheshwar Nath whispered in Daddyji's ear. "I had really better take her back to the hotel."

(When Mamaji heard this story, she was aghast that a Punjabi woman who was pregnant could be in England loafing about.)

"But then the yogurt dish is just the thing," Daddyji said.

To his astonishment, Mrs. Khanna thereupon got out of the car and came in for lunch.

Over the yogurt dish, she confided that she had had morning sickness and hadn't been able to eat anything all day, and that she was starving. But she did not explain why she had made such a fuss about lunching with him. Soon after lunch, the couple left.

The next morning, Basheshwar Nath rang Daddyji up and said he and his wife were eager to see the sights of London. Soon the three were sauntering down to Trafalgar Square and over to Piccadilly Circus. They took a taxi to the Natural History Museum, in Kensington, and from there a cab to Madame Tussaud's, where Mrs. Khanna was amused to discover that the English immortalized kings and robbers, the living and the dead alike. Daddyji showed her Napoleon. She took a step back.

"It's just wax, Mrs. Khanna," Daddyji said.

"Call her Sheila," Basheshwar Nath said.

"Yes, yes, please," she said.

Basheshwar Nath and Sheila asked Daddyji to come back to their hotel and have dinner with them in their room. Sheila didn't feel like eating much, so Daddyji ate most of her dinner. Sitting in their warm, comfortable hotel room and sharing Sheila's food made Daddyji feel somehow closer to them both—as if they were all members of a family sticking together in a foreign country. Yet now and again he could feel Sheila turning suddenly cold toward him.

The couple decided to prolong their stay in England and rented a house in Swiss Cottage. One day, Daddyji called on them there and found Sheila sitting on the lawn drying her hair. Daddyji discreetly tried to withdraw, but she saw him and, motioning toward a wicker chair next to her, called out, "He'll be back soon. Anyway, sit down. We're old friends."

She had long, thick black hair, which was loose and still quite wet. It glistened in the sun. Except for his mother and sister, Daddyji had seldom seen an Indian woman he knew with her head uncovered—certainly not with her hair loose and wet. And Sheila was so pretty. She was small—only about five feet tall. She had the healthy wheat-colored complexion of a Punjabi, and dimples appeared when she smiled. Though her voice was a little high-pitched and childlike, her manner was forthright and easygoing. It was the first time he had been alone with her, and he asked her why she had been so reluctant to meet him.

She started examining the ends of her hair. "Didn't you recognize me from Rawalpindi?"

"How could I recognize you when I had never met you?"

"Tell me, didn't you wear a salt-and-pepper worsted English suit in Rawalpindi?"

"It is a favorite of mine. It was tailored in Bond Street. Why do you ask?"

"Don't you know Dr. Sehgal, of Jullundur?"

"Of course, very well."

"Then don't you remember making an appointment with Mr. Chopra in Rawalpindi to meet us all at the cinema?"

It finally dawned on him that she was Mrs. Sehgal's cousin, the girl he had been invited to see at the cinema.

She served him some Ceylon tea with biscuits and chocolate cake, pouring a little milk in the teacup before she poured the tea. For a moment, he permitted himself to wonder what sort of wife she would have made him.

BACK IN INDIA after two years abroad, Daddyji was playing tennis at the Engineering Club in Lahore one autumn day in 1925, and as he was leaving the court he was stopped by Bakshi Ram Rattan and Principal Sain Das, who (as he told Mamaji) were two of the oldest friends of the Mehta family. Bakshi Ram Rattan had been the principal of the D.A.V. School, where three of Daddyji's younger brothers had studied. Principal Sain Das had known Daddyji's paternal uncle Bhaji

Ganga Ram from the time the two of them were students at D.A.V. College. Sain Das had gone on to become principal of D.A.V. College and had held that post for so long that "Principal" had come to seem part of his name. The two old family friends now told Daddyji that Durga Das Mehra, the famous advocate of Lahore, was interested in Daddyji for his eldest daughter, Shanti Devi, and that they had come with his formal proposal. They had known the Mehras almost as long and as well as they had known the Mehtas, they said, and they strongly urged the alliance. "We can't imagine a union of two better families," Bakshi Ram Rattan said.

Daddyji required just three things in a wife: that she be educated (that is, essentially, be fluent in English); that she be able to sing; and that she be pretty. Lately, he had been too busy with his work to give much thought to marriage. (That spring, there had been an outbreak of cholera in Kashmir, and Daddyji had been appointed health officer in Murree to keep the disease from spreading to the plains. And then, at the end of the summer, he had been posted to Montgomery, a place that was completely new to him.) Yet, because he was a gazetted, and therefore permanent, officer, twice England-returned, parents constantly sought him out as a prized piece of property that would guarantee lifelong security for their daughters. Principal Sain Das tapped his walking stick impatiently for Daddyji's answer, but Daddyji pleaded for time to consult his family about the proposal.

Daddyji went home and told Bhabiji and his sister, Bibi Parmeshwari Devi, about the proposal, and then he went over and told Sheila. (She was back in Lahore and had a baby boy.) Within a few days, the three women got dressed in their best clothes and took a tonga to the Shahalmi Gate house to look the girl over and, if they approved of her, speak to Babuji. The door was opened for them by Mamaji herself. She said, a little abruptly, "Who are you? What brings you here?" (She thought they had come with a proposal for Bhag-wan Das, and she assumed that tone because she fancied that matrimonial bargaining required it.) Bhabiji, Bibi Parmeshwari Devi, and Sheila pretended they hadn't heard her, because they didn't want to embarrass her by telling her that she was probably the girl they had come to see. Turning away, she said, almost to herself, as she led them to Babuji in the courtyard, "Coming to offer daughters and putting on airs."

They glanced at each other, taking note that the girl had a sharp tongue. Bhabiji and Bibi Parmeshwari Devi, who were used to village reticence, were taken aback. But Sheila thought that the girl was spirited and had city manners. By the end of their meeting with Babuji, Bhabiji had given her consent. They went home with the engagement sealed and the date of the wed-ding fixed for the seventh of December—six weeks later.

Daddyji returned to Montgomery very happy. He didn't worry about the choice of the girl, even though one day, back in the Engineering Club in Lahore, he happened to meet Des Raj, who, like Bakshi Ram Rat-tan and Principal Sain Das, was an old family friend (he had been a neighbor of Lalaji's from the time the family lived near Phoos Kothi), and who was now working as a librarian in the Punjab High Court, where he had frequent business with Babuji—and who said, "I don't know about the daughter, but if you happen to see the father's face, you will have such bad luck that you won't be able to find food for the rest of the day." Daddyji shrugged off Des Raj's remark as the idle chatter of an envious man.

VIII

MARRIAGE

T HE MORNING AFTER THE WEDDING NIGHT, MAMAJI, dressed in her *salma* suit, went to call on Bhabiji in her room.

Bhabiji greeted her new daughter-in-law by putting a gold chain around her neck and putting a sweetmeat in her mouth to sweeten it. "You have brought so many clothes in your dowry," Bhabiji said a bit later, sitting down at her spinning wheel. (She had been spinning cotton yarn when Mamaji came in.) "Maybe you can give the *salma* suit back to us. It will come in handy for my next daughter-in-law. There are four more daughters-in-law to come."

It happened that Daulat Ram, the brother next in age to Daddyji, had got married a few months before, ahead of his older brother; and his wife, Subhdran, was now standing in Bhabiji's room. She couldn't take her eyes off Mamaji, who was glittering from head to foot; Mamaji, for her first visit to her mother-in-law, had put on practically all her jewelry. "Maybe you can give back the gold bracelets, too," Subhdran said.

Mamaji immediately sent the *salma* suit back to Bhabiji, but she couldn't bring herself to part with the gold bracelets. If she did, she thought, the only token she would have left from her in-laws would be the gold chain that Bhabiji had put around her neck. Some time later, though, she did send the gold bracelets to Subhdran, and later still she sent the gold chain back to Bhabiji, in lieu of some of the money that Daddyji used to contribute monthly toward the upkeep of the family. Then Mamaji would often say to herself that the only token she had left from her in-laws was Daddyji.

❦

WHEN MAMAJI was a bride of just a week or so, Daddyji drove her in the Chevrolet to Anarkali, gave her some rupees, and took her into a shop. Although she was over seventeen, she had never seen the inside of a shop. When she had needed shoes or clothes, the *munshi* had brought to the house a suitcase full of sandals and high-heeled shoes, or saris and borders, and she had tried them on in the privacy of the *chaubara* and kept whatever she wanted. The *munshi* had packed up the rest in the suitcase and returned them. The haggling and payment had been left to the *munshi,* to Babuji, or to Bulaki Ram.

Now, in the shop, a strange man took hold of her foot and looked at it. He traced its outline on a piece of coarse brown paper, and then brought out shoe after shoe, sandal after sandal, and tried them on her.

"How do they feel?" Daddyji asked at one point.

She stared first at one foot, in an unfamiliar new walking shoe, plain, black, and ungainly, and then at the other foot, in a delicate new gold sandal. She said she liked the sandal very much but she was uncertain about the walking shoe.

Daddyji commanded the stranger to put the second walking shoe on her, and then he made her walk, clapping encouragement.

Mamaji stumbled around the shop, and they both

laughed over the way she walked in those shoes. She bought the sandals, and he insisted that she buy the walking shoes, too.

By the end of the morning, with Daddyji prompting her, she had also bought two plain, workaday cotton saris, two plain, workaday woollen shawls, and a purse for her rupees.

She thought she was going to enjoy being married.

THE FIRST TIME that Mamaji and Daddyji dined out after their marriage, it was with Basheshwar Nath and Sheila, at their house near Lawrence Gardens. Mamaji felt a little like the Punjabi rustic in her school skit who had arrived at the governor's house. All around her were bold, bright lights, mirrors, and shimmering curtains. There was no place to hide or retreat. And the men and the women, who did not belong to the same family, were in one room—the women sitting down, and the men milling about like kites flying above the rooftops of Shahalmi Gate.

After a while, Daddyji put his arm around her and escorted her into a whole room devoted to eating. She couldn't take her eyes off the table. The china was soft white with blue, green, and gold flowers painted on it, as if on a sari. The cutlery looked like many silver rupees laid end to end. And the water glasses threw rainbows on the tablecloth. All the guests sat down at a single table, and they ate as dexterously with the cutlery as with their fingers, and handled the china and glasses as if they were brass.

Mamaji watched Daddyji across the table and tried to eat with the cutlery as he did, all the while holding down a cough that kept rising in her chest. She had started sneezing under the wedding canopy, in the December chill, and the sneezing had developed into a cough and a cold.

After dinner, when Sheila saw Mamaji coughing, she handed her a glass of golden liquid. It looked like thin honey but had an off-putting strong smell, like a cough mixture.

"It's medicine. Drink it up," Sheila said, patting her on the back.

Mamaji held her breath and gulped it down.

Daddyji, a confirmed teetotaller, saw this from a distance. He rushed over and caught her by the shoulder, and said, "Hardly a week-old bride and you are already drinking brandy! Do you want to become a drunkard?"

She fainted.

Montgomery was a barren town—a sort of desert station, in the most arid part of the Punjab plain. Named after Sir Robert Montgomery, who was the lieutenant governor of the Punjab when the station was established, in 1865, it was essentially an administrative outpost. No one had a good word to say for it. The authoritative *Imperial Gazetteer* described it as "almost unequalled for dust, heat, and general dreariness." The station was situated on a tract between the River Ravi and the River Sutlej, and the British had recently started work on a network of canals to irrigate the region. When Mamaji arrived there, as a bride of a few weeks, Montgomery seemed to her to be a foreign country.

In Montgomery, Daddyji was provided with a commodious government bungalow of brick, with its own compound, beside a canal. It had once served as a dak bungalow (a house for travellers at a postal station), and travelling officers must have held court there, sitting in capacious wood-and-cane armchairs and dispensing justice, favors, and cold water to all comers. The bungalow had a wide veranda along all four sides, and it had particularly large rooms, large windows, and high ceilings.

All around the compound was open, empty space, with neither a wall nor a gate, neither a neighbor nor a friend. There were no hawkers or peddlers shouting up from the street; indeed, there was no street, no *gulli*, no staircase. From inside the house, one stepped onto the veranda as if into a public garden. Pigeons and doves were constantly flying in and out of the veranda as if they couldn't tell the difference between outside and inside. The house really seemed to have no walls, and reminded Mamaji of her wedding canopy; when she was standing inside the bungalow, she often felt as if she were standing outside. The silence of the compound—especially in the dark, when the birds were asleep—hummed in her ears like the "sha-ah-ahn, sha-ah-ahn" in a conch that a schoolmate had once held against her ear.

Now and again, a cloud would seem to fall on the horizon, and a dust storm would rise up and rush toward her. If she bolted the windows and doors against it, it would rattle and shake them, and sometimes it would fling them open, sweeping through the house as if it would carry her and the house along with it.

❦

ONE OF THEIR FIRST DAYS in Montgomery, Daddyji asked Mamaji to bring out the harmonium and sing. She looked at his expectant face and thought that he wanted to test her voice to find out whether it was worth training. She sat down on the floor and timidly pulled the harmonium toward her. She pumped the bellows as he looked encouragingly at her from an armchair, but, having never been trained in music, she did not know what to do next, so the only sound she was able to produce on the instrument was the hissing of air being forced out between the unpressed keys.

He said from the armchair, "Why aren't you playing the notes? Why aren't you singing? What is there to be shy about?"

She pressed down one key and made a brave attempt at singing, but felt short of breath and stopped.

It was obvious that she knew no music. For some days afterward, he tried to teach her, but it became clear that she had no aptitude. At last, in a fit of impatience, he kicked the harmonium aside. (In later years, the incident was so embellished in the retelling that in one version he flung the harmonium—a substantial instrument, weighing perhaps thirty pounds— right across the room, making it crash against the wall, and in another version it sailed through a glass window.)

She was frightened, yet relieved. Well, she thought, if he doesn't think I have a voice worth training, that's all right; if he doesn't want me to learn music, I certainly don't want to. She wouldn't have been surprised to receive a good thrashing on the spot. She felt that it would help exorcise the demon that all men had inside them. But he did nothing—just looked angry.

Daddyji had discovered on their wedding night that Mamaji was more or less uneducated, that she knew only Mrs. Humphrey's English. He had consoled himself with the thought that though she might not be able to talk to his European friends in good English, she would at least be able to entertain them with authentic classical Indian music, for he had assumed that, like most daughters of well-to-do Lahoris, she had had music lessons. "How I had looked forward to my house being filled with the sweet sounds of your songs!" he now said sadly. "I never thought I would be disappointed in my wife."

She recalled that one of her school friends had been returned to her parents the morning after her marriage because when the husband's sister and mother examined the bed sheet they hadn't found any blood on it. She feared that she might meet a similar fate, even though her fault was only that she couldn't sing.

"Do with me what you like," she said, "but don't turn me out, don't send me back to Babuji." She started sobbing.

Daddyji patted her. "What is there to be frightened of? This is your house as much as mine."

"No, you are the provider," she sobbed. "What are wives? They are like shoes. A man slips out of one and into another. I've heard that all the Mehtas are headstrong people. I've heard that you all get possessed by *bhoots* [demons] and become unmanageable."

"What nonsense you talk," he said. "It's Shahalmi Gate nonsense. You talk like a *shehran*. I was born in a village. We *paindus* don't think like that. You *shehrans* show the effects of your inbreeding."

Mamaji remembered now, as she often did, Tirath Ram's first wife; she could see the woman's face and hear her words. Tirath Ram was Babuji's colleague and neighbor—their houses had a common wall. He was a rich advocate, and yet after he had cast off his first wife to take a second one he would give the first wife only a *guzara* (pittance)—just a few rupees to ward off destitution. Even so, she would have to come and beg him for it. Every month, the poor woman would have to wait to get her *guzara;* she would often sit and wait with the women at Babuji's house, her face swollen with tears. "You know what a huge amount of money he makes," she would cry, "and yet he gives his poor wife only six rupees a month for bread and water, for clothes and washing, for kerosene to put in the lamps. For six rupees you can't even keep a cow in hay!"

"Sister, you were born unlucky," the women would say. "Unlucky women deserve nothing good, but that doesn't stop their tears."

Mamaji could never forget that *she* was born unlucky.

Daddyji took her in his arms and gently rocked her back and forth.

❧

DADDYJI would often mention his regret that Mamaji's education had stopped with the fifth standard—that she hadn't gone to college. She would bow her head and say that she couldn't count herself among either the lettered or the unlettered. He could do with her what he liked, she would say, but she begged him, with her forehead on his feet, not to send her back to Babuji. She had been told from childhood, "Remember, when a Hindu girl gets married, she must die in her husband's house."

He would rail against Babuji for hypocrisy as an Arya Samajist who was an educationalist with strangers' daughters but an orthodox reactionary with his own. "What about Lala Duni Chand?" he cried one night when they were in bed. "He's a neighbor of Babuji's and a barrister! He sent his daughter to a convent school and to college! If he could appreciate the importance of an education in English, why couldn't Babuji?" He added despairingly, "And so recently I was calling Babuji 'Father'!"

She cowered under the sheet, trying to take as little space in the bed as she could. In her mind, she was saying, "I didn't study. I failed. It was my fault. You studied. You are a doctor-sahib. What has my father to do with it? What has your father to do with it?" But the tongue in her mouth was numb—as if, with all her other faults, she must now also be mute.

He looked at her childlike face, which was quivering with tension. She was swallowing hard, trying not to cry. His face softened. "I'm sorry—I shouldn't have talked to you angrily," he said. "I put my foot on the stone, and there is no going back." He assured her that their feet were joined on the stone until death, and that Mrs. Humphrey's English was good enough for him.

MAMAJI AND DADDYJI had been married only a few weeks, and they were in Lahore on a short visit. Over dinner, Babuji said to Daddyji, "Bhagwan Das lacks self-confidence. He needs to get out of this house and prove himself. Can you help him to get a start in the District Court in Montgomery? I got my start in the District Court here in Lahore."

Mamaji had looked forward to her marriage as a means of escaping Bhagwan Das, and now, sitting between Babuji and Daddyji at dinner, she was sure that Bhagwan Das would soon be following her into her new home. But she felt she could say nothing about it. "A practice for my brother-in-law is no problem," Daddyji was saying. "All the magistrates in Montgomery are my friends."

In Montgomery, Daddyji took Bhagwan Das first to his friend Vidyadhar and then to his friend Balwant Singh; both of them were magistrates, and they immediately promised Bhagwan Das their patronage.

Bhagwan Das had been in Montgomery scarcely three days when Mamaji handed Daddyji a letter that she had folded and refolded many times. The letter was from Mataji. "What are you doing?" she had written to Mamaji. "You've taken him into your house, and this will lead to a great disturbance. You are a married woman—don't let him touch your happiness."

Daddyji demanded to know everything—what Mataji was talking about, how Mamaji's own brother could touch their happiness. He learned for the first time that Bhagwan Das was not her full brother but her half brother, and that Mamaji, though eight years younger than Bhagwan Das, was closest in age to him. She explained how he had lost his mother, his brother, and his sister, how he would beg for pity and sympathy, and how she and Mataji nevertheless hated to be in the house with him, because he terrorized them. She recalled how he would often follow her up to the roof and bar her way down the stairs, confiding in her even as he yanked her braid. She said that she couldn't run to Babuji, because of her *hauwa* of him, and that she couldn't count on her mother or her grandmother to protect her, because neither had had any *pichhchha*, or backing, since her grandmother was left a widow.

The more Daddyji learned about her past, the angrier he grew, at one point attributing Bhagwan Das's antics to the degrading *gulli* ways of the city. "In the village, even the touching of hands between full brothers and sisters was not permitted," he told her. "*Paindus* believe that girl and boy together are like ghi and fire."

"Among the *shehris,* men and women sometimes embrace when they meet," Mamaji said meekly.

"Yes, and in the West they kiss each other," Daddyji said angrily. "But for us Hindus a simple '*Namaste*' from a distance is best."

The next day, Daddyji came home and saw Bhagwan Das barring Mamaji's way to the veranda. Daddyji came up behind Bhagwan Das, put his strong tennis arm around the young man's neck, and pulled him out of the doorway. He ordered him to pack up, stood over him as he gathered his few things together, and marched him to the railway station.

For many days afterward, Mamaji feared that Bhagwan Das would wreak vengeance on her. But Daddyji told her that she now had *pichhchha,* and had nothing to fear.

After the Montgomery incident, Daddyji didn't see much of Bhagwan Das, who got married that April and, thanks to Babuji's friendship with the Chief Justice, Sir Shadi Lal, was eventually appointed a reader in the Law College in Lahore.

ONCE, while Daddyji was lying back in bed propped up on two pillows and Mamaji was at the dressing table fidgeting with a heart-shaped silver flask of kohl, he said suddenly that he hadn't known what tragedy was until the death of Lalaji.

How different he was from her, she thought. She couldn't remember a year when she hadn't seen someone—often a brother or a sister—committed to water or fire, the body, in her imagination, staring at her from river or pyre as if she were to blame in some way;

Mamaji and Om, Simla, 1932

she couldn't remember a year when she hadn't sat with Mataji and the other women up in the *chaubara* surreptitiously mourning the one who had died—crying softly and beating her breast quietly, fearful of being found out by Babuji and the Arya Samaj. Whenever she happened to see a child climbing up onto a table or sucking a sweet, she would think of her baby brother Pali, who had died while she and Mataji were holding him.

Since the wedding, Mamaji and Daddyji had formed certain theories about each other's background and family. He would tell her that the Mehras were submissive and resigned—why should they be so frightened of life and prone to nervousness? (In later years, he would joke that no sooner was one of the Mehra boys required to sit for an examination than he would come down with a stomach ache.) He insisted that even Babuji's rigidity was an attempt to hide nervousness.

Although she didn't say so, she felt that the Mehtas all boasted a lot. To hear him talk, they were always captains and never players, always the kind of people who got what they wanted, even if they had to cross oceans for it. He never seemed to tire of quoting Lalaji's favorite saying: "If you shoot an arrow to the sky, it will at least clear the top of the trees."

He would say, "The difference between the Mehras and the Mehtas is really the difference between most *shehris* and most *paindus*." He would point out that the Mehtas, in spite of having left the village, had retained the easygoing but proud natures and rustic values associated with *paindus,* but the Mehras, in spite

of having left the old city, had retained the brooding
nature and shifting values associated with *shehris*.
"There is a choice of just two ways to approach life—
fight or flight," he would say. "We Mehtas stay and
fight. You Mehras take flight."

He would often talk about his early childhood in
the village, describing the fresh air, the beehives, the
animals, and telling her how he would cut down a tree
early in the morning, when the dew was still on the
ground, and drag a branch home to his father's mud
hut, later to chop it up for firewood or fashion it into a
hockey stick. He had liked the freedom of running
about and thinking up simple games and simple sports.
He and his brothers would climb acacia trees and get
pricked by the thorns. The moment it rained, they
would run out into the field in just their drawers. To
him, there was something exciting about the very pre-
cariousness of village existence: one would start praying
for the monsoon rains a year ahead, and when the rains
came they would be either too early or too late, too
much or too little. Everyone was always looking up at
the sky and saying, "Brother, if there are good rains
this year, there will be a good harvest and we will all
eat well." It was like gambling with the gods. Once
the crop matured, in March and April, everyone would
begin praying for continuous sunshine. He would say
that in the city even the sky was closed in and divided
up by rooftops. But all around the village there were
only endless fields and open sky. He had grown up
thinking that only the sky was the limit to his wishes
and desires. He said that most *shehris* were out to get
what they could for themselves, without giving a

thought to the community, and so there were people without homes or food. Most *paindus,* by contrast, had to look out for each other, because they were like a family, each doing something that the others could not get along without, and each having his own function and his own place.

Listening to him, she felt he was a dreamer who ignored what was under his nose to look at something in the far distance. He talked as if the only people who starved lived in the *gullis,* when she knew perfectly well that it was starving villagers who came to the *gullis* for food. Besides, he had grown up in a mud hut, but she had grown up in a house with a courtyard and a staircase. And she was a Dha-ee-ghar. As she was handed into the victoria on her wedding day, a woman had muttered to herself, just loud enough for Mamaji to hear, "A brick of a tower has been put in the drain." Indeed, for centuries the Dha-ee-ghars had been the most exclusive of the Lahori Kshatriya subcastes, living mostly in the ancient cities and marrying mostly among their four family groups. (The family names had certain variations; for instance, some Mehras called themselves Mehrotra, others Malhotra, and so on.) Lately, however, because of Arya Samaj and economic pressures, they had been forced to marry into less exclusive Kshatriya subcastes, from the villages—like the Bunjahis ("Fifty-two Houses"), a subcaste consisting of a hundred family groups, the Mehtas among them. The woman's dark tower-and-drain remark had made Mamaji feel that perhaps she was marrying beneath her.

When he learned that she had been so terrified by getting her first monthly period at school, because she

didn't know anything about sex—as a child, she had believed that babies arrived in a trunk on the midwife's
back—he told her that in the village every child grew
up seeing dogs mounting bitches. He himself had led
Lalaji's cow to a neighboring village for mating with a
prized bull, and had ridden Lalaji's mare to a stud.
When he was barely six years old, he had stood by as a
calf was dropped, and had picked up an egg and held
it in his hand as a chick pecked its way out.

She was not impressed. That was just the way men
talked. Whatever he said, she felt she would rather
have the life of her mother than that of his, for she
could never forget what he had told her about Bhabiji:
that whenever he thought of her he saw her—as he did
every day of his childhood—bent over a smoking coal
fire, taking deep breaths and blowing on it, her cheeks
flushed from the strain. It made Bhabiji cough and rub
her eyes, yet she was so used to blowing on the fire to
keep it going that even when a bamboo fan was put in
her hand she would rather trust to her breath than to
her arm, which in any case was tired from lifting cal-
drons of food or stirring lentils. He would join Bhabiji
at the fire, adding his breath to hers, coughing, his eyes
smarting. He remembered telling Bhabiji that when
he had a wife he was going to get her a big bellows—
the kind he had seen blacksmiths use—or else go without food.

Daddyji said that Mamaji, as a *shehran,* had lived
a compartmentalized life and dwelt on people's social
positions and on caste distinctions. Her view of the world
—through no fault of her own—stopped at the next
wall, or, at most, the next *gulli.* She didn't even know

whether potatoes grew in the ground or on trees. People were shut in and everything was cooked and over-cooked, yet there was sickness—no wonder people were constantly preoccupied with their digestion and with home remedies. Children were forever being told, "Don't go out—you'll be run over by a tonga or a bicycle." They grew up afraid of life. Most *shehris* were always thinking of money, saving it up, hoarding it, using it to build things. They kept shop, so they knew exactly what one paid for one's merchandise, and what one could expect to get for it. They could even get along without women, for there were shops where one could eat. That was why Mamaji felt that a woman was a shoe that a man could wear and discard.

But she thought that Daddyji didn't know her side of it. He was such a simple villager that he hadn't even known for the first couple of months of his marriage that Babuji was a *dohaju*.

WHEN MAMAJI had been married only two months, she started worrying about being sterile. Daddyji took her to a hospital in Lahore, to consult an eminent woman doctor. "Your wife has an infantile uterus," the doctor said, in Mamaji's presence, and added something in technical language she couldn't understand. Suddenly, everything went dark for her. When she opened her eyes, her teeth were clenched and she couldn't open mouth. Daddyji was sitting by her, massaging her temples with his enveloping hand.

"Sometimes a classmate of mine used to faint," he

was saying softly. "If you massaged here"—he pressed
on her brow—"he would recover. Do you feel pain
there? You see how you took a deep breath? That
clears your head. You see, your supraorbital nerve is
here." He pressed on her brow again.

As he pressed, her jaw relaxed. He gave her some
water.

"Women are like shoes," she sobbed.

"What rubbish you talk," he said. "For us Arya
Samajists, women are goddesses and an integral part
of us. Look at my uncle Bhaji Ganga Ram. You know
that his wife, Chhoti Bhabiji, is childless—she's had
thirteen miscarriages—but has she been turned out, has
she been shown the door?"

He might be able to bring her out of her hysterical
fit, but there was no bringing her tears under control.
Her weeping finally stopped only after he had taken
her to a second gynecologist, who said that all her condition required was some knee-elbow exercises. Even so,
she didn't go back with Daddyji to Montgomery that
day or that week. She spent days in the *chaubara* with
Mataji, who would massage the area around her navel
for hours at a time, and feed her *suji halwah*, in order
to align something she called "the childbearing nerve"
with the navel. The childbearing nerve was elusive.
Sometimes it seemed to be on the left, sometimes on
the right. In any case, it was hard to feel. Mother and
daughter worked on it until, one morning, Mataji announced that the childbearing nerve was finally in
place and Mamaji should go home to her husband.

Within the next two months, Mamaji conceived.
She had never been happier. (Twenty-five years later,

Mamaji's third daughter, Urmila, had trouble conceiving, and Mamaji tried Mataji's cure on her, with equally good results.)

SHE WANTED to cook for him, but in Montgomery the kitchen was a separate building, some distance from the bungalow, and near the servants' quarters. Anyway, he had a cook and a bearer, and they considered her mere appearance at the kitchen door a reprimand. For them she was the "memsahib," whose place was inside the house, and whose only function was to give orders. She wanted to wash his clothes, but there was a resident *dhobi* (washerman). One day, she started rewashing his sleeping suit in sweet-smelling Sunlight soap. He saw her and said, laughing, "If you wash clothes, the *dhobi* will die of hunger." So, once she had adjusted to the place, she mostly ate and slept and went on long walks with him—in her walking shoes—along the canal, each time as incredulous as she had been when she was first told that the canal was not God's creation but something the British had thought up and brought there.

One day, she went out for a walk with the wife of his friend Vidyadhar. As she and Mrs. Vidyadhar were strolling back toward the house, plucking marigolds along the way and sticking them in each other's hair, she was stunned to see him standing on the veranda, looking at her as if a *bhoot* had got inside him. She had been reaching up to make sure the flower behind her ear was in place, and her hand stopped in midair. Before she knew it, Mrs. Vidyadhar had slipped away, and he had come down the steps and was standing over her. He looked at her so severely that her earring fell off. (The earring may not have been fastened properly, or she may have loosened it while she was arranging flowers in her hair, but she felt certain that his look had yanked it off her ear.) "Why weren't you here to receive me?" he demanded. "I've been here half an hour, and, for all I knew, you might have fallen into the canal or been run over by a lorry. I just sent the bearer on a bicycle to look for you!"

He had not been expected for another hour. He had told her to be independent, to make friends, to get fresh air. He was always telling her not to be so housebound, not to be so timid. But she said nothing in her own defense, simply waited patiently for his rage to spend itself—as she knew it soon would—reflecting that he wanted her to be independent as long as she stayed by his side.

It seemed to her that he didn't want to let her out of his sight. If he went on tours of inspection, he took her along in the car, at first having her hold the steering wheel while he worked the pedals, then having her sit behind the wheel. Rolling along the road with her hands on the wheel, she would feel self-confident, but when the time came to stop the car she would get flustered, and he would have to throw his leg over hers and slam down the brake. If he went to the club to play tennis, as he did practically every day, he would sit her down in a chair next to the court and would keep coming over to her to explain the game. If he stayed on at the club—or went to a friend's house—to play bridge, as he often did, she would wait for him with the other wives, many of whom were older and treated her like the group's mascot.

Sometimes, he would go to the club alone at four o'clock, play some tennis, and then settle down to a game of cards. He would come home late, and she would heat up his dinner for him and listen to him tell about his winnings and losses, his good hands and silly mistakes. She would listen to him with complete concentration, liking the fact that he couldn't keep anything to himself—in the Punjabi idiom, "in his stomach"—when *she* could keep the sorrows of the whole world inside her. She thought that perhaps it was because he was afraid of nothing that he never worried about saying anything to anyone, while she was always afraid of consequences if she didn't keep everything to herself.

❦

SHE LOVED TO EAT, especially *maltas* (oranges)— pulpy but juicy, red, and sweet. Sometimes, they would go over to the place of a friend who was famous for growing *maltas*. They would walk around his groves, testing oranges from each of the trees, and when they found a tree whose oranges they particularly liked, Daddyji would pay the gardener five rupees and ask him to give them two or three dozen oranges from that particular tree. As they waited for the gardener to pick the fruit, they would sit under a tree, and Daddyji would sing to Mamaji a childhood song, in a voice that was little more trained than hers:

Take the wisdom from the Tree,
O man,
Take the wisdom from the Tree,
O man.

Whoever throws a stone at you
Give him fruit, O man.
Take the wisdom from the Tree.

Summer or winter,
Whatever the hardships, endure.
Never cry in woe.
Take the wisdom from the Tree.

When they got home, he would cut the oranges open with his Rogers Sheffield pocketknife—"made in England"—and watch her suck them while he ate with her, until most of the oranges were gone.

ONCE, in exasperation, he cried, "Whatever I say, you just say yes!" He must have immediately repented of his outburst, because he then tried to make a joke of his remark, touching her hair and saying, "If it is nightfall and I say, 'The day is risen outside,' you are to say, 'Yes, the day is risen and the sun is shining.'"

"Yes, sir!" she said, in English, with a laugh.

In the beginning, she had felt that everything he said and did was right, and that everything she said and did was wrong. To an extent, she still felt that, and, indeed, never contradicted him. In front of him, she was as submissive as Mataji was in front of Babuji, but when he was out of the house (when, as she thought of it, his back was turned), she would rush about the house self-importantly, issuing orders to the servants, and would pray to the gods to protect her from his anger even while she was sabotaging him in little ways: spending only four rupees for vegetables and fruit when he had given her five, and hiding the extra rupee for the day when she was turned out of the house, like Tirath Ram's first wife.

Once, Daddyji happened to return home unexpectedly from the office for a file he had forgotten. He caught Mamaji sitting on the bed cradling a clay idol of Durga Mata and singing to it. He could hardly have heard more than a few notes, because she stopped her singing the moment she saw him; even so, he looked at her sadly. "Such superstitions don't become you," he said. "You're the daughter of an Arya Samajist and the wife of an Arya Samajist."

After that, she kept her prayers private, like the secrets of the *chaubara*. At the same time, she redoubled her efforts to become a student of his moods. She extracted information about him from her in-laws. She discovered that what he called her "vein of superstition" had in fact been the lifeblood of his own family, and after this she would now and again quietly remind him that as children Lalaji and his brother Haru Ram, and Bhabiji and her brother Gulab Mal, too, had all worn heavy gold hoops in their ears, believing them to be lucky links in "the chain of life." Or she would get him to tell her how Bhabiji used to sprinkle holy Ganges water on him whenever he had been accidentally touched by a Muslim or an Untouchable, and then she would ask innocently, "How did she keep the bottle refilled? How often were there pilgrims going from your village to the Ganges? Didn't they have their own bottles to fill?"

Or she would say, "Just like you, we all believed that the earth was balanced on the horns of the Great White Bull. We used to say that whenever the bull moved his head—you know, whenever he twitched or turned—he shifted the weight of his burden and caused an earthquake."

Or she would ask, when she and Daddyji were settling down to sleep on the veranda on a moonlit night, "What was that prayer that Bhabiji and her mother used to say to Chanda Mama [Moon Uncle] when they saw it rising? How did it go?"

Although he must have heard the prayer a hundred times, he couldn't repeat it. But her question was rhetorical, since she had grown up hearing the same prayer:

> Blessed thou, O moon, bring us happiness,
> Give us peace and blessings to all.

He had told her that Bhabiji and her mother would stay inside the evening of the fourth day of the new moon, because they thought that seeing the moon on that day brought bad luck.

She reflected that, however much he might scold her for being superstitious, she had something in common with his mother and his grandmother.

❧

SHE HAD ALWAYS SEEN MATAJI going around with a big ring of keys clipped to the waist of her sari—keys that constantly rattled and jangled as Mataji did her

housework. Now she had a ring on her own sari, with
a key to the storeroom, to her Singer sewing machine,
to her cupboard. As she went about the house, a jin-
gling sound accompanied her, like the sound of ankle
bells she had once heard on a dancer in Shahalmi Gate.
Although the keys made her feel secure, her bunch of
keys still seemed far smaller than Mataji's, and partly,
she felt, that was Daddyji's fault.

"In this house, you are never to lock a door," he
once told her.

At the time, she was sitting with a little notebook
in her lap and adding up with a pencil the prices of her
morning purchases of fruits and vegetables, just as she
remembered seeing Bulaki Ram do. But when she
heard Daddyji's words she put aside her notebook and
pencil.

"You need never keep accounts, either," he was
saying. "I want to keep an open house, without either
locks or accounts."

She put her keys and her notebook away in her
chest of drawers.

For many weeks, she did not go near the notebook.
Then she realized that there were many things he did
not approve of and yet did not object to if she did them
in private, in his absence—for when he found her out,
he would only laugh at her feminine ways. For the
time being, she left her keys in their drawer, but she
resumed her household accounts.

At the beginning of August, when Mamaji was
five months pregnant, Daddyji's family came from Lahore to stay with them in Montgomery for a month. It
was the first time that Bhabiji had come to stay with

Mamaji, and Mamaji was apprehensive about having to look after her mother-in-law, but she welcomed the chance to take the measure of Daddyji's brothers, most of whom he—as the oldest son and an earning member of the family—had been supporting with monthly contributions. Except for Daulat Ram, who now had a job in Lahore and couldn't come, they were all students and were all there on holiday: gullible Balwant, twenty-seven; truculent Raj Kanwar, twenty-five; studious Romesh, twenty-two; and handsome Krishan, eleven—the baby of the family, whom Daddyji had more or less adopted. Bibi Parmeshwari Devi's oldest son, Dharam Bir, seventeen, whom Daddyji was bringing up like one of his brothers, had also come.

When they had been in Montgomery only two days, Bhabiji said to Mamaji, "Daughter, have you seen my gold shirt studs?" Mamaji remembered picking up the gold studs from the chest of drawers and tying them up in the end of her veil for safekeeping before going to sleep. The end of the veil where she remembered tying the knot was puckered and wrinkled, but the studs were gone. She had lost her mother-in-law's studs! In a panic, she turned the house upside down looking for them, but they were nowhere to be found. Next morning, Mamaji reached into her jewelry box for her diamond earrings. They were missing. Then she couldn't find the gold brooch fashioned in the shape of a chinar leaf which she habitually pinned on her sari. Then Balwant complained that he couldn't find his pocketknife, and Romesh that he couldn't find his fountain pen.

When Raj Kanwar heard of the missing property,

he confronted Mamaji accusingly and said, "Who is it? Who has the gall to steal Bhabiji's studs when I am living in the house?" He considered everyone in the house a suspect, and undertook an investigation, beginning with perhaps the most defenseless person of all, the fan-puller.

The fan-puller was a skinny eleven-year-old boy whom Mamaji had noticed hanging around the club looking for a position and had brought home. She had taken him in hand. She had made him a pajama and kurta of white muslin, and got him a cap to keep his hair from falling into his eyes. She had taught him to stand up straight, to look alert and neat, to speak properly. He had become so attached to Mamaji that he would follow her around the house, stopping whenever she stopped, looking at whatever she looked at. Every time she sat down on the veranda, he was at his station, pulling and letting go the rope of the fan so rhythmically that she was lulled into fancying that it creaked and swung automatically.

Raj Kanwar now picked up the double-barrelled gun that Daddyji, in the English manner, kept in the house, and aimed it at the fan-puller, who was at his post on the veranda, as if he were a hardened dacoit caught in a robbery, rather than an eleven-year-old waif.

"Where are the studs? Where is the brooch? Where is the fountain pen?" he shouted.

"Which studs, Sahib, which studs?" the fan-puller cried.

"You see these two barrels? Look at them!" Raj Kanwar thundered.

The boy at first tried to hold his ground, but then hid behind Mamaji, who was almost as frightened as he was. He looked at Raj Kanwar's fierce frown and at the black gun, and then, suddenly becoming very cool and worldly, said to Raj Kanwar, "Put down the gun, Sahib, and follow me."

By now, Raj Kanwar's brothers had gathered, and they all trooped, incredulous, behind the fan-puller, who took them to his quarters, jumped up on his cot, and brought from behind a rafter studs and cufflinks, brooches and bangles—all the things they had noticed were missing and some they might never have missed.

Raj Kanwar was ready to march the boy down to the local police station at gunpoint, but Daddyji wouldn't hear of it. The little boy continued to pull Mamaji's fan and to get instruction. Now, however, he also had to clean out and dust the rafters of his quarters daily, with Mamaji watching from the door.

Early in September, Daddyji's family returned to Lahore, and Mamaji's family arrived to visit and then to take her back with them for her confinement.

One night, when Mamaji was in bed on the veranda—it was still too warm to sleep inside—she thought of getting up and bolting the back door, but she was afraid that Daddyji would scold her. She dropped off to sleep.

Suddenly, she sat up in bed. All around, servants were shouting, "Thieves! Thieves!"

Everyone rushed into the house. All Mamaji's saris and Daddyji's suits were heaped up on the floor. Daddyji's dress trousers had been used as a torch, and the house stank of burned wool. The whole floor was streaked with telltale ashes and muddy footprints, and there were drops of candle tallow.

Mamaji thanked Ram that after the fan-puller incident she had put all her jewelry in a bank locker. And she was triumphant. "You see, we should have locked the house," she said to Daddyji.

"But we are missing only three things," he said, having completed the inventory. "Mataji's trunk, which was locked, and your Singer sewing machine, which you had locked, along with my cricket bag, which they probably didn't know how to open. They were clearly looking for your jewelry."

"You are always right," she said, with a smile. But she took out her keys and clipped them to her waist. Afterward, she was never seen without them.

SOME FIFTY YEARS after Mamaji and Daddyji were married, they were in the bedroom of a little house they had built in New Delhi. It was during the winter holidays, and many of their seven children—including me—and fourteen grandchildren were gathered around them. One of the children was slumped in an armchair, another was stretched out on the floor, a third was half asleep across the foot of the bed; in fact, almost every available sitting or lying space in the room seemed to be occupied. Some of the youngest grandchildren were running about playing tag or riding a big Alsatian dog named Caesar. The subject of Montgomery and the birth of the oldest child, Promila, came up, and Daddyji realized that the day of their golden anniversary had almost slipped past them. Mamaji, who was straightening her saris in the cupboard, laughed, and brought out a packet of letters from the first year or so of their marriage, when they had sometimes been apart.

In those days, Mamaji had looked upon Montgomery as a forlorn place, where she was camping out with an all-powerful man. She had difficulty pronouncing the English name Montgomery, so she called it "the new place," "that place," "the station," in much the way she referred to him—whom custom forbade her to call by name, even out of his presence—by such epithets as "the dear," "the long-lived," and "thee." Moreover, in those early days of marriage she had often been homesick and unwell. She missed Mataji, so whenever she could, she went to her in Lahore; the city was only a few hours from Montgomery by his Chevrolet or the Karachi Mail. Moreover, at the time of Mamaji's first confinement, in the winter of 1926, she was away from Daddyji for about three months, including the traditional forty-day lying-in period after delivery. During these intervals of separation, they wrote to each other almost daily. Through the years, she had been able to preserve some of his letters, in their envelopes, carrying them with her from place to place like her jewelry box. (Many of his other letters to her and all of her letters to him, along with Montgomery and Lahore and their home and practically everything else, had been lost to Pakistan at the time of Partition.) In her hesitant English, she now read out to the gathered children and grandchildren—to whoever would listen —Daddyji's few surviving letters to her. Both of them laughed so much over the letters that she could scarcely read and he could scarcely hear what was being read; and at times their eyes teared so much with their laughter that it was hard to tell whether they were laughing or crying. We children, listening to the letters, joined in much of the laughter, and felt no embarrassment at being with our parents during such an intimate moment—perhaps because, among other things, the passage of time and the recent history of India had turned Montgomery into a remote memory.

Mgy
July 12, 26

My Sweetest Love,

I am glad to learn that you have reached Lahore safely.

I remember you very very much and your child-like talk. You are really a baby and I love you, your talks and everything of yours.

In December next I will have two babies, one you, and the other little one.

Take care of yourself and do not jump or run. Take complete rest if tired and you must not faint.

With love and thousand kisses,

Your own darling,
Amolak

Montgomery
July 26th, 26

My Own, My Darling, My Love,

I read your sweet letter over and over again, and felt very happy, all the feelings of being tired were gone.

The house looks so sad and lonely without you, that I did not like to stay and went out to Balwant Singh's where the bridge party had collected.

The lawn looks very green after the rains, and the trees seem washed green & beautiful. Birds are chirping this morning on all sides and the weather is pleasant but what use are all these without your smiling face, without your sweet talk, without your grace, without your company and without your child-like habits.

Really "no life without a wife" is true, and I am very anxious to get you back here.

It is 7 o'clock in the morning and I am sitting out in the lawn but all the time I am thinking of you and you alone. I want to go to the canal but I do not like to go without you.

If you were here, you and I would have gone on the canal to the falls and would have brought some lemons and together we would have prepared the lemon squash. Now who would give me lemon squash?

I will go to Dipalpore tomorrow and then hope to come to Lahore next Sunday.

Hoping you are keeping good health and that the "baby" is doing well.

With love and thousands of fond kisses,

> Your own loving
> darling
> AMOLAK

> Montgomery
> 1 November 1926

DEARER THAN MY DEAREST HOPES, SHANTI, I GREET YOU IN THE NAME OF GOD,

I have received your letter full of love. It made me feel very happy. I will now go to Calcutta in January or February—the order has come not to go to Calcutta in November—so now I will be able to show you and the "baby" the city. It's my intention to take ten days leave then and show you and the "baby" Delhi, Benares, Agra, and Lucknow—all these cities.

Perhaps I'll come to Lahore on Divali day. If I come, whether you come back with me to Montgomery or not will be up to you. My own wish is that you come back with me. Without you, my heart is absolutely not in the place. But, of course, all will depend on your health.

Tomorrow I will have to go on tour, again.

The chicks are really quite fetching. Five of them are black and one is white. All day long, they cheep, cheep, cheep. They seem very good-hearted.

You don't know English, and I don't know Hindi, how can I write a long letter in Hindi? [This particular letter is in elementary Hindi, but the rest of the letters in the packet are in English.]

With love and kisses,

> Your own,
> DARLING

> Montgomery
> Dec. 3rd, 26

MY SWEETEST LOVE, MY OWN,

I received your loving letter today. I am glad you saw Mrs. Shave [an obstetrician]. I think Mrs. Bonner [a private nurse] is very expensive and I will ask the Lady Health visitor to attend to you for a week or so. You may send for all the things from Juggat Singh & Sons [chemists], and I will settle about the price myself.

You have written that Babuji gave me some money and that I did not tell you.

Babuji did *not* give me any money but that morning he promised to send me Rs 500 & he has sent me a cheque for Rs 500. I have also received your Rs 200. I am collecting all this money do you know for what?

It is a secret. I will tell you in February 1927. I am *not* collecting this money to go to England, you don't wish me to go to England, do you?

I will bring two canisters of Ghee when I come.

I do not know why I wake up every morning at 4 or 5 A.M. & then I am hungry of love and food. I want you every minute, now I sleep inside where we used to sleep last winter & I take my meals in bed with *razai* [quilt] over my knees. How last year we used to eat together! I am longing to get you here. Your storeroom is now complete & a door has been put into it also.

The hen & her chickens are growing, they play about amongst the flowers all day and are very pretty.

The vegetable garden is all green & nice, parrots & birds chirp all day, & the weather is very nice indeed, but all this does not look nice to me without you. "No life without a wife." I am not getting good food. Milkhi is gone on 10 days' leave & I have a new cook.

With love, kisses & kindest regards,

Your most affectionate,

AMOLAK

P.S. I can't wait to tell you the secret, dearest Shanti. I am building you and the "baby" a bungalow.

Montgomery
[Undated]

MY DEAR LOVED ONE, SHANTI, NAMASTE,

During the nights here, it is very cold these days, and I feel even colder sleeping alone. If you were near me, how much better I would sleep! And yet, I'll have to bear two months like this, and these months will prove very difficult.

The house is being white-washed all over, just now. If you want a room done up in any special color, do write. Otherwise, I will have the rooms done in off-white as before.

The white sofa and armchair have arrived. The white looks very nice in the room.

Today the Governor is here. Tomorrow he goes to Okara. And the day after, Dipalpore. I will go along with him just to keep him company.

Khawja-Sahib went back to Lahore by the Mail yesterday, and I too long to come to Lahore.

With love, kisses and kisses,
Your loving husband,
AMOLAK

Montgomery
Dec. 8th, 1926

MY DEAREST, MY OWN, MY DARLING,

I have received your loving letter of yesterday. You have written that the "baby" has taken a lower position, this means that it will be about two or three weeks after that the delivery will take place. The pains also are not important because the pain in the back is a sign—and not ordinary pains.

Therefore, I think it will be about the 25th Dec. and I will be there on the 18th Dec.

I am going to Okara tomorrow & will arrange with the Lady Doctor.

You should do as you like with your gold bangles, I have no objection.

When you get pains in front and in the back let me know.

Keep yourself happy and cheerful, and do not worry, everything will be all right.

With love & kisses,

Your most affectionate own,

AMOLAK

Montgomery
Dec. 17th, 1926

MY DEAREST & SWEETEST,

I will leave Montgomery tomorrow at about 3 P.M. & reach Lahore at about 7 or 8 P.M. Milkhi has come back but is still ill and yet, the food arrangements are quite good.

I have received your loving letter of yesterday. Anxiously waiting to meet & kiss you & embrace you.

Do not worry about English. Hindi is good & I like it.

With love and kisses,

Your own darling,

AMOLAK

Montgomery
Dec. 31st, 1926

MY DEAREST & SWEETEST LOVE,

I arrived here quite safely yesterday and everything is in order. The bungalow is progressing nicely and now one can make out the limits of each room. We shall have five big rooms, three bathrooms, two small rooms, and there shall be a veranda in front and behind. If I had any money later on I will also make a kitchen, a garage & servants' quarters but that will be seen.

Lt. Col. Sodhi & Mrs Sodhi the father and mother of Mrs. Puri are here & I dined last night at their place and played bridge. I won Rs15.

Write to me all about the little darling girl. [Mamaji had been delivered of a baby girl on December 22nd.] How many times do you feed her? Does she get up at night? How is she growing? Don't forget to write every detail. Kiss her for me & give her my love.

With love & thousand kisses, get these from the baby, I am,

Your own darling,

AMOLAK

Montgomery
Jan. 4th, 1927

My Dearest & Sweetest Love,

I hope you & the baby are doing splendidly. I received your loving letter but though your letters are welcome, I want to receive you & the baby, and when I come I will bring you back with me. You must be prepared to come. I am so lonely and I want you so very much.

The canal is going to close on the 6th inst. & the work at the bungalow will have to stop. We will finish it after I come back from Calcutta. So far no orders have come for Calcutta. Munshi has come back. I did not pay the tonga-wallah. I took him at 8 A.M. I left him at 8:30 when I just caught the Karachi mail, pay him -/10/- [annas] for one hour.

I hope the baby does not trouble you much at night. Who sleeps in your room at night? Write to me fully.

With love & kisses to you & the baby,

Your affectionate & loving,

AMOLAK

Montgomery
January 12th, 1927

My Dearest & Sweetest Loving Shanti,

I have again come back without you. I thought I would bring you back but your mother I could not refuse, she was so kind and I did not like to disappoint her.

199

I have got all your loving letters and thank you for the same.

The little "dolly" I want to bring here and play with. I love both the mother and daughter. Of course I love the mother the most; and mother loves her baby most.

I have not received any orders about Calcutta so far. The work at the building has not been stopped and the progress is very good indeed. The steel beams have arrived from Karachi and will be put up when the walls are ready.

Write to me soon and a long long letter & write all about yourself and the "dolly."

With love & kisses,

Most affectionately yours,

AMOLAK

AT FIRST, the dolly—or Promila, as they named her —did not urinate, and Mamaji feared for her life. After twenty-four hours, she finally did urinate. Mamaji experienced her first feelings of relief and tranquillity since going into labor. She felt that her main goal in life had been attained, for she had grown up hearing Mataji say, "Once you have a man's child, he is tied to you by a silken thread. For that reason, it's much more important to be a mother than just a wife."

Mamaji now had a new routine, defined by watching over the baby—nursing her, putting her to sleep, washing her clothes. Daddyji, who hated to go away from her or Promila, even on short tours, would lecture her about everything: how to hold the baby; how to burp her; how to put the diaper on her so that it was loose and gave her the most freedom to kick. If Mamaji even hinted at disagreement, she would only prolong the lecture. She began to console herself by thinking that if he had married an educated woman, who could speak English and sing, that woman wouldn't have lasted in his household for ten days. She would have waved her hand, said "Ta-ta," and walked out. Maybe he was lucky to have someone who didn't talk back and was always prepared to do what he told her—in front of him.

After Promila's birth, Mamaji felt confident that she could have children, but now she became anxious about bringing forth only daughters. That silken thread, she feared, might break unless she had his son.

As Daddyji was driving Mamaji back to Montgomery after her confinement in Lahore—Promila was then forty days old—he said to her, "You remember that surprise I wrote to you about?"

" 'Making a new house with bare feet,' " she said shyly, quoting a Punjabi saying. She knew that he had almost no savings, and that his responsibility for educating his brothers would go on for years—Krishan was just in third standard. How could he think of building a house? She had, of course, thought of marriage in terms of having a house of her own, but she had long since decided that her husband was a strange man who seemed to have no interest in holding on to possessions. And now he had built a house as a surprise. (I have recorded in my biographical portrait of my father, "Daddyji," that he and Mamaji jointly planned and built the house. That is how Daddyji remembered it at the time I was writing, probably because at that point in his married life he could scarcely imagine building a house without having her at his side.)

He was telling her that he had completed the Montgomery house in just two months. He had been able to get all his supplies very quickly: bricks and cement had been freely available; then he had had the good luck to get, for roofing, some old wooden railway sleepers (sleepers were the ties used to keep railway tracks aligned) that had been lying rotting in the stables of one Colonel Cole. "The Colonel is so busy breeding horses that he didn't know what treasures he had lying in his stables," Daddyji said. "He was delighted to get rid of the sleepers. He even provided me with a lorry to carry them away! I had the sleepers sawed through, painted to protect them from white ants, and placed end to end on a steel girder. I covered them with cement, and I covered the cement with five inches of mud, and I covered the mud with tiles. There was the roof."

She listened to him keenly, thinking all the time that the laborers must have robbed him blind. They must have put too much sand in the cement, or sat around smoking a hookah when they should have been working. She wished she had been there to supervise them.

"The whole house cost me only ten thousand rupees," he was saying. "I raised the money easily—with our little savings, with a loan from Basheshwar Nath, and with a mortgage from the Punjab National Bank. Look, there is our house!"

She has never forgotten her first view of the house. The orange light of evening gave the whole building the warmth of burnished brass. On one side, in the distance, was the canal; on the other was the compound of the deputy commissioner. In front was a big tennis court, as if he had built himself his own small club.

She stepped onto the veranda, with Promila asleep on her shoulder.

"The veranda goes all around the house," he said. "It is so wide that we can put up as many of our relatives as we like, and we can all sleep out here through rains and storms. Sleeping here is like sleeping outside, except that you are sheltered."

She followed him inside. He showed her the drawing room, the dining room, the two bedrooms, all quite cavernous and all quite forlorn. The house smelled of whitewash, and it felt open and empty—there seemed to be no cozy corner. She missed the pervasive smell of ghi and incense and the constant sound of children running and squabbling—things that she had from childhood associated with a home. But then at the back of the house she came upon a plot of land for an orchard and a vegetable garden, lying fallow, waiting for her hand. She could picture it full of rosebushes and fruit trees—of lemons, mangoes, and *maltas*. Beyond the garden were the chimneys of the kitchen and the servants' quarters.

"Whom will I talk to? Whom will Promila play with?" she asked herself. In the distance, she heard crickets and frogs, chirping and croaking, in the heavy Montgomery silence, which she had still not got used to. It seemed to her that she and they were all trapped in the "sha-ah-ahn, sha-ah-ahn" of an inland ocean.

Promila woke up and started crying for milk.

❧

"Now THAT WE HAVE PROMILA," he said to her as they were bumping along in the car to the club one day, "we need a car that will ride smoother. We've had this Chevrolet only two years and it's already falling apart."

She shifted the sleeping Promila, who was now nearly a year old, to her other arm. The car jolted, and Promila woke with a start and began to cry.

"We really must get a new car," he said.

The car was part of her dowry—almost as dear to her as her wedding jewelry and her saris—and for a moment she wondered whether, if the car went, she could be far behind. But then she cradled Promila in her arms and felt better.

He had often complained to her about the car, saying, "I'm sure Babuji must have tried to pinch pennies, or else why would he have bought a year-old model— and a demonstration one at that?"

She had tried to intimate to him in a roundabout way that Babuji was knowledgeable about victorias, which were all that Lahoris needed in order to get around, but not about cars, which were only new toys for the England-returned. Anyway, the fault might not be with the car at all but with the Montgomery roads, which he had often complained were full of bumps and pits.

A few days later, he came home and announced that he had got permission from the deputy commissioner to raffle off the old car. As he explained what a raffle was, she reflected on one more difference between the Mehtas and the Mehras: the Mehtas, from a large subcaste, were always trying something new and outlandish, as if to proclaim to the world their individuality, their distinctiveness, while the Mehras, from a small subcaste, held to the old and ordinary ways, as if to announce to the world their inbred indifference to it.

In spite of herself, she was soon engulfed, like Daddyji, in the excitement of the raffle. He was one of the kings of the district, and all the people under him—the sanitary inspectors, the sweepers, the village leaders—were busy selling raffle tickets at a rupee each. Many people who didn't even own a cow bought a ticket for the Doctor-Sahib's motorcar. After all, having a car was even better than having a Singer sewing machine. A car moved by itself, without the need even of tracks.

Daddyji collected, altogether, fifteen hundred rupees.

On the appointed evening, a little band of officers gathered at the club. Daddyji dropped the counterfoils into his felt hat and took the hat over to the deputy commissioner. The deputy commissioner shut his eyes, fished out a counterfoil, and, reading off the piece of paper in his hand, announced, "One, one, one, two."

The officers looked at the tickets in their hands, crumpled them, and tossed them on the floor, laughing, once it was clear that none of them had won the car.

The winning number was traced to a rich landlord who lived in Okara, twenty-three miles away. He arrived the next morning in a Ford with a driver, and, as Mamaji looked on from the steps of the veranda, he jumped into the Chevrolet, bouncing on the seat and slamming the door as if it were a hard-wearing lorry, and not her father's fragile gift. He drove away without even pausing to look back at her.

❧

FIVE MONTHS after the birth of Promila, Mamaji became pregnant for the second time, and in the course of her pregnancy she was again often in Lahore. The separation from Daddyji again prompted many letters back and forth, but again only a few of Daddyji's survive:

27-7-27

MY DEAREST SHANTI,

I am sorry Promila is giving you trouble but after all she is a child and loves you very much.

I dined with Col. and Mrs Forster last night and came back here at 11.30 P.M. It was raining and for the first time I took *Rickshaw*.

I do not like to sit in the Rickshaws. [He didn't like the idea of coolies working like animals.]

I have been very busy and have not played any Tennis or Bridge except yesterday.

You may go to Kasauli with your parents. What about your warm clothes? You can send Jagtu [a servant] to Montgomery to bring your clothes etc.

If you go to Kasauli you must be very careful and follow the advice of Mrs. Shave.

Let me know what things you want me to bring for you or Promila.

With love and kisses,

Your affectionate
AMOLAK

On February 19, 1928, Mamaji was delivered of a second daughter, who was named Nirmila. Daddyji was in Lahore for her birth, but had to rush back to his work in Montgomery immediately.

Montgomery
March 7th.28

MY DEAREST AND SWEETEST LOVE,

I arrived here safely but I can not tell you how lonely I feel.

You are probably not so sad as I am because you have Promila and the little baby to play with. I have no body, not even to talk to.

I will stay here for three more days and will then go out on tour and remain out till the 25th inst.

I have agreed to rent the bungalow to Patel Cotton Co. from 1st September at Rs 110/-/- per mensem. Thus we can spend summer here and will see what happens in winter.

I went out for tennis today and we could not make four for bridge so I am home early and doing office work.

I hope your temperature is normal in the evenings. Babuji has not sent me a card about you.

If you can not write ask him to write to me.

With love and *thousand* kisses to you and *one* kiss to Promila & one to the baby.

Your Loving Husband,
AMOLAK

About this time, Daddyji was told that in the winter he would probably be transferred to Lahore as its district health officer.

IX

MEHTA FAMILY

I N THE AUTUMN OF 1928, WHEN MAMAJI AND
Daddyji had been married about three years,
they were attending a christening in Lahore, to
which Daddyji had just been transferred from
Montgomery as district health officer. Savitri
Khanna, the child's mother, was the daughter
of Principal Sain Das, and she came up to Mamaji after
the ceremony and said, "We all grew up like the fingers
of one hand, but since our marriages we've scarcely
seen each other. Why don't we buy land together here
in Lahore and build houses next to each other?"

The child, who had just been christened by having
all his hair rudely shaved off, was bawling so loudly in
his mother's arms that Mamaji couldn't hear what was
being said, and Savitri Khanna had to repeat her suggestion.

"We have barely finished building a house in
Montgomery," Mamaji said. "The money-knot of my
sari is empty."

But Daddyji overheard her, and said, "A house in
lonely Montgomery is no match for a house in Lahore.
Let's get some nice land here, on Temple Road, and
build a new house. I may not have any money to my
name, but I carry my luck with me."

Within days, Daddyji had found a piece of land on
Temple Road, hardly a minute's walk from where
Babuji and Mataji were now living, in a bungalow on
Mozang Road. (They had moved from the Shahalmi
Gate house only a few weeks after Mamaji's marriage.)

He and Mamaji bought one portion of the Temple Road land; Savitri and her husband, Hari Dev Khanna, also bought a portion; and Principal Sain Das bought the rest. Mamaji sold her dowry jewelry and her silver tea set, Daddyji sold the Montgomery house, and they borrowed some money at interest from Savitri and Hari Dev Khanna; then they started building their house.

The house was completed in November of 1929, just in time for Mamaji to give birth to her third child there. Mamaji was sure that the completion of the house in Lahore augured good luck. But the delivery turned out to be a difficult one—she had a hemorrhage and had to be given a transfusion—and the child was a third daughter. When Mamaji saw the baby, she felt that the shadow of her bad luck would follow her to the cremation ground. She turned her face to the wall.

Just then, Bhabiji came to see the new baby, so Mamaji turned around. Mamaji felt sure that she would see in her mother-in-law's eyes a look of disapproval, or, at least, dismay, because the wife of her eldest son was capable of producing only girls. She had grown up hearing that on such an occasion a mother-in-law bared her teeth, warning of dire things to come. Instead, Bhabiji looked at the baby and broke into a beatific smile. "She's the prettiest baby I've ever seen," she said, laying the baby across her lap. "She's just like her father. I always wanted a second daughter, and she will be a sister to him."

"Bhabiji, she's our daughter, too," Daddyji said, with a laugh, and he took the baby. He immediately named the child Urmila, to accord with Promila and Nirmila.

The three girls were born within the space of three years. Mamaji had scarcely finished breast-feeding one baby—she breast-fed most of her children until they were six months old—before another baby was on the way. But, to Mamaji's unceasing amazement, the three were entirely different.

Promila was delicate and restless almost from the day of her arrival. The climate of Montgomery didn't seem to suit her. She sneezed a lot, and when she was barely two months old she came down with pneumonia. "She's going," Mamaji thought, and she clutched the crying baby to her shoulder, feeling the baby's forehead and feet every few minutes to see if the fever had abated. Daddyji, like many doctors, was reluctant to treat his own child, and both he and Mamaji placed their trust in the district civil surgeon, who lived across the road. He stopped by every hour or so, as much to counsel and comfort Mamaji and Daddyji as to treat the baby. Promila recovered quickly but remained thin and irritable. Mamaji took her to Babuji's house in Lahore, thinking that Lahore's slightly warmer climate would improve her health. But everyone at Babuji's house was constantly picking her up and playing with her, and, as Mamaji later put it, "the social climate of Lahore didn't suit her." When Mamaji and Promila had been in Lahore only a few days, Daddyji was ordered to go to Calcutta for three months to take a refresher course in the treatment of leprosy; besides being district health officer, he was serving as leprosy

officer for the Punjab. He took Mamaji and Promila—
Mamaji had never travelled far outside her little world
of Lahore and Montgomery—with him on the train.
Promila loved being on the train. She smiled and gur-
gled and slept all through the day and a half of the
journey. But when they reached Calcutta she kicked
up a fuss, as if she didn't have any use for the noisy
metropolis.

Nirmila, as a baby, was chunky and easygoing. She
seldom cried, and seemed to grow up by herself. She
could lie in her crib for hours waving her arms and
kicking, giggling and getting fat.

Urmila seemed to sense from the very beginning
that her being a girl was a disappointment, and she
grew up a fighter. She was a healthy, energetic baby,
the prettiest of the three girls, and almost from the first
she was very particular about who might hold her.
When she was a little older, if she didn't like the look
of someone reaching out for her she would vigorously
push the person away, and if that didn't work she was
not above boxing the person's ears, but always with the
most winning smile.

❧

WHILE MAMAJI WAS STILL RECOVERING from her
confinement with Urmila, most of Daddyji's relatives
in Lahore moved in, so that the new house became the
home of a traditional Indian joint family. She and
Daddyji now had living with them Bhabiji; four of
Daddyji's younger brothers; three of his sister Bibi
Parmeshwari Devi's teen-age children; and one of

Daddyji's first cousins. Daddyji, using a cricket term she didn't understand, insisted on calling the family "the home eleven," when she could count at least fourteen in the house on any given day. Mamaji began to feel—rightly or wrongly—that in Daddyji's affections Bhabiji was first, then his brothers and close relatives, and then their own children, and that she came last. No matter how often he told her that he loved them all equally, she couldn't believe it, because of the way he seemed to allow his brothers Balwant and Raj Kanwar and his cousin Jaswant to treat her.

Balwant, Jaswant, and Raj Kanwar were big, tall, rambunctious fellows in their twenties. At Government College, which they were all attending, they were captains of the swimming and rowing teams and had become known as the Invincibles. Balwant and Jaswant had failed their B.A. examinations. Raj Kanwar had passed, but only on a second try, and was now studying law. All of them could talk themselves out of any situation. (At the time Raj Kanwar failed his B.A. examination, he didn't tell Bhabiji. When, after a month or so, she found out, and asked him about it, he said nonchalantly, "What is there to tell about failing? I would have told you if I'd passed. A good mother like you deserves only good news.")

Mamaji felt that the three boys had been completely spoiled by, among other things, Daddyji's way with money. Ever since Daddyji had taken on the responsibility of supporting the family, he had refused Bhabiji nothing. If she asked for five hundred rupees, he produced five hundred rupees and put them in her lap. If she asked for seven hundred, he produced seven

hundred. No sooner would she get the money than
Balwant, Jaswant, and Raj Kanwar would crowd
around her clamoring for money to pay fees, to buy
books, to get haircuts. She would give them what they
asked for, but more often than not they would squander
it on cigarettes and poker and, instead of going to college, loaf like teen-agers in Lawrence Gardens—crack-
ing jokes, passing the time of day, staring longingly at
the birds in the sky because the birds had wings.

Mamaji felt that Balwant and Jaswant were really
simple and pliable, and by themselves would not have
given her any trouble, but in the company of Raj
Kanwar they were unmanageable. All three were older
than she was, and rarely missed an opportunity to tease
her—as though she were their younger sister instead of
the wife of the head of the family.

If she bought a basket of pears, they would gobble
them up, belch, and then complain about them.

"Those pears were like rocks!"

"She doesn't even know how to choose fruit."

"What can you expect from a mere child?"

If one day there wasn't a meat dish at a meal, they
would nip at Mamaji's heels. They particularly objected
to *dal* (lentils).

"*Dal, dal, dal,* all we ever get to eat in this house is
dal. Is that any way to feed the Invincibles?"

Once, when she thought the Invincibles were out
of the house, she went up to the sideboard, fingered a
bunch of bananas, and chose the ripest one to mash for
Nirmila. Raj Kanwar came up behind her and bellowed, "Give me that banana! Do you want to waste

such a good banana on a baby? She spits it out anyway!"

Another time, she was in bed with abdominal pains. She had developed them from skipping rope at her sister Pushpa's birthday party, where, in the excitement of the moment, she had forgotten that she was still convalescing from Urmila's birth. The doctor had prescribed complete bed rest. Daddyji was all solicitude, but after he left for the office in the morning she heard Raj Kanwar in the next room announce, to the laughter of his acolytes, "She's in bed because she thinks she needs rest day and night."

Then Raj Kanwar summoned a servant with a shout: "Tulsi! Bring hot water immediately!"

"In a minute, Sahib," the servant replied, from Mamaji's room.

"What!"

"Sahib, Mistress is in bed. I'm changing Baby Nirmila's clothes."

Raj Kanwar rushed in, snatched Nirmila out of Tulsi's arms, set her down on the floor, and shoved the servant toward the kitchen.

Mamaji, observing the scene from her bed, was too petrified even to call out to Nirmila, who was screaming, until she could hear Raj Kanwar out on the veranda, contentedly singing as he shaved:

> Walk, walk, walk like a general,
> Talk, talk, talk like a king,
> And the world will belong to you!

When Mamaji was alone, she brooded and seethed

about the Invincibles, scheming to best them in the next encounter, but in front of them she either laughed off their complaints or demurely bowed her head. Once, however, when she heard Raj Kanwar giving Bhabiji a rapid-fire accounting of a hundred-rupee note he had taken from his mother, she spoke up.

"I spent seven rupees on books—right?" Raj Kanwar told Bhabiji. "I gave five rupees to the fruit vender —right? I gave two rupees to Tulsi for bicycle repairs —right? That makes thirty—right?" Bhabiji—trusting, as always—was concentrating on her spinning, and didn't say anything, so Raj Kanwar went on boldly, "Twenty rupees went for fees—right? So here is your balance of thirteen rupees." Bhabiji took the thirteen rupees and blessed him, in her usual way.

Mamaji knew that the Invincibles had the in- genuous Bhabiji wrapped around their fingers to the point where they could make her see lilies and lotuses in the thorns of an acacia tree, yet she found herself saying, to her own horror, "Bhabiji, that makes only thirty-four rupees. He owes you sixty-six rupees."

Raj Kanwar glanced at her, and she thought that she had never seen an angrier man in her life. He said to her under his breath, "You wait. I will make pudding of you." Then he looked straight at Bhabiji and said in a loud voice, "She's a mere child—what does she know about anything?"

"You should speak respectfully to your eldest brother's wife," Bhabiji said, resuming her spinning. "Give her a proper accounting of the hundred rupees. She's very good at household accounts."

He didn't say anything then, but when he and

Mamaji were out of Bhabiji's hearing he turned on her.

She stammered, "After all, the money comes from Doctor-Sahib's pocket, and I have a right—"

"Right?" he bellowed. "I'm his brother! I'm his blood! She's my mother! Who are you? You want to separate brother from brother, mother from son?"

Whenever she found Daddyji in a good mood, she would complain to him about the Invincibles. He would listen calmly and then say, "You should settle it yourself. Just behave like the eldest brother's wife—don't get into squabbles with them and start *tu-tu, main-main* [you-you, me-me]—and they will respect you."

Yet, try as she would to do what Daddyji had told her, Raj Kanwar always managed to find an opportunity to make a new scene. Such scenes may not have been as frequent or as severe as she later remembered, but each stood out in her mind, as frightening in memory as the "tuk-tuk" of Babuji's walking stick in her childhood.

DADDYJI AND MAMAJI HAD A QUARREL one evening. Later, they couldn't remember how it had begun—only that some small complaint about Raj Kanwar or Bhabiji, about bananas or money, had flared into his making wounding comparisons between her and Bhabiji: Bhabiji was gracious to her fingertips, charitable and forgiving; Mamaji was a born malcontent, ungenerous and carping.

"You don't want me to educate my brothers!" he shouted. "You don't want my brothers in the house!"

She cried, "You can keep your brothers! You can have your joint family without me!"

He caught hold of her arm and took her across to Babuji, on Mozang Road. He left her there.

Her father lectured her. "Don't you know there are no quarters for you here? Whether he keeps you or throws you out or beats you, you have to fulfill all his wishes. You're not a child, you're a woman of good sense. Go home and behave like a good Hindu wife."

He quoted to her this Punjabi quatrain:

> Yours is a life without help,
> The same is your story:
> Milk under your veil,
> Always water in your eyes.

She bent down and touched his feet—encased, as usual, in highly polished black leather slippers—and then walked out of his house, crying quietly to herself behind her veil.

Daddyji was sitting in his new car just outside their house, waiting for her. He leaned across the seat, opened the door, and motioned to her to get in. He drove for some time in silence. She had no idea where he was taking her or what he would do with her. Finally, he stopped the car. She looked up. They were on the bank of the River Ravi. It was the monsoon season. The river was up to the top of the bank, and the current was swift. There was a full moon. He drew her veil aside. He said he felt that the world was at his feet. He was somebody in his own town, and was able to provide for his children, for his brothers, for his nephews and nieces, for Bhabiji, for her.

"I can't live in the same house as Bhabiji and her family," she said, forgetting Babuji's words. "I want to live in a separate house. I really need a house of my own."

He quoted a Punjabi saying:

> Those who have not been born of your blood
> Come into your house
> And separate the real blood brothers.

Then he said, "I could never have imagined that *my* wife would separate blood relations. But if you are determined, I will get you your own house. Bhabiji is perfectly capable of bringing up the boys and seeing to their education." He turned away from her and looked at the river, and added, in a cold way that sent chills through her arms, "I have no choice. I will have to live wherever you and our children live. But if we do break up the joint family, remember one thing—you and our children will never be able to see Bhabiji and my brothers again. Think about it."

For a moment, she thought he was only threatening her, but then she remembered that she had heard of many households where mothers-in-law and daughters-in-law stopped talking to each other, stopped walking together. She started crying.

He patted and embraced her. "Make your heart a little bigger," he said. "What does it matter if Raj Kanwar eats the baby's banana? You can just go out and buy more bananas." He tried to make her laugh. "I will always give you the money for more bananas." Her face remained stiff with tears. "I have never begrudged you money," he continued. "Lalaji used to say,

'Only get married if you are in a position to give your wife fifty rupees when she asks for five. You might give her only ten or fifteen, but you should be in a position to give her fifty.' I am the son of that father, and I am in a position to give you fifty rupees."

By the end of the evening, they were laughing, and as they were driving home he quoted to her a Persian saying of Lalaji's which had become, in effect, his own motto:

> To the patient and confident,
> No difficulty is difficult.
> Let a man not lose heart.

ONE OF THE EARLIEST SURVIVING PHOTOGRAPHS of Mamaji after her marriage shows her in the courtyard of the Temple Road house, kneeling behind Bibi Parmeshwari Devi's daughter Vidya and combing her hair. Vidya, a rather studious-looking, frail young woman, has a pained expression on her face. The photograph was taken in 1929, when Vidya was seventeen years old and was living with Mamaji and Daddyji. Some six years earlier, Vidya had contracted tuberculosis of the bones in her wrists after drinking milk from a tuberculous cow. As a result, her wrists seemed always to be covered with handcuffs of oozing sores, and her hands were deformed. She had difficulty doing the smallest thing for herself—washing, combing her hair, dressing herself, even eating. It was accepted that because of her hands no one would marry her and take care of her, and she would have to make her own way in the world as a spinster, so Daddyji had brought her from Jullundur, where her father was a petty official, to Lahore to educate her. (At the time, her two older brothers, Dharam Bir and Prakash, were also living in the house, so that they could be educated in Lahore.) At first, because of the pain in her hands, Vidya wrote with difficulty and was unable to concentrate on her studies. The more helpless she became, the more Mamaji was drawn to her. Occasionally, at night, Mamaji would tell Daddyji what she had done for Vidya that day: how she had nursed her and tended to her. He would listen, but then quote to her adages of his childhood: "Do a good deed and then throw it in the river," and "He who does a good deed or a favor and talks about it wipes it away."

(In December of 1977, Vidya, who was the only girl in the family who never married, and who had dedicated herself to a career of teaching and administration, retired, at sixty-five, as principal of a women's college in Jullundur, where she had become well known as a strict disciplinarian and moralist.)

ONE DAY, a friend of Bhabiji's stopped by and said that she had a girl in mind for Raj Kanwar. Daddyji had helped Raj Kanwar get into the police service, where his domineering disposition, his nearly six-foot frame, and his powerful build were serving him well.

Raj Kanwar was much excited by the proposal, and immediately asked Mamaji, as his "best friend," to go and look the girl over for him. Mamaji was touched by his request, but she felt that, whatever part she played in his marriage, she would be put in the wrong. If she gave her approval of the girl and the marriage wasn't a success, Raj Kanwar would be out to get her. If she withheld her approval and Raj Kanwar subsequently made a bad match with another girl, he would blame Mamaji for having prevented him from marrying this one. She begged off, and he boldly set forth by himself on a momentous mission into the old city, where the girl lived.

Many hours later, he swept into the house, calling to Mamaji, "She's beautiful! And do you know how many silver platters of sweetmeats they had? Twelve! She's comely! And do you know how many silver bowls of condiments they had? Twenty-eight! And you should have heard her voice!" As he talked, he jumped up and down, making Promila and Nirmila laugh uncontrollably; they apparently thought he was putting on a special show for them.

Raj Kanwar asked Bhabiji to send for the *shagan* immediately and make arrangements for the wedding then and there. But Bhabiji wanted Balwant, her third son, to get married before Raj Kanwar, her fourth son; she had still not got over the fact that Daulat Ram, her second son, had got married before Daddyji, her first son, and so had made people whisper that maybe there was something wrong with Daddyji. Moreover, Daddyji had just set Balwant up in a tailoring shop, and she felt that Balwant was now quite as eligible a bachelor as Raj Kanwar. Bhabiji went to Raj Kanwar's prospective mother-in-law and explained the situation to her.

The prospective mother-in-law immediately began touring the *gullis* talking up the virtues of Balwant, whom she had never met, and in a matter of days she had found a girl for him—of the right caste and of good appearance. The girl's father was dead, and her widowed mother, who had brought her up in reduced circumstances, was eager to have her daughter marry a man of good family, even if he did only run a tailoring business.

When within a few weeks Mamaji saw two of the Invincibles—one after the other, Raj Kanwar after Balwant—get on their wedding horses and ride away from the house to fetch their brides, she gave thanks to God Ram. Now they would have their own wives to tease and to find fault with, then their own children to frighten, and, in time, their own separate homes to rule. (Jaswant eventually married, too, and Daddyji got him a job as superintendent of a tribal settlement outside Lahore.)

Balwant and his wife, Sheila, turned out to be well matched. They settled down almost like brother and sister. But Raj Kanwar's "beautiful" and "comely" wife, Janki, turned out to be a different matter. Though she looked half his size, she had twice his fire. Often, he would make a great noise about how her mother had dazzled him with silver platters and silver bowls, and had never let him get a good look at her. Each time, she would push him out of the house and say, "Go be a policeman with other women!" Every second day, he would threaten to send her back to her mother, and every second day she would threaten him with his paternal uncle, Bhaji Ganga Ram, for she had heard

Bhaji Ganga Ram say that no blood relation of his could turn out a wife and remain part of the family.

Before long, Janki got pregnant and, one day, stormed out of the house to her mother.

Some months later, after Janki was delivered of a son, she and her mother came to Raj Kanwar and laid the baby at his feet.

"Kick him if you like, but he's yours," Janki said.

Raj Kanwar hesitated for a moment, then bent down, picked the baby up, and fondled it. He took Janki back.

Mamaji was not surprised. She had thought all along that Raj Kanwar could not bear the silence of Janki's absence, and must be missing the fights he had got used to. Indeed, he and Janki were soon following their old pattern of spirited married life.

Around this time, Daulat Ram, Balwant, Raj Kanwar, and their younger brother Romesh banded together with Bhaji Ganga Ram and Mukand Lal, Bibi Parmeshwari Devi's husband, and bought some land across Temple Road from Daddyji's house, for separate houses of their own. Romesh, who had qualified as an architect, was going to oversee the project, and he drew up plans to build a separate, self-contained flat for Bhabiji in his own house.

Mamaji greeted the news with deep relief. Each of the brothers, she told herself, would now have his own place, his own wife, and his own children to look after, and the wives and children would have one another to fight with. The Mehtas would finally have a little village of their own—already they were calling it Mehta Gulli—in the center of Lahore. Day after day, as she

Mamaji and Daddyji, Simla, ca. 1934

watched the walls and roofs go up—the structures standing shoulder to shoulder, in the manner of a village lane, but looking new and *pukka,* in the manner of a Lahore *gulli*—she reflected on how fortunate she was that Daddyji had built their house before Mehta Gulli was thought of, so that, although their house was close by, it was outside the colony and therefore independent of it. She was finally going to have a house of her own in Lahore. But, much to her surprise, the building of Mehta Gulli and the departure of Daddyji's family made the house feel almost empty, and she began missing the early years of her marriage, when Raj Kanwar and the rest of them had caused her heart to beat faster with dread, and when she had spent wakeful nights scheming ways to trip them up and to get even with them.

X

RAI BAHADUR

E VERY MORNING, MAMAJI WOULD GATHER PROMILA, Nirmila, and Urmila and dress them up in pink, or orange, or green. She would give the end of her sari to Promila, who was well on her way to mastering a sedate walk and could be depended upon to stay close; she would catch hold of Nirmila's hand and practically drag her, to keep her from picking up a rusty horseshoe or a sharp-edged bottle top and putting it in her mouth; she would seat Urmila, her lordly daughter, in the pram. In this way, the four would set off to spend the day with Babuji and Mataji in their bungalow on Mozang Road. There, while Mamaji closeted herself with Mataji and Malan in the safe-room—it was their bungalow version of the *chaubara,* and contained a safe—Mamaji's three younger sisters would fall upon the little girls with kisses and sweets and take them either out on the lawn or up on the roof, where they could make as much noise as they liked without disturbing Babuji and his visitors, on the veranda. In the safe-room, the three women—grandmother, mother, and daughter— would spend most of the day gossiping and looking over the jewelry and saris for the dowries of Mamaji's younger sisters. Now and again, Mataji and Mamaji would stash away a little money saved from their household purchases, in case, like Malan after her husband's death, they should be abandoned to the mercies of the world.

Early in 1926, Babuji had sold the Shahalmi Gate

house and bought and moved into the Mozang Road bungalow. It was surrounded on all sides by bungalows, so the area had the atmosphere of a fashionable suburb; it stood a quarter of a mile to the west of Lawrence Gardens, so it had clean air; and it was a couple of houses to the east of Mozang Chowk (*chowk* means "square" or "intersection"), so it afforded easy access to both the Indian bazaar that lay to the south and the Western shops that lay to the north, along the Mall. The bungalow, an open colonial-style structure on a twelve-hundred-square-yard plot, had been built by a nawab on a princely scale some years before, with spacious private grounds and a tennis court. Like a Lahori notable, Babuji furnished the veranda with capacious wood-and-cane sofas and chairs that had slats under the arm rests which could be swung out to serve as leg rests; and all around the veranda he installed full-length roll-down bamboo shades to keep the sun out. Again like a Lahori notable, he furnished the drawing room with long, comfortable divans, many brass tables and *pan* boxes, and brass standing spittoons, and the dining room with a big dining table and chairs, a matching sideboard, and sets of Western china and cutlery. (All this furniture, silver, and china had come in the dowry of Bhagwan Das's wife, Sumitra.) At one end of the dining room, he installed a Western-type sink, with running water and with a makeshift drainpipe that emptied into an open drain outside. He filled the rest of the rooms with dressing tables, mirrors, and big beds; there were also dozens of charpoys, which could be put down anywhere. The only visible reminders of the Shahalmi Gate house were an old wall clock and some framed school certificates.

Babuji felt he had a special aptitude for planning, building, and remodelling houses. He first cleared away the tennis court and built a small cottage, which he rented out to a prosperous friend—one M. R. Khanna. Next, by the wall that formed the back boundary of the property, he built another cottage, even smaller, which he rented out to another friend—one Gandharva Sen Kashyap. (Within a year of his putting up the cottages, they had paid for themselves, and he was receiving twelve per cent interest on his original investment.) He bought some land adjacent to Lawrence Gardens and built on it a bungalow to rent out. Next, he built an annex for Bhagwan Das and his family, quarters for the servants, and a stable for a cow. Finally, he sank a tube well and installed an electric pump, for a private water supply, and put in a lawn with flowers in pots all around it.

The back boundary wall of Babuji's property was one of the boundary walls of Mehta Gulli. It was scarcely five feet high, and all the children were constantly scaling it to get back and forth between Babuji's house and Mehta Gulli. Babuji, watching them from the lawn, took special pride in the fact that he was surrounded by relatives and friends and yet had his own choice piece of property.

The Mozang Road house was unmistakably the residence of a member of the new Lahori Hindu propertied class. The members of this class were not wellborn, like the maharajas and nawabs of the hundreds of semi-independent princely states that made up the so-called "Indian India," but, rather, had risen by dint of their own efforts and gone on to become *babus* and the like, who helped the British govern their colony, the so-called "British India." If the Shahalmi Gate house had been a halfway station between the old world of Babuji's father and the new world of Babuji's children, betokening a man still struggling and making his way, the Mozang Road house was the destination reached by a man who had taken leave of his father and was preparing himself to watch his children go forth.

BABUJI had developed cataracts that were deemed inoperable. He stopped going regularly to the Punjab High Court and spent most of the day on his veranda, where he busied himself with his affairs. The *munshi* would attend to his correspondence and to the files. A house servant would stay within earshot, at the ready for any order. A water carrier would parade up and down the yard in front of the veranda morning and evening, sprinkling water from a sheepskin to settle the dust. On the lawn, within sight of the veranda, a gardener would be training vines, cutting the grass, and watering the flowers in their pots. Although Babuji couldn't identify many flowers by name, he would now and again shout instructions to the gardener to put fertilizer on this one or to trim that one.

Morning and afternoon, Babuji read the newspapers and wrote letters to their editors on issues close to his heart: the superstitions of Hinduism, which thwarted the country's progress; student indiscipline, which undermined the national character; the need for hard work, which was the best way for young men to better their prospects. He received visitors—rich and poor—who came to him for private loans and to arrange mortgages.

Babuji ascribed the change in his fortunes to his past diligence at the law, to his prudence in investment, and, above all, to the principle "Economy is a necessity but austerity is a virtue." Indeed, in his new splendor, Babuji did not change his old, simple ways. Unlike other Hindu gentlemen, who, as they rose in the British world, shed Indian clothes for Western trousers and jackets, he kept to the patriotic Indian dress of his father and his Arya Samaj associates. He generally wore a white turban, a coat with a closed collar, and pajama trousers, and, depending on the weather, black socks and laced shoes or just slippers. His dress varied only to the extent that in winter his coat and pajamas were of wool and in summer they were of cotton. Unlike Westernized Indians, he never smoked or drank, never played cards or other games, and never went to the cinema, or even to parties—unless they were given for a special reason, like a wedding. He never made any British friends, and he never joined a club. He prided himself on having no vices and no idle hobbies.

Babuji did, however, keep a car, and he had a driver, Salig Ram, who served him for twenty years, driving a succession of different cars: first a green Citroën, which was part of Sumitra's dowry; then an old Austin; then a newer Austin. Babuji had come to a car too late in life to even think of learning to drive.

He tended to regard the car as a kind of victoria, the principal difference being that instead of facing backward as he rode, he faced forward. All his children, both sons and daughters, who were of school or college age went to the best schools and colleges, and were ferried back and forth in the car. Now and again, in the evening, they would crowd into the car with him, and he would take them to Lawrence Gardens. He would have Salig Ram drive the car around the gardens very slowly—almost at the pace of his remembered victoria—so that they could all take the air.

Most of the time, however, Babuji kept to his morning and evening constitutionals to Lawrence Gardens and back. In the course of them, he might meet some friends, and they would walk around the gardens together, tapping their walking sticks to emphasize a point or register an objection.

One evening, Sir John Maynard—who, next to the governor, was the ranking officer of the province—approached Babuji in Lawrence Gardens and asked him if he would like to be nominated for the Legislative Council of the Punjab. "Your services to Punjab University are well appreciated," Sir John said. "The government would like to show its gratitude."

"All my life, I have held to the principle that I will not hold a political office of any kind unless I am elected to it," Babuji said.

Sir John, despite having been turned down, complimented Babuji on being a man of principle, saying, "My experience of Indians is that they will do anything for advancement—they have no character. I thought all

along that you were an exception, and you've confirmed me in that opinion."

Another evening, around the anniversary of the
founding of Punjab University's law college—an important day for Babuji, because he had been one of the
founders—he met Sir Shadi Lal in Lawrence Gardens.
Sir Shadi Lal, who lived near Mozang Road, was the
first Indian Chief Justice of the Punjab High Court,
and he and Babuji were close friends. Sir Shadi Lal
looked around him to make sure that no one could
overhear, and then said, "I would like to recommend
you for a title. You don't have any objection? You will
accept?"

Babuji kept walking and registered no particular
surprise. "Shadi Lal, what title do you have in mind?"
he asked.

"I could recommend you for the title of Rai Sahib."
Rai Sahib was a fairly common title.

Babuji, without taking so much as a moment to
think about the offer, said, "No, thank you. If it should
be offered to me, I would not accept."

"Why not?" Sir Shadi Lal asked, taken aback.
"Your fame is too local to catch the eye of His Excellency the Viceroy, who alone can bestow a higher title."

Babuji knew that his being in private practice, as
opposed to government service, had meant giving up
the prospect of a knighthood, which only the Crown
could bestow. But he didn't see why he couldn't aspire
to the title of Rai Bahadur, which was the highest one
in the gift of the Viceroy, the Crown's representative in
India. He said as much to Sir Shadi Lal. "Contractors

are walking around with the title of Rai Sahib," Babuji said. "I have been in public life for twenty-five years. If you want to recommend me for a title, let it be for Rai Bahadur."

Sir Shadi Lal cagily said nothing more, but complimented Babuji profusely on being a leading member of the High Court bar and a leading light of Punjab University.

For about a year and a half, Babuji heard nothing more about the matter. Then, one evening, on another walk—near the end of 1927—Sir Shadi Lal said that he had recommended Babuji for the title of Rai Bahadur. Sir John Maynard had supported the recommendation and sent it on to the governor, who had supported it in turn and sent it on to the Viceroy. The Viceroy had accepted the recommendation. Perhaps even that evening, Babuji would be officially informed that his name was included in the list of titles to be awarded that year. And in due course the news would be released to the press.

"Brother, accept my heartiest congratulations," Sir Shadi Lal said.

The two men stopped and embraced, awkwardly tangling their walking sticks.

BABUJI and Sir Shadi Lal had but to meet to start discussing local politics and comparing notes. One evening, Sir Shadi Lal turned to Babuji and said, "Congratulate me, brother. Today, I cooked the goose of two Punjabi Muslims. You know about the vacancy for a Muslim judge on the High Court? Well, His Excellency the Governor called me in and asked me what I thought of Sir Mohammed Iqbal and Khan Bahadur Shah Nawaz—the two Muslim candidates he was considering for the vacancy. I said, 'Who doesn't know Iqbal, our greatest Urdu poet? And certainly everyone in government knows Shah Nawaz, and his work as a member of the Punjab Legislative Assembly. Either of them would be a distinguished choice for the bench. But, Your Excellency, why don't you interview them both? Then we can discuss which of the two is better suited for the bench.' I then went to Iqbal and told him that the governor would be interviewing him for the judgeship, and that his main rival was Shah Nawaz. I took him by the arm and said, 'Iqbal, when you see the governor, be sure to tell him what kind of man Nawaz is—that he visits prostitutes.' Then I went to Shah Nawaz and told him much the same thing: 'Be sure to tell the governor that Iqbal visits prostitutes and writes couplets for them.' At the interviews, each of them outdid himself in throwing dirt on the other. The governor said to me afterward, 'What awful men those two are!' Today, I got the governor to appoint a good, compliant Muslim of my choosing, from Allahabad, to the judgeship."

"You made a grave mistake, Shadi Lal," Babuji said, striking the ground with his walking stick for emphasis. "Iqbal and Nawaz are prominent Muslims and well qualified. If you had got one of them appointed, he would have been indebted to you for life. You would have had a prominent Punjabi Muslim in your pocket."

"I have the Allahabad judge in my pocket. What more do I need?"

"But you have two powerful Punjabi Muslims as your enemies."

"Let Iqbal and Nawaz cut each other's throats. Punjabi Muslims deserve each other."

The issue of whether Sir Shadi Lal deserved Babuji's congratulations for cooking the goose of two Punjabi Muslims preoccupied the two men for a long time. It was not resolved until some years later, when Babuji and Sir Shadi Lal were in the summer capital, Simla, and went to pay a courtesy call on Sir Fazli Husain, another prominent Punjabi Muslim whose ambition to become a Muslim judge of the Punjab High Court had been thwarted by Sir Shadi Lal.

In the course of the visit, the subject of Punjab politics came up, and Sir Shadi Lal asked Sir Fazli Husain, "Can you do something about Chhotu Ram? He's downgrading fellow-Hindus badly."

Sir Chhotu Ram was in Sir Fazli Husain's Unionist Party, which included both Hindus and Muslims. Born a peasant, Chhotu Ram never forgot—even after he had been knighted—how his father had been harassed by village moneylenders. In fact, he was blighting the careers of Hindu moneylenders—exposing their nefarious activities and helping to institute harsh laws against them.

Sir Fazli Husain smiled at the mention of Chhotu Ram's name and said, "If you, Shadi Lal, can produce a 'good, compliant' Muslim from Allahabad for the judgeship, then I, Sir Fazli Husain, can give birth to a Chhotu Ram from among the Hindus."

After Sir Shadi Lal and Babuji had left Sir Fazli Husain, Babuji said, "If you had put one or two powerful Punjabi Muslims in your pocket at the time of those judgeships, you would have had a card to play today in the matter of Chhotu Ram."

Sir Shadi Lal shrugged, tacitly acknowledging that, after all, he hadn't deserved Babuji's congratulations on the cooking of that goose.

Sir Fazli Husain's remark about giving birth to a Chhotu Ram was repeated by his private assistant, who had overheard it, and it became part of the folklore of officialdom.

XI

COUPLES

M AMAJI AND RASIL DATED THEIR INTIMATE FRIEND-
ship from the delivery of Urmila, when Rasil
gave blood for Mamaji's transfusion. After that,
the two women felt that their lives were braided
together—that if someone touched a hair on
the head of one, the other would feel it. They
started calling each other "sister."

Rasil would often come to the house and sit with
Mamaji on the swing and knit. Sometimes she would
come with Sheila Khanna, who was a friend of both of
them, and sometimes come without her, but invariably
she would bring her dog, a big white Alsatian. (Daddyji had often cautioned Mamaji against Alsatians, saying that they were descended from wolves and were
apt suddenly to exhibit wolfish tendencies. He said that
the dogs could no more bear the climate of the hot
plains than the British themselves could but that the
British had kept them anyway, as an emblem of their
foreignness.) Rasil had named her dog Milton.

The friendship between Mamaji and Rasil had begun just before Urmila's birth. Mamaji had said to
Daddyji, "I have met a new friend, at Sheila Khanna's
house. Her name is Rasil, and she has invited us to tea
tomorrow. She and I are very different, but I already
feel close to her."

"Rasil!" Daddyji exclaimed. "I know about her
and her husband. People are always gossiping about
her. Her husband is a rich businessman, and I know he

does not have a good name. It's best for us to keep our distance from people like that."

"We don't have to go and have tea with her," Mamaji said, to please him.

"Since you have accepted their invitation, we should go through with it," Daddyji told her.

The tea turned out to be a big affair. Mamaji unself-consciously made her way through a crowd of shimmering saris and elegantly tied turbans of the finest muslin. She went straight up to a tall, erect, very fair-skinned young woman with a haughty manner but an apprehensive look, who was standing next to an elderly black gentleman with a potbelly. Mamaji threw her arms around the young woman.

The woman was Rasil, and the man, who looked to be almost twice her age, was her husband, Fatumal. (The couple's identity has here been disguised.)

Mamaji and Daddyji sat down on a sofa with Sheila and Basheshwar Nath Khanna. Rasil started to serve them tea, and Fatumal looked on, fidgeting. She spilled some tea on the tray. Fatumal reached over, snatched the teapot from her, and poured out the tea.

Sheila kept up a running patter. "Now that you are living in Lahore, we should form a group," she said warmly to Daddyji. "We know you are a member of the Gymkhana Club, but what about favoring us by joining the Cosmopolitan Club?"

Daddyji was not very eager to belong to the Cosmopolitan Club. For one thing, the Gymkhana Club had excellent facilities for both tennis and cricket—his two favorite sports—while the Cosmopolitan Club had

facilities only for tennis. For another thing, the Gymkhana Club, which had originally barred Indians, had
started accepting a few well-placed Indians (Daddyji
was one of the first), while the Cosmopolitan Club,
which had been started by some prominent Indians in
response to the Gymkhana Club's original policy, still
barred Europeans—something that Daddyji didn't like.
In any case, he did not want the expense of belonging
to two clubs. Sheila, however, was insistent, and, in a
moment of weakness, Daddyji agreed.

"That's good," she said. "Since they are both in
Lawrence Gardens, you can go to the Gymkhana Club
and pretend to be an Englishman, and then come across
to the Cosmopolitan Club and be one of us natives—
both in the same evening!"

After tea, when most of the guests had left, Rasil
sat down with a harmonium and sang a song about a
hill girl and a parrot. Then Daddyji was coaxed into
reciting some Urdu couplets of Iqbal.

On the way home, Daddyji said, "We are not in
the same class as Rasil and Fatumal. They are high-
society business types, not our kind of people at all."

Mamaji nodded, but nonetheless got him to acknowledge that Rasil, with her unusual combination
of Indian and European looks, would be considered a
great beauty anywhere.

As it happened, Mamaji and Daddyji couldn't
avoid seeing a lot of Rasil and Fatumal, for they were
always around Sheila and Basheshwar Nath, and were
also frequently at the Cosmopolitan Club. And Daddyji
had started going to the Cosmopolitan Club increas-

ingly often, because, although it did not have cricket, its tennis courts were as good as the Gymkhana Club's and, more important, its bridge was better.

Fatumal had got himself elected to the Cosmopolitan Club by making a large donation toward the construction of a club building. The day he first walked into the club, a member had exclaimed, "By Jove, do I see an honest-to-goodness *chamar* coming through the door? What next? An Englishman?" (*Chamar* is slang for Untouchable.)

"So you think you've elected a *chamar*," Fatumal said, chuckling. "Well, even in South India, where our brothers are as black as Africans, they look upon me as a *chamar*. One evening, I was taking a train back from Madras to Delhi and saw that the second-class compartment was so full that there was no room for me. I stood at the door of the compartment and announced over the clatter of the station, just the way the *chamars* announce themselves when they are taking a public conveyance, 'Here comes a *chamar*. All wellborn people, look out.' Everybody moved over, and I had a whole seat to myself. Actually, I'm not a *chamar*. I am a Kayasth [member of a business subcaste] with the skin of a *chamar*."

Some of the clubmen stamped their feet and thumped the tables in delight, until one of the less demonstrative ones shouted, "Silence! Is this a club or a dancing-monkey show?"

The club members never tired of telling the *chamar* story and making remarks about Fatumal's appearance. He had kinky hair, a crooked nose, a narrow forehead, and beady eyes, in contrast to most of the members, who were fair-skinned Punjabis with straight hair, straight noses, broad foreheads, and large eyes. He was often the subject of club jokes because instead of sitting down at one of the bridge or poker tables, where the men, in the sign language of bidding, tested each other's characters, Fatumal would sit at one of the ladies' tables and play gin rummy or flush, giggling and bantering with the women. Moreover, he didn't take part in a single outdoor sport. Members made up stories in which he was sitting on a pile of ill-gotten gold, counting and re-counting his spoils, while he held on to his beautiful wife by her long hair as she struggled to get away.

Rasil stood out in the club, too—but for her beauty. Members' wives were always casting envious glances at her. She had the milky complexion of a European but the demeanor of an Indian. She had the classic features associated with the original, martial Aryan settlers of the Punjab, but she always wore *swadeshi* (homespun silks and cottons)—a custom associated with Mahatma Gandhi, who had made *swadeshi* a symbol of nonviolence, racial equality, and national pride. Her clothes seemed to say that, despite her European complexion, she was at heart an Indian nationalist. She had large eyes that were the greenish blue of the sea. Some members said that they were cold and empty, and others that they were warm and full. She had long, straight, thick auburn hair, which she tied up in a bun at her nape, and never wore loose in public. Some members' wives, looking at the size of the bun, claimed that her hair was long enough for her to sit on, and others that she used fallen hair to enlarge her bun—that her real hair must come down only to the small of her back. She had rosy cheeks and very pink lips. She had one noticeable imperfection, which seemed only to set off her beauty: she had a nasal voice. It had probably started out as the affectation of a pretty child, and had stuck. Whatever the contradictions of Rasil's appearance, club members and their wives saw in her the romantic legends of the hills, where she was born. They talked of her as "the hill girl"—the kind of woman whom maharajas and nawabs of little hill kingdoms kidnapped and fought over, imprisoned and strangled, in the throes of absolutist passion.

In the club, people referred to Rasil and Fatumal as White and Black or as Beauty and the Beast.

THERE WAS ABOUT RASIL something at once haughty and vulnerable, which made people afraid to inquire closely into her past. But certain facts about her were common knowledge, and they provided a sort of focus for the constellation of fancies about her.

Rasil was born, around 1901, high in the Himalayas, in a Sherpa village just inside the border of Nepal. Before she had learned to walk or talk, her mother died of a chill. Her father remarried and migrated to the Punjab, where he found a job as a watchman in the hill station of Dalhousie.

One day, when Rasil was in fifth or sixth standard in the local Arya Samaj school and was walking home in the afternoon, a police sub-inspector stopped her on some pretext and, in full public view, handcuffed her and dragged her to his house.

For weeks, Rasil's father went from one Arya Samaj home to another, trying quietly to enlist help; he knew that if he tried to rescue her himself he would be jailed on some trumped-up charge. But he got nowhere, because people thought that he had given his daughter to the sub-inspector for some money or favor and was now trying to make trouble.

In the meantime, the sub-inspector was promoted and transferred to Amritsar, near Lahore. Rasil's father followed him. There he eventually gained the ear of the president of the local branch of the Arya Samaj, Dr. Gian Kaul, who had been trained in Britain and was sympathetic to the problems of the poor. Dr. Kaul got the deputy commissioner to arrest the culprit and liberate the girl.

The ordeal had left Rasil shattered, and she wouldn't let her father come near her. Dr. Kaul told him that she was probably ashamed to face her stepmother, and he offered, as a shelter, the nearby home of his father, Rai Bahadur Munmohan Kaul. Rasil's father accepted the offer, because he was afraid that Rasil, as a supposedly ruined woman, might be spurned in his community and he might never be able to arrange a marriage for her.

Rai Bahadur Munmohan Kaul brought Rasil up as his own daughter, engaging private tutors for her in English and in music, teaching her the manners of a lady and the skills of the sitar. He would regularly send her to Dalhousie to visit her father, whom the good Rai Bahadur had put on a pension, and who, after Rasil had gone to Amritsar, had fathered a second daughter, named Shoni. With each visit home, Rasil felt more of a stranger. In time, she stopped going to Dalhousie altogether, and even brought her stepsister to Amritsar to live with her.

No one could later remember how, exactly, Fatumal came to marry Rasil. But around 1920 he had been a widower "in the market" for a young, decorative wife who might give him lustre and, at the same time, be a second mother to his sons, Ravinder and Varinder. He liked what he had heard about Rasil, and then, when he actually saw her, he was so overwhelmed by her beauty that he insisted on an almost immediate marriage.

Fatumal, who had not gone beyond secondary school, had spent a few months with an accounting firm. His little training had enabled him to get a job as a lower-level accountant with the railways—a minor, nonpermanent government post. He was singular in having had an offer of promotion early in his career and having refused it, wryly observing, "There is greater scope for my small talents as a simple accountant." Everyone in the department knew what he meant. As an accountant, he dealt with contractors who provided the government with wooden railway sleepers. Procuring these sleepers was a complicated process: the government leased the public deodar forests in the Punjab Himalayas to the contractors; the contractors hired laborers to cut down the deodar trees and chop them into logs, to pre-season and mark the logs, and to float them down the mighty Punjab rivers to the plains;

other laborers collected the logs downstream and made them into railway sleepers, which the contractors finally sold to the government. At many stages in the process, there were opportunities for a shrewd accountant to make money, since it was the accountant's job to recommend contractors, to take inventory of the logs, and to certify the quality of the sleepers. Over the years, Fatumal made a fortune by giving out lucrative contracts in return for "considerations." (He shared some of these "considerations" with his superiors, who eventually named him to the post of senior accountant and helped him get the title of Rai Sahib.)

Fatumal and Rasil had a modest Arya Samaj wedding in Lahore, where they were honored as models of modernity and religious reform, caste and class strictures having been set aside.

Fatumal was not very particular about his own dress, but he bought Rasil expensive saris, shoes, and handbags, and adorned her with huge, eye-arresting diamonds, so that her ears and her fingers and her neck sparkled with the light reflected from her jewels. He took her to Europe, and she came back with the coveted designation of England-returned.

It happened that before Rasil married Fatumal, Dr. Kaul had proposed Rasil as a wife for Daddyji. In 1920, when Daddyji was preparing to go to England for postgraduate work in medicine, he had sought out Dr. Kaul in Amritsar to ask him about his British experiences. "Instead of going to England, why don't you settle down here?" Dr. Kaul had said, looking Daddyji up and down appraisingly. "We could help you to set up a private practice and also arrange a marriage for

you. I have a very pretty girl in mind. She's just nineteen and very accomplished. Her only drawback is that
she has a somewhat checkered past." Daddyji had
changed the subject; he was not interested in getting
married to anybody—he was going to England.

When, many years later, Daddyji learned that the
girl Dr. Kaul had spoken about was Rasil, he told the
story to Mamaji. She exclaimed, "I have always known
that Rasil and I were born under the same star!"

MAMAJI used to accompany Daddyji to the Gymkhana Club during their first months in Lahore, and
sit and watch for hours as he shone on the tennis courts
or at the bridge tables, but just as he started spending
more of his time at the Cosmopolitan Club she started
having less time to go with him, because of the children. From the veranda, she watched him leave for the
office in his car early in the morning, and from the
bedroom, where she waited up for him, she heard the
car coast into the small driveway late at night. She
seldom saw him in between.

Rasil, however, saw him often at the Cosmopolitan
Club. She was one of a very few Indian women who
were bold enough to take up tennis. She pioneered the
custom of playing tennis in a sari, and even played in
mixed doubles, despite the objections of conservative
club members, who said, "If they have mixed doubles
on the courts, what's to stop them from having mixed
doubles off the courts?" Daddyji would often play with
Rasil, in singles and in doubles. At first, he played with

her because she was often the only woman standing about the tennis courts and she couldn't find a partner; the men were hesitant to team up with a woman. Later, he played with her because she had proved to be one of the best tennis players at the club; by then, many of the men not only accepted her presence on the court but sought her out as a partner. Partners for the annual tennis tournament were drawn by lot, and Daddyji drew Rasil for the first mixed-doubles match. The draw evoked much comment in the club. Tennis players said, "Dr. Mehta carries his luck with him wherever he goes."

When it got too dark to play tennis, and the mosquitoes became so thick it was anguish to sit outside, the members would retreat inside the screened and Flit-sprayed club building and play cards. In the beginning, Rasil would look over someone's shoulder or reluctantly consent to be a fourth at the bridge table. Before long, however, serious bridge players were competing for her as a partner, and within a few months, a card-room prodigy, she had graduated to Daddyji's table, the hub of the most serious bridge in the place. She often played as his partner, intuitively understanding his game.

❦

In March, 1931, Daddyji attended the annual meeting of the All-India Leprosy Association in New Delhi. There he found himself seated next to Major General Sir John W. D. Megaw, who, as director general of the Indian Medical Service, was the highest-ranking officer present. (General Megaw had military rank because, like all officers of the Indian Medical Service, he was subject to call for military duty.) The two had last met when Daddyji was doing the leprosy course at the Calcutta School of Tropical Medicine, of which Megaw, then a colonel, had been director. Megaw now remarked on Daddyji's chair, for it was marked with the name of Daddyji's superior, Colonel Clifford Allchin Gill, director of public health in the Punjab, who had been slated to represent the Punjab branch of the Leprosy Association. Daddyji told him that Colonel Gill had fallen ill and had asked Daddyji to take his place. The meeting between Daddyji and General Megaw was thus a fluke, but it turned out to be momentous.

"We have been looking for a suitable organizing secretary for the new King George Thanksgiving (Anti-Tuberculosis) Fund," General Megaw said. "It's a year's appointment to an ad-hoc post. I think you are the right man for it, but I will have to consult Sir Fazli Husain, chairman of the Anti-Tuberculosis Fund Subcommittee of the Indian Red Cross Society." As the meeting hall was filling up, he quickly explained that he was a member of the board that had established the new Fund, and finished by saying, "Tomorrow, go and see my colleague Colonel H. H. Thorburn."

Colonel Thorburn, honorary secretary of the Fund and surgeon to the Viceroy, had his offices in the Indian Red Cross Society building, which housed the staffs not only of the Indian Red Cross but of the Anti-Tuberculosis Fund, the Lady Chelmsford League of Maternity and Child Welfare, and the All-India Leprosy

Association—all of whom, Daddyji felt when he went to see Colonel Thorburn, seemed to be living together under one roof like a happy family of medical social workers.

"How much do you know about the Indian Red Cross?" Colonel Thorburn asked, waving Daddyji to a chair.

"I know some of its history," Daddyji said. "I know that the government presented you with the land for this building, and that the Nawab of Junagadh presented a purse for putting it up."

"Yes, but you might say the Red Cross Society was actually born when Their Excellencies the Viceroy and Vicereine established a sizable fund in 1915 to supply and distribute blankets, clothes, soap, and other necessities to the soldiers of the Great War," Colonel Thorburn said. "In the beginning, the director general of the Indian Medical Service ran the war fund himself with the help of only a few clerks. Later, in 1920, they became the core of the Indian Red Cross Society when it was officially formed, under the patronage of the Viceroy and the Vicereine."

"But, sir, how did the Anti-Tuberculosis Fund come into being?" Daddyji asked.

"As you may know, the King-Emperor recently recovered from a serious illness," Colonel Thorburn said. "In gratitude for His Majesty's recovery, His Excellency the Viceroy issued an appeal for an All-India Thanksgiving Fund to alleviate disease and sickness in India. Maharajas, nawabs, and private citizens have shown their gratitude by contributing almost ten lakhs of rupees to the fund. It has been decided, with His

Majesty the King-Emperor's blessing, to spend the money on only one disease—tuberculosis. In order to keep administrative expenses to a minimum, His Excellency the Viceroy has asked the Red Cross Society to administer the money with the help of a subcommittee to be named for the Fund."

(When Daddyji later recounted to Mamaji what had happened in New Delhi, all she heard through his words was the mention of emperors and viceroys, maharajas and nawabs. She imagined him shifting to Delhi one day and hobnobbing with them in palaces and big office buildings, trying to cure the racking, hacking cough she had grown up hearing all around her in the *gullis* and bazaars.)

Colonel Thorburn leaned back in his chair and asked Daddyji what he thought was the best way to go about alleviating and preventing tuberculosis in India.

"The money could be spent building expensive sanatoriums, on the European model, in the hill stations," Daddyji answered, choosing his words carefully, "but that would be completely impractical—there are just too many poor Indians with tuberculosis."

"Go on," Colonel Thorburn said encouragingly.

"I think the most effective use of the money here would be to concentrate it all on prevention—to establish local dispensaries, to give intensive courses in medical colleges on the disease and its prevention, and to organize provincial and state anti-tuberculosis associations."

Colonel Thorburn looked pleased, and asked Daddyji for his qualifications.

Daddyji told him that as a Rockefeller Fellow he

had studied tuberculosis at the King Edward VII Tuberculosis Institute in Cardiff in 1924, and that later, when he was named district health officer in Montgomery and in Lahore, he had been made the provincial leprosy officer, because of his tuberculosis studies. (The two diseases are related.) As leprosy officer, he had gained experience of leprosy asylums and leper colonies.

"How I wish I had known about you earlier!" Colonel Thorburn said.

The next day, Daddyji was offered the post, provided that his department in the Punjab would agree to let him come on deputation for a year.

As soon as Daddyji returned to Lahore, he took his application for deputation to Colonel Gill.

"This comes as a rude surprise," Colonel Gill said angrily, barely looking at the application. "I won't forward your application. I'll tell them in New Delhi I can't spare you." He added gently, "Ever since you returned from your Rockefeller Fellowship, I have been looking forward to a time when I could make you an assistant director of public health, and now here you are, wanting to run away from the Punjab."

"Colonel Gill, you know I've always wanted to work in the All-India service."

"I must think about my department, and not about your castles in the air."

Daddyji walked out of Colonel Gill's office and started pacing dejectedly around the wide lawn outside.

Colonel Harry Malcolm Mackenzie, the new inspector general of civil hospitals in the Punjab, came out of his office on the other side of the lawn and, seeing Daddyji, strolled over to him.

"Amolak Ram! What are you doing these days?"

They hadn't seen each other since Daddyji was at medical college, where Colonel Mackenzie had been one of his teachers.

Daddyji unburdened himself to his old teacher.

"Is that so?" said Colonel Mackenzie. "Now I remember that a couple of months ago General Megaw wrote me a D.O. [demi-official letter] to inquire if I could recommend someone for that post. I couldn't think of anyone. But, of course, you are an excellent choice."

Colonel Mackenzie asked Daddyji to wait, and went directly into Colonel Gill's office. He was senior to Colonel Gill in the service, and, in fact, reviewed annual confidential reports on him. After a few minutes, the two colonels sent for Daddyji, and Colonel Gill handed him the application with his recommendation.

Daddyji assumed his new duties in New Delhi on April 1, 1931, but he stayed there only a week, for on April 7th the entire government moved to Simla for the six summer months. "I expect good things of you, Dr. Mehta," Colonel Thorburn said on Daddyji's first day. Daddyji saw in the remark a hint that if he proved himself in the post he might be asked to stay on longer than a year, and so remain in the All-India service, which was known for having the crème de la crème of officials, who lived in the cosmopolitan atmosphere of New Delhi and Simla, the winter and summer capitals. He looked forward to an extended absence from the provincial service, which was equally well known for having petty-minded officers, and for posting officers to out-of-the-way places. Moreover, along with a salary of seven hundred rupees a month—the equivalent of his Punjab salary—Daddyji was to receive a twenty-per-cent deputation allowance; the post was therefore not only a very distinguished one but also among the best-paid posts in the service.

MAMAJI didn't immediately join Daddyji at his new post, because she was then in the final month of her fourth pregnancy. She stayed back in Lahore, but in the annex of the Temple Road house; the main house was already occupied by a Muslim tenant, who had moved in with two wives and two sets of children. Mamaji could see the veranda of the main house, where the family ate, from the terrace of the annex. At first, she was horrified by their eating habits, which Hindus regarded as unclean: the children would all eat meat, rice, and lentils out of a single pot with a ladle, which they all licked. Later, she came to marvel that the two wives seemed to live together without any bickering or show of jealousy; that their husband didn't seem to favor one over the other but treated them as if they were alike in all respects; and that she couldn't even tell which children belonged to which mother.

Mamaji went into labor in the early morning of the twenty-fifth of April. She recited the sacred syllable "Om" between contractions, hoping thereby to bring forth a son. Daddyji arrived from Simla just in time for the delivery. He held the baby near her pillow, and she heard him say, "Look! The girls have a brother." She opened her eyes and saw for herself that the pink little creature in his arms was indeed a boy. She called out "Om!" and it was decided then and there to name the child Om Parkash (Light of the Sacred Syllable).

Daddyji had to rush back to Simla, but he returned to Lahore early in June, after Mamaji had completed the prescribed forty-day lying-in period, and drove the family—the girls in the back seat, and Mamaji and Om in the front—to Simla. The journey was an arduous one, and although they took a couple of days to make it, Mamaji and the girls could later remember little about it except the last section, which was on a hill road, a seemingly interminable corkscrew. Promila, Nirmila, and Urmila seemed to be sick through all the ninety-odd dizzying miles of the hill road. The girls had never been happier than when they reached Simla and learned that they would not have to set foot in the car again until October, when they were to go down to New Delhi; with the exception of the three ranking officers of British India in residence— the Viceroy, the commander-in-chief of the Army, and the governor of the Punjab—no one was allowed to use a car within the precincts of Simla.

Mamaji and the girls were astonished and excited by everything about the new place. The children, especially, enjoyed being in the hills; they had never seen hills before. Often, in the mornings, Mamaji would hire three donkeys that had children's saddles (criblike structures), and would put the girls in the saddles on them, and, with Om in her arms, walk ahead of the donkeys up one of the two circular roads—the Lower and the Upper—around Jakko Hill, the highest hill in the station. The girls would laugh, and talk to the

Family group, Lahore, 1935
Top row: Lakshman Das, Daddyji, Bishan Das
Middle row: Dharam, Mamaji with Ved,
Pushpa, Babuji, Mataji, Kaushalya
Bottom row: Vimla, Nirmila, Promila, Urmila, Om

donkey-wallahs, who would walk along and prod the donkeys with sticks. On the way, the little caravan might meet a white sahib and memsahib in their riding habits, trotting elegantly side by side on ponies, or might meet an Indian couple trying to imitate the English example, except that something would inevitably be wrong: the man's breeches would be too big for him, or missing some buttons, or the woman would be in a sari, sitting sidesaddle as if on a couch, or the man would be constantly glancing behind to make sure that his lady had not fallen off her horse. At the sight of such a couple, Nirmila would almost double up with laughter. At the top of Jakko Hill was the temple to Hanuman, the Hindu monkey god, where a colony of friendly monkeys lived. Mamaji and the children would spend the day watching the monkey tamasha. There were baby monkeys, mother monkeys, father monkeys, all dancing attendance on a king monkey and a queen monkey, who sat on thronelike stones. The courtier monkeys would make offerings of a banana or some toothpaste or a box of cornflakes—which they had purloined from the bungalows below—to the royalty. The king monkey could spend two hours spreading the cornflakes on the ground, or throwing handfuls of them on his head and then eating them as they came down on his nose.

DADDYJI had taken temporary accommodations halfway up Jakko Hill while he waited for Mamaji to come and look for something more central, near his office, which was in Simla's Red Cross building—a big old two-story cottage, called Sherwood, on the Mall. Although Daddyji and Mamaji met everybody in Simla within a short time—the official family was quite small, and there were few places to go, so one could run into practically everybody in the course of a day—almost their only close friends were Tara and Harish Chander, whom they had known in Montgomery. (That year, Harish had come to Simla as superintendent of the post office.) One day, the four happened upon a beautiful, commodious cottage called Glenarquart. It stood at the foot of a hill, on a plot four hundred yards square, and had its own hard tennis courts. It was not far from the Mall, the most important meeting place in Simla, and it was also on the way to Annandale, a huge level ground—in the middle of the woods—on which were a golf course, a racecourse, a hockey field, and a football field, and where some kind of tournament was nearly an every-weekend affair. Although the season's rent for Glenarquart was three thousand rupees, and neither Mamaji and Daddyji nor the Chanders had planned to spend more than a thousand rupees for the season, the moment they saw Glenarquart they decided to take it and share the rent.

At Glenarquart, Daddyji and Mamaji ostensibly settled into the upper-middle-class life of the British raj. In addition to the indispensable sweeper for the floors and lavatories, they now had a cook, a bearer, an office peon, who also helped around the house, and an ayah for Om. Daddyji—who could never forget the sight of his mother and his grandmother keeping the fire in the kitchen going by blowing on it for hours at a time, while their eyes smarted from the smoke and their faces grew red with the effort—would often tell Mamaji to sit in a chair like a queen and give orders. But when he wasn't there she would make forays into the kitchen or descend to the native bazaar below the Mall to pick out the fruits and vegetables herself, much as her grandfather had done. The servants, she found, were all but useless unless there was someone to direct them and nag at them, and they were constantly underfoot. Either the bearer was complaining to Mamaji about the cook or the cook was following Mamaji around with some tale of horror about the peon. The ayah was only in her teens and was such a simple hill girl that having her there was like having another child in the house rather than a real helper. The servants were always at Mamaji for keys to the storeroom, orders for meals, money for shopping. She couldn't imagine what sins she had committed in previous incarnations to deserve such a collection of clowns for servants.

To have a house in Simla, with its salubrious climate and its quiet hill life, was to issue a general invitation to relatives, and, indeed, a train of Daddyji's relatives and of Mamaji's were constantly arriving at Glenarquart and staying for weeks or months. The house became a little camp. Mamaji had many charpoys put down in one room downstairs and more put down in a room over the kitchen. There was bedding all over the floor. Children slept two to a bed, head to foot, tickling each other and laughing until they quarrelled. Everyone lined up all day long to have a turn in the bathroom or at the table. There seemed to be no gap between breakfast and lunch, lunch and tiffin, tiffin and dinner.

On the whole, the unmarried boys visiting Glenarquart—Mamaji's brothers Dwarka and Lakshman; Daddyji's brothers Romesh and Krishan; and Bibi Parmeshwari Devi's three sons, Dharam Bir, Prakash, and Dev—were not as rowdy and troublesome as Raj Kanwar and company had been. They spent most of their time in the room above the kitchen trying to study, playing film music on the gramophone, dancing with each other. Sometimes, when Mamaji was in the kitchen, there was such jumping and pounding overhead that she was afraid the ceiling would collapse. If she went upstairs and shouted at the boys, they would tease her and try to include her in their antics. She would threaten to report them to Daddyji, and then they would quiet down quickly. She enjoyed having them around, especially at dinner, when they got together and told stories. How they made her laugh! For weeks, they kept her amused by talking of a friend of Daddyji's who had come to stay at Glenarquart for a few days. He had just returned from England and had brought back with him a very la-di-da English air, which suited him as peacock feathers suit a crow. The first day he was there, Mamaji had served him a *jellabie* (a kind of sweetmeat). He had just stared at it.

"What's the matter?" Romesh had asked, stifling a giggle. "Have you forgotten what a *jellabie* is?"

"My dear chap, I don't seem to have a knife and fork with which to eat it."

No one had ever heard of eating a *jellabie* with a knife and fork. Part of the fun of eating it was to get one's fingers sticky with *jellabie* syrup and then lick them.

The boys had shouted, "Bearer! Bring a knife and fork on a tray! The England-returned sahib can't eat his *jellabie* without them! Peon, bring gloves and an umbrella for the England-returned sahib, so that he can feel at home!"

Whenever the boys told the story, they embellished it, adding hat, raincoat, rubber boots to their shout, and they and Mamaji would all laugh until they could hardly breathe or swallow.

The boys also talked incessantly in the same vein about an eventless trek to Narkanda. Narkanda, twenty-one miles north of Simla, on the main road to Tibet, was at a height of about nine thousand feet. Bhabiji, Mamaji, the girls, and Om—in Mamaji's lap—had travelled there mostly in rickshaws, Daddyji on horseback, and all the boys on foot. It was so remote from everything, and had such sheer slopes of snow and drops and precipices on every side, and such light, heady air, that they felt they might as well be in Tibet, "the roof of the world." When they got back, the boys would tell strangers, "We usually go to Tibet for our picnics," and the strangers would sometimes be taken in. The credulous strangers would become the subjects of further stories, each more outrageous than the last, with which to regale Mamaji at the dinner table, and make her laugh so much that the distance between her, as Daddyji's wife, and them, as her charges, would dissolve.

❧

In SIMLA, Mamaji saw less and less of Daddyji. Every day except Sunday, his day at home, he would get up at eight and, within a matter of minutes, shave, bathe, dress, have his breakfast, and be off. Sometimes she and his brother Krishan, who was sixteen, would walk with him to the office. For the rest of the day, she knew of Daddyji's whereabouts mostly by what she had come to think of as his habits. Around noon, he would send his peon to fetch lunch, and she would give the peon a thermos bottle of tea and a tiffin carrier she had packed with more or less the usual Anglo-Indian fare: chapattis, meat cutlets, and vegetables—perhaps one boiled and one fried in ghi. When it was five o'clock by the watch on her wrist, she could picture Daddyji getting up from his desk and going off to play tennis with one friend or another before settling down to bridge at his new club, the Chelmsford, with Mr. Hayman. (All she knew of Mr. Hayman was that he was a widower whom fate had robbed of the comforts of home life.) On Saturdays, the office would close at one o'clock, and Daddyji and his cardplaying friends would have a Western-type lunch at Davico's restaurant and would again settle down to bridge. Weekdays or Saturdays, she would seldom see him before midnight. She would wait up for him, because, as a good Hindu wife, she could never think of having her meal before giving him his. He would often scold her for being so old-fashioned, but to little effect. As soon as he came in, she would set out the meal, which the servants had kept hot, on a folding table next to the bed, and, sitting on the bed, they would eat it together. They were usually asleep by twelve-thirty or one.

In the morning, she was up before he was. Though by the time she arrived in Simla the hill rains had set in and it was cold, she would get out of bed in an unheated bedroom, take a cold bath in an unheated bathroom, get dressed in an unheated dressing room. The only fireplace was in the drawing room, and it took some time to get the fire up. Then, too—because the young ayah for Om was not competent but Mamaji couldn't bring herself to get rid of her—she took some of the ayah's work upon herself. Sometimes, right after her bath, she would wash the children's clothes in cold water. Whenever Daddyji saw her shivering in the morning cold, he would remind her of the English custom of taking bed tea, which helped one retain the warmth of the bed after one had got up, but she did not pay much attention. (In the plains, she had sometimes taken bed tea, but somehow she had got out of the habit in Simla, where she needed bed tea most.) He would also tell her that hill people didn't bathe for days at a time, and she didn't need to bathe often, either, but she felt that she couldn't sit down to her morning prayers unless she had first purified herself with a bath. She didn't seem to realize that summer in Simla could at times be colder than winter in Montgomery or Lahore. The cold, damp wind would sweep down the hills and go right through her sari. Once, as Daddyji and Mamaji were walking on the Mall, they met a woman friend who touched Mamaji's bare shoulders and cried, "Shanti! How is it you are not wearing a sweater?" Daddyji ran his hand over Mamaji's arm and said, "She doesn't need a sweater. She has lovely, healthy skin that keeps her warm." He didn't worry much about her coming down with a cold, because she appeared to be naturally healthy.

Mamaji wasn't sure exactly when, but she developed bronchitis. A cough would start up at any time of the day or night, and she would be convulsed by it. Some time later, she caught what she called a stomach chill. Everything she ate would give her a stomach ache. She went off all food except grapes and grape juice—a home remedy that Mataji had often used, because grapes were said to be the most digestible and nourishing of foods. However uncomfortably the grapes and the grape juice sat on her stomach, she thought she had no choice— partly because grape juice was said to be good for making mother's milk and she was breast-feeding Om. She had breast-fed all her daughters. How could she not breast-feed Om, her Prince of Wales? Whenever Daddyji remarked on her loss of color and weight, she would smile and say that it was just the Simla climate. She made light of her symptoms, because she didn't want to alarm him. But Daddyji happened to stay home from the office one day, and he noticed that she did not take either breakfast or lunch but instead ate one grape after another. She hadn't told him about her grape remedy, because she knew he would disapprove.

"I had no idea that you were eating nothing but grapes," he said to her in astonishment. "You can do serious harm to yourself that way." After that, she began eating regular meals at regular times, and even weaned Om, who was four months old, but her health didn't improve. Doctors were consulted, and their unanimous diagnosis was that she had an ordinary case of hill diarrhea. They said that in the rainy months

many people from the plains who had come to Simla
for the first time contracted hill diarrhea, which sometimes lasted right through the season.

Daddyji prescribed the injections and pills of modern medicine. Babuji, who was staying with them, prescribed the herbal chutneys and powders of Ayur-Vedic
medicine. She blindly accepted the treatments of both,
without telling either about the prescriptions of the
other.

As it happened, Rasil and Fatumal had started
coming to Simla that same season, and had taken a
house called Windmere Lodge, next door to Glenarquart. Rasil and Tara took turns looking after the
house and the children for Mamaji, but gradually Rasil
came to do everything, because Tara was preoccupied
with her own children and with Harish, while Rasil
had no children of her own and was alone most of the
time. (Fatumal was little more than a bird of passage in
Simla, coming up for a week and then going back
down to the plains for a few weeks to look after his
"business interests"; and Rasil's stepsister and the
younger of her stepsons were both at boarding school,
while the older stepson was away in government service.) Rasil helped prepare Mamaji's meals, bought her
medicines, kept her charts. Always accompanied by her
Alsatian, Milton, she would arrive in time to give the
girls breakfast and give Om his bottle, and would usually stay to oversee the children's lunch. She would go
home for a nap and return at teatime. Sometimes she
would bring a little ivory statue of Krishna playing his
flute, a little silver bowl for holy water, and an incense
stick. She would sit down in one corner of a room with

her prayer things, and pray for Mamaji's recovery in warm, fervent words while Milton sat panting beside her. Sometimes she would also play the sitar for an hour or so to soothe Mamaji. Her touch was delicate, yet so firm that she had but to pluck the top strings to set off a rush of chimelike resonances in the bottom strings. Her playing was slow and moody, each note lingering in the ear the way the smell of the rose scent she wore lingered in the air.

Whenever Daddyji heard her sitar, he would say to her, "Your hand puts me in mind of Lalaji's wistful hand on the sitar. Lalaji, you know, was a little taciturn, but once he sat down with the sitar he was as soft as his music, and even the crows seemed to be affected by his playing."

To Mamaji, he would say, "I didn't get music with you, Shanti, but, thanks to your friend, our children have a musical atmosphere to grow up in."

One evening, Fatumal stopped Daddyji on the Mall and said, "Doctor-Sahib, if you continue in your Delhi-Simla job, it would give Rasil and me great pleasure if you and Shantiji would share Windmere Lodge with us next season. It would mean only a modest, a very modest, increase in your rent. As you know, this season we have been sharing our bungalow with the Lalls, but they have decided not to come to Simla anymore."

Daddyji put him off. As he later told Mamaji, he didn't want to get involved, because the fellow always seemed to have ulterior designs. "We will simply find ourselves in Lall's shoes," he added.

Lall ran a motor firm in Lahore and was the Indian agent for Ford Motors in the Punjab. He had given Fatumal a Ford at cost, and Fatumal, when he wanted to show Rasil Europe, had prevailed upon Lall and his wife to go with them, in part because Lall's Ford connection gave him a call on certain amenities, like a car. Lall, for his part, found Fatumal useful because of his widespread business connections. But Fatumal and Lall were constantly quarrelling, because each was always worried about being tricked into giving more than he received.

Eventually, Daddyji put aside his reservations and decided to share Windmere Lodge with Rasil and Fatumal after all. Later, he was never able to explain to Mamaji the reason for his decision. It might have been something as indefinable as the spell of Rasil's music or something as practical as the fact that Tara and Harish had taken a house of their own and Daddyji could not afford to keep Glenarquart by himself. In any case, the decision meant still greater involvement with the strange rich couple, in violation of his own dictum: "The truth is that neither the friendship nor the enmity of the rich is agreeable."

In October, Mamaji and Daddyji shifted to New Delhi, which that year was having one of its coldest winters. The wind would blow across the Delhi plain and rush through the airy, open houses, which were built for the heat of the summer rather than for the usually mild winter. They found accommodations on the upper story of a house whose ground floor was occupied by a family of Madrasis. The people downstairs would cook strong-smelling food, leaving whole chilis simmering in pots in the oven for entire days. Mamaji felt suffocated by the smell of the cooking if she shut the doors and windows against the wind. But if she opened the doors and windows to get rid of the smell, she froze. It seemed that every time she took a breath she felt either the burning sensation of chilis or the cold of the wind settling in her chest. The bronchitis that she thought she had finally shaken in Simla returned with new strength.

Daddyji sent Mamaji and the children to Babuji and Mataji in Lahore, hoping that Mamaji would recover in its gentler winter. There she consulted an old woman in Mozang Chowk, who prescribed daily doses of an herbal laxative. Mamaji used the woman's laxative for two weeks, then gave it up, because instead of improving her bronchitis it made her so weak that she started having fainting spells. Next, she went to see a practitioner of Hindu medicine, who examined her and pronounced that the trouble was with her phlegm, which he said had solidified in her chest. He prescribed a "thinning potion," and she took that for some time. She finally gave his medicine up, because it only made her nauseated. She tried several Western doctors and their medicines with no better results. Eventually, her bronchitis went away, but it left a permanent mark— she began having asthmatic attacks.

DADDYJI submitted the annual budget for the Anti-Tuberculosis Fund in April, 1932, at the end of the first year of his Delhi-Simla job.

Sir Fazli Husain, who, as the Viceroy's Executive Councillor for Education and Health, had to pass on it, called Daddyji in to his New Delhi office and fixed him with a penetrating look. "I've just got the consent of the government of the Punjab to allow you to stay on for a second year. Are you happy with your Delhi-Simla job?"

"Yes, sir."

"By the way, I want to compliment you on your budget," Sir Fazli Husain said, looking down at the budget before him on his desk.

"Sir, if I may say so, I'm having some difficulty in balancing my domestic budget," Daddyji said rather cautiously.

"Why should that be?"

"I'm receiving only a twenty-per-cent deputation allowance over and above my Punjab salary of seven hundred rupees a month. I cannot get government accommodations, and the rents for private houses in Delhi and Simla are so steep that I cannot find suitable accommodations for the right rent."

Daddyji waited for a reply, but Sir Fazli Husain kept his own counsel. Later, when Daddyji told Mamaji about Sir Fazli Husain's silence, he said, "Not for nothing is he Executive Councillor to the Viceroy." But when the budget of the Anti-Tuberculosis Fund came back from the Viceroy's office it had an added provision of one hundred and fifty rupees a month for house rent for the organizing secretary.

❧

MAMAJI and Rasil enjoyed living in the same house. The weather of the second season in Simla, in contrast to the first, was balmy and agreeable, and they would sit in the sun for hours at a time, knitting and gossiping—the children out of sight in the care of the ayah and the other servants—and feeling that they were two women of leisure. Every morning, at breakfast, they would ask each other, "What is the program for today?" It was more of a greeting than a question, because the program was always just about the same: a stroll along the Mall; a little shopping, which included a bag of sweets for the children; coffee and ice cream at Davico's restaurant; lunch at home; a nap; another stroll along the Mall; and, often, a social function in the evening. Rasil was seven years older than Mamaji and more experienced in fashion, and at first Mamaji relied on Rasil's advice about what colors suited her, and what kind of sari she should wear, with which blouse and shoes, for a particular occasion. Mamaji had noticed that Rasil parted her hair in the center, and that this made her eyes look even larger than they actually were. Mamaji had always parted her hair far to the left, but she shifted her part to the center. Gradually, with a little reassurance from Rasil, Mamaji started taking pride in what she recognized as her own natural sense of color and occasion.

For Mamaji and Rasil, their turns around the Mall were rather like the turns of the planet, getting them from sunrise to sunset, from week to week of the season. The Mall, a little valley bounded on all sides by hills, was a few hundred yards' stretch of level walk. As they strolled along it, they would go past Christ

Church, a Gothic-style building of rough-hewn mountain stone, and would often remark on its cold, forbidding aspect and on the castelessness of the Christians, even if they *were* English. No matter how often they saw the nuns who ran Christ Church College, they would comment on the plainness of their habits, and on the sad expression of the few Indian nuns who were sequestered there. They felt much more at home when they went into Kali Mandir (Goddess Kali's Temple), with its bustle of people, its sound of chanting, and its smell of incense, or when they descended from the Mall into Lakkar Bazaar (Wood Market), where they were surrounded by little stalls, and the shopkeepers hawked everything from garishly painted hobbyhorses and toy engines to carved wooden lamps and tables and lacquered walking sticks.

In the evening, Mamaji and Rasil might go with a party of friends to the Green Room, a beautiful small building of chiselled stone on the Mall, which was used for amateur theatrical productions. Built by the government around the turn of the century, and painted green inside and out, it was a private theatre where talented government officers and their wives staged, for their own amusement, English plays, like "The Comedy of Errors" and "The Importance of Being Earnest." The Viceroy and the governor, who, as ranking officers, were the patrons of the arts, would attend the performances with their wives, and later Simla's official family would remember the season by what the Viceroy or the Vicereine had been heard to say about someone's performance, such as "Jackson and Das were excellent as the twins."

Just about Mamaji's and Rasil's most important outing was to the monthly tea party of the Ladies' Chelmsford Club, which was held in Davico's ballroom, a hall above the cinema. Wives of all high-ranking military and civil officers and of the few Simla society notables, along with begums, ranis, and maharanis from neighboring hill principalities, would come to the tea. Some ladies, who were in purdah, came wrapped from head to toe in shapeless cloaks; others, not in purdah, came in flatteringly wound saris or fashionable frocks. Some arrived in private rickshaws, others in rented ones. A row of rickshaws waited on the side of the road for the return journey; indeed, on the day of the tea party hardly a rickshaw could be found free. Not much happened at these teas. There was a receiving line, and everyone was announced, was presented to the Vicereine and the governor's wife, milled about for an hour or so talking about the weather and admiring everyone else's clothes, and went home. But everyone worth her salt showed herself there. The only occasion that surpassed the monthly tea was the annual reception, which was given by the Viceroy and the Vicereine at the Viceregal Lodge. The Vicereine at the time, Lady Willingdon, had noticed Mamaji at one of the tea parties and had been impressed by how pretty she was. Later, she had been heard to remark on Mamaji's and Rasil's way of moving. "Why can't all Indian ladies carry themselves like these two lovely ladies?" she said. When Mamaji was presented to her at the annual reception, the Vicereine motioned to her to linger by her side in the receiving line. She went on greeting other guests and directing them to the Viceroy. Now and again, in the middle of her duties, she turned toward Mamaji and smiled at her. Although Mamaji felt that her English wasn't good enough for her to converse with the Vicereine, they got to know each other so well through smiles and nods at the first reception that subsequently Mamaji and Daddyji were sometimes invited to smaller tea parties at the Viceregal Lodge.

The Viceregal Lodge was a huge Victorian heap high on a prominent hill a few miles up a macadamized road from the portals of Christ Church. The lodge surveyed its own extensive grounds. The house was the domain of Lady Willingdon, for it was a tradition that each Vicereine could redo the rooms as she liked. Lady Willingdon had done hardly anything to the lodge, but what little improvements she did make—like new mauve curtains in the drawing room—were talked about and admired for most of one season. That season, everyone wore a mauve sari or a mauve necktie; everyone carried a mauve parasol and a mauve purse or sported a mauve handkerchief or a mauve lapel flower. An annual tennis tournament was held on the grounds of the Viceregal Lodge, which were the domain of Lord Willingdon. Invitations to this tournament were as avidly coveted as invitations to any gathering at the Viceregal Lodge.

The Viceroy's aide-de-camp kept a roster of good tennis players for convening the tennis tournament. Daddyji and Rasil, who was one of only two or three women on the roster, were invited to play in mixed doubles that season. As a rule, in Simla as in Lahore, Daddyji avoided mixed doubles, because he was not much good at the net. He usually played singles, be-

cause ever since he took up tennis, in his teens, he had
fashioned his game after that of the perennial Indian
tennis champion, Mohammed Saleem—returning every
ball from the baseline, using the tactics of passing shots
and lobs, and depending on his opponent to make mistakes and give him the game. But Rasil was such a good
doubles player that whenever she was Daddyji's partner his play was inspired. At that season's Viceregal
tournament, Daddyji and Rasil reached the semifinals,
and lost only to players with a national reputation.

At a special party at the lodge after the tennis
tournament, Lord Willingdon asked a few guests who
were standing around him, including Sir Fazli Husain
and Daddyji, "Have any of you seen the figures of the
1931 census?" The census report had just come out.

"Yes, Your Excellency," Sir Fazli Husain said,
with an officious bow. "The figures show a marked increase in India's population," he went on, and he added
slyly, "Your Excellency, Mr. Gandhi exhorts our people
to abstain and not to produce any more children, because they would only swell the number of Indian
slaves in the British Empire. The figures show how our
people go about obeying Mr. Gandhi."

There was general laughter, and the Viceroy
looked pleased at the implicit compliment to the Empire.

Daddyji almost blurted out that Sir Fazli Husain
was trying to ingratiate himself with the Viceroy at
the expense of truth—that everyone knew that the reason for the rise in India's population was the success of
public-health measures in controlling epidemics. But
Sir Joseph Bhore, a member of the Railway Board,

and his wife came up just then. Daddyji later remarked to Mamaji, "If Sir Joseph and Lady Bhore had not come up at that moment and engaged Lord Willingdon in conversation, my tactlessness would have cost us our invitations to the Viceregal Lodge, and probably any extension in my job."

"Rasil would never have forgiven you," Mamaji said, for Rasil's invitations were dependent on Mamaji's and Daddyji's.

At the end of that second season in Simla—in October, 1932—Mamaji and Daddyji again shifted to New Delhi, and this time they found a large, pleasant house next to the hockey field of the Modern School.

❧

THE officers junior to Daddyji in the Health Department in the Punjab hoped that he would refuse to return to the department if he was asked to, because that refusal could be grounds for depriving him of his seniority, and hence of his promotion to assistant director of public health. And if he should be denied his promotion, one of them would automatically supersede him, even though he might eventually return to the Punjab. In March, 1933, at the end of his second year of deputation to the central government, they hit upon the scheme of dispatching to General Megaw a formal departmental request for Daddyji's return.

General Megaw, however, being familiar with such bureaucratic machinations, saw through the scheme and brought the letter to the attention of Sir Fazli Husain, who immediately sent a demi-official letter to

Sir Firoz Khan Noon, the Minister of Health in the Punjab, asking for a deputation of Daddyji's services for three additional years—until April, 1936. Sir Fazli Husain's request was a command, and Sir Firoz Khan Noon acquiesced. At the same time, Sir Fazli Husain doubled Daddyji's deputation allowance, from twenty to forty per cent of his salary in the Punjab, the increase to take effect immediately. Daddyji ordered a crate of mangoes for Mamaji and the children to celebrate his good fortune.

IN LATER YEARS, Daddyji would warn his children against taking up cards. And still later, when he himself had stopped playing cards regularly—with age and with growing children, the importance of his club diminished in comparison with the importance of family and home—he and Mamaji would sit together and talk about how he had got started on cards in the first place.

"The cards were your club wife, just like Rasil," Mamaji would say. "And the Hayman Group was your club family."

All along, Mamaji accepted his playing cards the way she accepted his club companionship with Rasil, because, as a Hindu wife, she felt she had no choice in the matter. Anyway, she knew the whole story of his "marriage" to cards—a marriage that had preceded his marriage to her.

Although he had received his first bridge lessons when he was a student in London, in 1920, from his tennis mentor, Mohammed Saleem, he had not

Malan, Lahore, 1937

thought of playing bridge as a socially necessary accomplishment until, on his return to India, he read a matrimonial advertisement: "Wanted for an England-returned barrister: A convent-educated, English-speaking, beautiful Brahman girl who can play bridge." A few days later, he had dropped in on a leading advocate in Rawalpindi. "What about making a fourth?" the advocate asked. Daddyji hesitated, and the advocate exclaimed, "What! An England-returned bachelor with such a remunerative first job, and you don't jump at the chance to make a fourth? Where have you been living—in the university halls of England or in the village stables of the Punjab? Don't you know that bridge is the only refuge we educated have from heat, dust, and rampant ignorance?"

Daddyji, however, did not take up bridge seriously until he was in Montgomery waiting to be confirmed in his department, when he needed the recommendation of the assistant director of public health, Dr. Abdul Rehman. Dr. Rehman, who was an avid bridge player —the game at that time was auction bridge—judged the intellectual calibre of his subordinates by the calibre of their bridge. Daddyji had no difficulty getting the recommendation, because, as it turned out, Dr. Rehman was a less than average player. But by then Daddyji had become fascinated by the game.

Later, in Lahore, Daddyji again encountered Saleem. Saleem, a barrister, was a senior advocate of the Punjab High Court and an elegant bachelor around town. Daddyji's bridge game caught Saleem's eye, and after that there was for Daddyji no escape from a nightly round of bridge at Saleem's table—at the Cosmopolitan Club or at Saleem's second home, the Punjab Association Club. Daddyji usually won, and he became known for being as lucky as he was skillful in his play.

When Daddyji took his Delhi-Simla job, he became a member of the Chelmsford Club, which had facilities in both cities. It was patterned after the National Liberal Club in London, and was thus designed to provide opportunities for discussion and association between Indians and Englishmen, but by the time Daddyji became a member it had lost most of its original interracial impetus; its Indian members seldom showed up, because they had little use for clubs, and its English members preferred to spend most of their time at the grander Imperial Gymkhana Club in Delhi or at the exclusively English United Service Club in Simla. But the Chelmsford Club was kept alive as a monument to British good intentions.

The stalwarts of the Simla Chelmsford Club, known as "the select circle," never played bridge for stakes of less than five rupees for one hundred points— four or five times Daddyji's limit in Montgomery or Lahore. They were constantly looking for a fourth, because there was a dearth of rich bridge players, and, once they learned that Daddyji was an outstanding bridge player, they persuaded him to join the table and let his partner "carry" him—absorb his losses in return for taking his winnings. At first, Daddyji, eager to do well for his partner, tended to overbid his hand, but he soon caught on. He discovered that there were only two outstanding players at his usual table, and that the third had a lot of money but no particular acumen. He calculated that, given the odds of two good players and one bad one, in the long run he should be able to win. He decided to run the small risk of losing money he did not have for the winnings he might pull in. He started "carrying" himself, and also started winning.

In time, Daddyji switched from auction bridge to contract bridge, and was inducted into "the inner circle" of "the select circle"—into the so-called Hayman Group, which was notorious in clubs all over India for its unequalled stakes and for its fast-paced games, played late into the evening both on weekends and during the week. The leader of the group was Mr. Hayman — the "Mr." was so much a part of his name that it might as well have been his first name. He was born in Madras, of mixed English and Indian parentage, and, although he could have passed himself off as English, he always gave his nationality as Indian. (In contrast, another member of the group, a Hindu gentleman who would have liked to have Mr. Hayman's option of being English, had anglicized his obviously Indian name, Tandon, to Tannan, on the pretext that it was easier for Englishmen to pronounce.) The regulars of the group were all about twenty years older than Daddyji, but within a few weeks of his joining them his name was linked with theirs.

Mr. Hayman—a widower with one grown daughter, who was married and did not live near him—spent most of his time at the club. When he was not playing bridge, Daddyji would find him sitting in the cardroom with a peg of whiskey in his hand, absently looking toward the door while he waited for a game to get under way. After a brilliant career in the Audit and Accounts Service in the central government, he had become head of Audit and Accounts and director of labor for Indian Railways, ending up as a member of the Railway Board—an important appointment, with a princely salary of four thousand rupees a month. He was a born gambler, and invariably offered to take any stranger for a partner and to carry him. He was clearly delighted if that stranger happened to be a woman, but the regular members of the group were all men. He played with great concentration, consuming peg after peg of whiskey. His game was erratic—sometimes brilliant, sometimes slapdash. But he was consistently sportsmanlike, both losing and winning with grace.

With the passing of the years, Daddyji realized that money and winning had become more important to the Hayman Group than the game or than sportsmanship—the group had abandoned contract bridge for poker, because it was more of a gamblers' game—and that his energies, which might better have been devoted to science and research and family life, were being siphoned away. Moreover, he was becoming a bit concerned about the notoriety he had gained as a cardplayer: in New Delhi, the Hayman Group forgathered at the Roshanara Club, where the winnings and losses were charged to the monthly bills of the members, so that they couldn't easily be kept private, and, to Daddyji's chagrin, his enormous winnings were talked about outside the club as well as in.

❦

ONCE, in the Simla season of 1933, Daddyji came home from the club earlier than he was expected, and walked quietly into the house to give Mamaji a pleasant surprise. He found her sitting at the dining table and staring at a big sheet of paper on which were spots of saffron paste and a picture of the elephant god, Ganesh. She tried to roll up the sheet in time to hide what she was doing, but he had seen it.

"What nonsensical superstition is this in my house?" he asked, laughing.

"It's Om's horoscope," she said. She quickly finished rolling up the chart and, at the first opportunity, hid it.

That night, fearing that Daddyji's remark about the horoscope might bring the evil eye upon Om or upon the family, she took a handful of red chilis and circled them in the air over Om's cot, and then, before going to sleep, she prayed to Ganesh not to punish Daddyji for his insult or send her more afflictions. But soon afterward she was confined to bed with a low-grade fever and a persistent cough, which she secretly attributed to the evil eye. She had been having breathing trouble and asthma for some time, and now she started coughing up phlegm with blood in it. The doctors whom Daddyji called to attend her began suspecting tuberculosis, and they put her through a series of tests. Although the tests proved negative, the strain of the symptoms and of the worry left her feeling dispirited. The very thought of being sick and bedridden brought tears to her eyes.

She and Daddyji were sharing Windmere Lodge with Rasil and Fatumal for another season, and Rasil would sit by Mamaji's bedside and try to amuse her by playing bezique or just talking, in preference to going

to the club. For some time, Rasil had been trying un-
successfully to have a child, and lately she herself had
become preoccupied and moody. Often, she would simply give up her attempts to cheer Mamaji, and cry, too.
"Shanti, I wish I were sick instead of you," she would
say. Sometimes Rasil would leave the room suddenly,
as if it were too painful for her to sit with Mamaji.
Then Mamaji would feel abandoned and frightened,
especially since Daddyji seemed to be always at his club.

Daddyji grew alarmed by her continuing illness
and took her to the Dharampur Consumption Hospital,
in the plains, for further tests. There Dr. F. S. Master,
the superintendent of the hospital, examined her
thoroughly, taking, among other things, a fresh set of
X-rays and a specimen of sputum. Then he drew Daddyji aside. "I find nothing incriminating," he said,
speaking as one doctor to another. "Does she have a
long history of colds and coughs?"

"I think she caught a cold under the wedding
canopy," Daddyji said. "We were married in December
in Lahore, and it was very chilly that day. Then she
had a little cough off and on through the first year of
our marriage, but I was posted in Montgomery at the
time and I attributed the cough to the Montgomery
dust storms. I don't know what she told you, but she
now believes that she never had a cold until she came
to Simla."

"I can't find anything wrong with her physically,"
Dr. Master said. "But she seems very sad. If you can get
her to talk about why she is sad, you may find that
many of her symptoms will disappear."

"I myself have often thought that some of her

symptoms were more in her mind than physical," Daddyji said. "When we first got married, and she thought she couldn't conceive, she had several hysterical fits, with the classic symptoms—a fainting spell and a locked jaw. The interesting thing is that the moment she conceived, her fits and her symptoms disappeared. In fact, she is never so healthy as when she is pregnant. She doesn't remember those fits now, of course."

When Daddyji had finished talking, Dr. Master nodded sympathetically, as if he were used to patients who forgot their own histories. "Well, then, you know what to do as well as I—try to lift her spirits," he said.

Soon after Dr. Master's examination, Mamaji became pregnant for the fifth time. (It was the official beginning of the writer of this narrative.) There had been a three-year hiatus between her pregnancies—the longest so far—and the moment she knew she was pregnant again she began to rally.

WHENEVER FATUMAL was in residence at Windmere Lodge that season, it seemed he couldn't do enough for Mamaji and Daddyji. He would go down to the native bazaar himself, with a servant, to choose chickens—a great delicacy in India—for dinner. Then he would stand around in the kitchen supervising the cooking of the chickens, frequently tasting the curry to make sure that it had just the right balance of spices. He would set aside an especially mild portion for Daddyji, who didn't like chilis, and the rest of it he would make good and hot. Daddyji and Mamaji began to wonder if Fatumal had something up his sleeve. The chicken dishes seemed to augur a request for a favor.

One day, Fatumal came up to Daddyji on the veranda. He shifted his bulk from foot to foot, waved his hands, and seemed to be having trouble getting his words out. "If you have no objection, would you consider having Mr. Hayman to a tea party and introducing me to him?" he asked.

"Of course. We'll have him to tea any day you like," Daddyji said, taken aback at Fatumal's making so much of such a simple request.

"One more minute of your time, please," Fatumal continued, in an obsequious manner. "Could the tea party be in our side of the house?"

"Of course, if that's what you want," Daddyji said. "Your side, our side—it's all the same."

On the day of the tea party, Fatumal waddled around the house all day, seeing to it that the best pastries were bought, that the best savories were cooked, that the best china was laid out, and that the servants put on their best tea manners. At tea, he pressed one delicacy after another on Mr. Hayman, and afterward he requested Daddyji and Mr. Hayman to do him the honor of convening the Hayman Group at his house the following evening. When the group met there, Fatumal saw to it that Mr. Hayman's glass was never empty, and that Mr. Hayman noticed the label of the expensive bottle of whiskey from which he was pouring. As Mr. Hayman was leaving, he complimented Fatumal on his hospitality.

The very next day, Fatumal said to Daddyji, over a special chicken dinner, "I am about to retire. I have had my innings, and I have served the government faithfully. I doubt if any official in my department could find fault with my service as an accountant."

Daddyji said he hoped that Fatumal would be properly recompensed at retirement with a good provident fund.

"My provident fund comes to nearly two lakhs of rupees," Fatumal said. "But in life you must have something to keep you busy. Even having money is less important to me than having something to do."

Mamaji almost laughed in her veil.

"I want only one thing now from the government and from life," Fatumal continued. "I want a contract from the railways for an exclusive food concession at the Delhi station." Then he mumbled something about Mr. Hayman.

Suddenly, the reason for the chicken dishes, the tea party, the card game, the whiskey became clear to Daddyji.

"I've looked into the matter," Fatumal went on, "and certain high officers in the railway department can grant such contracts in special circumstances."

Daddyji found himself saying, in spite of himself, "Could Mr. Hayman help?"

"You have put the idea into my head, and what a good idea it is!" Fatumal exclaimed.

Later, when Daddyji reproached himself for suggesting an appeal to Mr. Hayman, Mamaji reminded him how Rasil had looked after her during her illnesses, and said that, whatever he might think of Fatumal, they were all friends.

Daddyji went to see Mr. Hayman in his office and

told him about Fatumal's request for the concession. Mr. Hayman immediately made a note on his desk pad, and said, "Rest assured, the case will receive favorable consideration."

In due course, Fatumal got his concession.

Not long afterward, Daddyji and Mamaji were walking along the Mall. They saw Fatumal coming toward them, followed by a servant with a couple of plucked chickens.

"I wonder what he wants now," Daddyji said.

"I don't know how Rasil got caught by this *chamar*," Mamaji said.

That evening, over chicken curry, Fatumal said, in his most disarming, offhand way, "A tip from an old man, Doctor-Sahib. You should buy a house in Simla, rent it out, and pledge its income to your wife and children. A house in Simla is the best insurance policy for this uncertain life."

Daddyji didn't think much of the suggestion. He felt that an interest in summer property was a concern fit only for the rich, and that his best investment was the education of his children and his relatives. Anyway, he had no money to spare; he was in government service, with just enough salary to get by on.

"Rachel's Folly is on the market," Fatumal was saying. "The agent tells me that the owner is a European, who would prefer to sell it to another European. But, Doctor-Sahib, someone of your position and status in the world might be able to persuade him to sell it to you."

"I know that house well," Daddyji said. "It was built by an English architect for his family, at the insistence of his wife, Rachel. A house like that will fetch a good price. But who has the money to buy such a house? I certainly don't."

"Then you could buy the house for me, and in return I'd sell you a plot of land on the property at cost, and you could build your own house on it when you do have the money. You could pay for the plot of land when it was convenient—as they say, 'payable when able,' " Fatumal said.

Later that night, Daddyji told Mamaji he was tempted by the idea—it would be nice for them to have a place of their own in Simla one day.

She said she was against entering into any business arrangement with Fatumal. "Fatumal will get you to buy the house for him and then keep all the property for himself," she said. "He's the kind of man who will cook a chicken for you when he wants something from you, but when he has what he wants he will eat the chicken himself and go away."

"You're just partial to Rasil," Daddyji said. "You've been happily eating his chicken dishes all this time."

The next day, Daddyji made inquiries at his club and learned that the owner of Rachel's Folly had entrusted the sale of the house to the secretary of the United Service Club. Daddyji called on the secretary, an obliging, fair-minded Englishman, who turned out to be a believer in equal rights for Indians. Daddyji took the secretary into his confidence.

"Look here, Dr. Mehta," the secretary said. "It is true I've given my word to the owner to sell Rachel's Folly to a European, but that commitment holds only until noon of the seventh of October, the last day of the season. If a European buyer doesn't turn up by then, I can sell the house to you in good conscience. Once it is sold to you, no one can say anything about it, and you can do with it what you like."

Daddyji presented himself at the secretary's office on the morning of the designated day. As it happened, no bid had been received from a European. When, at the sounding of the official noon hooter, there was still no bid, the secretary sold the house to Daddyji, who, as had been arranged, was acting as proxy for Fatumal. The following day, Daddyji, Fatumal, and the secretary went to the registration office, and Rachel's Folly was officially registered in Fatumal's name. On their way home, Daddyji congratulated Fatumal on the acquisition of such a valuable and desirable property, and added that, for his part, he would put up a decent-looking cottage on the plot of land Fatumal had promised him.

"What promise?" Fatumal exclaimed, as if he'd never heard of the idea. "A new house on my property? The house would be an eyesore and ruin the value of the property. I wouldn't think of it. I may look like a *chamar,* but I'm not going to behave like a *chamar*— with my Rachel's Folly."

When Daddyji told Mamaji what had happened, she said, "Your trouble is that you trust everyone. I would have got something in writing about the plot of land before I lifted a finger to help a *chamar* who wants to live in an Englishman's house."

"I would have helped him anyway, whether he had offered me the plot of land or not," Daddyji said. Then he remembered Mamaji's remark about Fatumal and the chicken dish, and he laughed, saying, "We have escaped the worse fate of having that scoundrel for a neighbor for the rest of our lives."

❧

JUST as Mamaji and Daddyji were settling into New Delhi for the winter of 1933–34, Daddyji fell ill. At first, the doctor's diagnosis was influenza, brought on by fatigue. Mamaji didn't understand much about influenza, but she understood instinctively that he had got sick by tiring himself out. For many months, he had been hard at work organizing the First All-India Anti-Tuberculosis Conference, and then, after it opened —in October, in New Delhi—writing up its proceedings, reading a paper, and collecting and editing papers of other specialists and workers. When he hadn't had to stay late at the office or at the conference, he had been playing cards far into the evening at one or another of his clubs. In the *gullis,* she had heard of married men having mistresses; she had even lived in the same house as a Muslim tenant who had two wives. But she had never heard of any woman having as much power over a man as cards had over Daddyji.

The doctors tried several treatments for his influenza, but none of them had any effect. He started passing some spongy matter from his bladder. Then he started talking in his sleep, and there were times when he was delirious. Mamaji wanted to take him to Lahore, to Babuji's, to try the remedies of practitioners of Hindu and Muslim medicine, but when she suggested the move to him he wouldn't hear of it. He said that he would be well soon, and that he had to oversee the publication of the proceedings and papers of the conference. In the end, however, he was forced to take three months' leave, and to go to Babuji's house.

The diagnosis of the practitioners whom Mamaji consulted in Lahore was that a mysterious moon force was working through Daddyji's system. They prescribed powerful charms in lieu of herbs and potions—which they knew he could not be tricked into swallowing, even in his semiconscious, weakened state. The Western doctors in Lahore suspected that he had colibacillosis. They said that his was an exceptional case—that although the *coli* bacillus rarely becomes pathogenic, in his case it had produced toxins, which had affected first his bladder, then his brain. They started intensive treatment for colibacillosis.

On the first morning of spring in 1934, five months to the day after he became ill, he was dozing in Babuji's bedroom, which had been given over to him. Suddenly, Mataji woke him and said, "Congratulations! Shanti has given birth to a second son. Mother and child are in the safe-room, both asleep."

An hour or so later, when it happened that no one was sitting by his bedside, he raised himself, put on a dressing gown and slippers, and, for good measure, wrapped a blanket around his shoulders. Then he walked like a ghost through the house, and, before anyone knew it, he was in the safe-room and had picked up the baby (me) from Mamaji's side.

It was from the birth of the baby, whom they eventually named Ved Parkash, that both she and he

Babuji, Lahore, 1939

later dated his recovery. Within a few weeks, he had bounced back and had returned to his job.

❧

THE SIMLA AIR, that fourth season, seemed to have a new, uplifting clarity, and, for the first time in some months, Mamaji and Daddyji both felt well. Their friendship with Rasil and Fatumal faded. Fatumal, having got his concession and Rachel's Folly, had little further use for Daddyji; Rasil, disappointed at not having been able to bear a child, withdrew from clubs and society for prayers and meditation, and was increasingly content to remain in the sanctum of Rachel's Folly. Mamaji felt more in command of her own life without Rasil always in the house, and she realized that Rasil's presence had put some indefinable constraint on the understanding between her and Daddyji. Daddyji, too, felt freer without Rasil's company, and he realized that her presence on the tennis court and in the club, however exciting and challenging, had been disquieting to his home life. Above all, Mamaji and Daddyji both felt that Fatumal's chickens, however delicious, had placed them in the debt of someone they had never liked and would never have chosen as a friend if it hadn't been for Rasil.

In the club, too, there was a change, and it had to do with a change in Mr. Hayman's fortunes. Lady Willingdon had invited Mr. Hayman to dinner one Saturday, but he had become so engrossed in his card game that he forgot about the invitation. The next day, the Vicereine's social secretary wrote to him conveying the displeasure of the Viceroy and the Vicereine and demanding an explanation.

Mr. Hayman, as a rule the picture of equanimity, was distraught. In his reply to the social secretary he reminded him that the employees of both the Great Indian Peninsular Railway and the Bombay Baroda & Central India Railway had been on the verge of a strike, and he said that he had been following the labor negotiations by telephone and had become so preoccupied with them that he had completely forgotten about the honor of dining at the Viceroy's table. He begged the secretary to convey his sincerest apologies to the Vicereine and the Viceroy. Mr. Hayman knew that the excuse sounded lame, but it was the best one he could offer.

It was understood that the Viceroy forgave the discourtesy, but the Vicereine did not, and she ordered that Mr. Hayman was never again to be asked to the Viceregal Lodge. And he never was. From that moment, his career with the government seemed to be under a cloud. (A couple of years later, he took an early retirement and accepted the job of chief accountant at the Tata steel plant in Jamshedpur, in Bihar.)

IN TIME, Daddyji's own career with the central government also came to a close. When he went back to work after his illness, he proposed to the Anti-Tuberculosis Fund Subcommittee that it sever its connection with the Indian Red Cross Society Committee and become independent. "I would like to transform the Fund from a stepchild of the Indian Red Cross into a national tuberculosis association," he said at a meeting. "At the moment, many members of our subcommittee are also members of the Red Cross Society Committee, and for them tuberculosis is only one of many interests. But with an independent membership we could devote ourselves entirely to the prevention and cure of tuberculosis." The proposal was immediately embraced by the Indian members, who felt that a new, independent body would indeed be more effective, but spurned by the English members, who felt that any attempt to split up the omnibus Indian Red Cross Society was a form of secession. The debate degenerated into a bitter racial question, which preoccupied the subcommittee for the next several years. Daddyji became disillusioned and decided to rejoin his department in the Punjab, and at the end of the winter season of 1936–37, after six years in New Delhi and Simla, the family returned to Lahore to live. Looking back, he feels that if he had not raised the question of separation and tangled with the English members of the Indian Red Cross he would have been able to stay in his Delhi-Simla job and retire with an international reputation and a good provident fund. Looking back, Mamaji, for her part, feels that those English members cast an evil eye on the family, for the end of Daddyji's Delhi-Simla job was the beginning of what Mamaji sees as their real troubles.

XII

BROTHERS AND
SISTERS

O F THE ELEVEN CHILDREN BABUJI FATHERED WITH Mataji, only six survived: Mamaji; Dwarka, a son, born in 1912; Lakshman, a son, born in 1915; Dharam, a daughter, born in 1918; Pushpa, a daughter, born in 1922; and Vimla, a daughter, born in 1925.

Dwarka, as a child, was untidy, and left his shoes, his clothes, his books wherever they happened to drop. He attended the D.A.V. School and barely scraped through. He went on to Government College and passed his B.A. examination only on a second try. For a couple of years, he was cheerfully idle, and then Gandharva Sen Kashyap, a middle-aged man who had been Babuji's tenant in the back cottage, said to Babuji, "Give me this boy and I'll make something of him. I will put him in business." Babuji said, "Take him."

Dwarka enthusiastically went with Kashyap to Delhi, where he started out living with Mamaji and Daddyji, and then shared a house with Kashyap in Darya Ganj, just inside the wall of Old Delhi. Their first business venture together was the purchase of a small forest. They expected to make a lot of money from the timber, but the forest caught fire. Next, they bought some machinery and started a factory for making borders and pipings for saris. But they knew little about running a factory and less about women's tastes, and the factory went bankrupt. Dwarka tried for a time to refloat the business, but Kashyap struck out on his own and started a factory for making envelopes.

Dwarka liked the idea of making envelopes and wanted
to become Kashyap's partner again, but Kashyap said
that enough was enough, and he wouldn't have Dwarka
in the business unless he could help raise ten thousand
rupees of new capital. Dwarka applied to Babuji for the
money, and received a few lines in reply saying, "Nothing doing. Stand on your own two feet or come back
and live with me. I now have enough money so that no
son of mine need work." Dwarka lingered in New
Delhi, where, when he was not struggling with the
business, he spent his time at the Roshanara Club (Daddyji had got him elected to it), playing tennis, dancing
with the ladies, and having a peg or two of whiskey.
But before long he ran out of money and went back to
Lahore.

Lakshman, as a child, was tidy, serious, and something of a goody-goody, and he was given the nickname
Pandit, which stuck to him for life. He went to the
D.A.V. School and then to the College of Commerce,
where he received a Bachelor of Commerce degree on
his second try. He became a clerk in the Punjab National Bank, of which Babuji was a director at the time.
He was conscientious and hardworking, and did well
at his job. He left the bank to become secretary of and
a partner in the Central Life & General Assurance
Company, Ltd., after Babuji bought a share in the company and became its chairman. A few months later,
Babuji and the company's owner, Veda Veyas, had a
falling out over Veyas's decision to run for public office
and to divide his time between politics and business.
Babuji resigned from the insurance company, and even-

tually got his money out; Lakshman returned to his post in the Punjab National Bank.

Dharam was a somewhat plain, slow girl, who in demeanor resembled Mataji. She failed her F.A.—First Arts—twice (by Dharam's time, women's education was more fashionable than it had been in Mamaji's time), and Babuji thought that it would be best to try to marry her off quickly. Dwarka suggested a Delhi friend of his named Jagmohan Soi, a son of the chief electrical engineer for the Delhi Corporation, saying, "Being a failed F.A. himself, I don't think he would object to marrying a failed F.A." Daddyji and Mamaji looked Jagmohan Soi over for Babuji and liked him, but Daddyji wrote to Babuji, "The boy has a bald spot on which the skin looks grey and infected." Babuji wrote back and asked Daddyji to make inquiries about the infection and, if it didn't seem a permanent condition, to make a formal offer of Dharam to Jagmohan Soi. The skin blemish turned out to be only untreated ringworm. Jagmohan Soi agreed to marry Dharam on the strength of Babuji's reputation in Lahore and his own meeting with Daddyji and Mamaji. But when he finally met Dharam, in New Delhi—she and the family had come there for the engagement ceremony—he was so disappointed in her looks that he tried to back out. His maternal uncle took him aside and gave him a tongue-lashing. "Have you ever heard of a Kshatriya going back on his word?" he said.

It took Jagmohan Soi about two years to bring himself to the point of getting married to Dharam, but on the appointed day he went through the ceremony like a Kshatriya gentleman. He was fat and jolly, and one of his main interests was to make the rounds of the bazaars, pick out the fattest rooster he could find, cook it himself with a lot of spices, and make a meal of it. Dharam made it one of her main interests to watch him cook his rooster and help him eat it.

A year or so after Dharam and Jagmohan Soi were married, he started a neon-sign business in New Delhi, and for a time Dwarka worked with him, ignoring a Punjabi adage that went "Brothers-in-law can no more get along in business than cocks in a cockpit." It turned out that the two indeed could not get along. Dwarka went back to Lahore for the second time, and Jagmohan Soi moved to Calcutta and went on to become one of the barons of the Indian neon business.

Babuji became exercised that a younger daughter had got married before his older son, and he started showing Dwarka a parade of tall, comely girls, but Dwarka had difficulty settling on any of them.

"I can't make up my mind," he would say. "I don't want to get married. I'll be as unlucky in marriage as I have been in business."

"You will get married," Babuji would say.

And in 1941, at the age of twenty-nine, Dwarka finally chose a girl, named Santosh. She was short, as Dwarka was. (All Babuji's children except Lakshman were short.) "I think Santosh's being short is an advantage," Dwarka said. "We can see eye to eye." But after they got married he and Santosh had a daughter who was astonishingly small even for a baby. (In fact, the couple had three children—all daughters—who were all very short.)

Mataji, Lahore, 1941

Babuji made inquiries, and discovered that two short people almost always produce short children. After that, one of the first questions he would ask about a prospective mate for any of his children was "How tall?" and when the time came to choose a bride for Lakshman—he was married a year after Dwarka—Babuji found him the tallest girl he could. Lakshman and the girl, Sureshtra, went on to have two tall sons.

About the time of Lakshman's marriage, Babuji found a husband for Pushpa. She was the prettiest of his daughters, with long, thick hair. Babuji found for her a rich, very handsome Punjabi named Payare Lal Tandon, who lived in the industrial town of Cawnpore and, as a partner in a firm of chartered accountants, was a member of a small gentry there. Payare Lal helped to settle Dwarka by putting him on to a job in Cawnpore with the British-India Corporation. (Dwarka worked in its big brushmaking concern, and eventually rose to become manager of that concern.) Payare Lal, however, turned out to be something of a playboy, and Pushpa's marriage was the unhappiest one in Babuji's family.

Vimla, who became a sort of companion to Promila, had an easygoing, simple nature. She would say anything that came into her head. Very pretty, she grew up to be spoiled, good-humored, and rather naïve. The family considered her to be one of a kind until she married a man who seemed to be just like her.

XIII

CHILDREN

W HEN DADDYJI AND MAMAJI RETURNED TO LAHORE in 1937, Promila was ten years old. She was tall and thin, and, for an Indian, had very fair skin. She had gone through stages of being in turn like Mataji and like Mamaji, but was growing up to be a sort of understudy to Daddyji's sister, Bibi Parmeshwari Devi. Like Bibi Parmeshwari Devi, Promila was sedate and proper, and was always conscious of her position in the family and of her health. She felt that, being the oldest, she always had to be good and behave responsibly. She went about her household duties with a minimum of fuss, and cultivated a relaxed manner, gently cajoling the servants and the other children to do her bidding. She was very particular about when she went to sleep, when she got up, when she had her meals. If she was awakened from her afternoon nap before she had had the full hour she felt she needed, she would find a chance to make up the missed time with a second nap. Her chief fault as a child was that she was finicky about what she ate. She would push aside any dish with greens in it. If Mamaji forced her to eat a spoonful of squash, which she didn't like, Promila would make a face, cough, and get up from the table. No matter how often she was told that if she didn't eat all her vegetables her teeth would fall out, it did no good. (She grew up with a couple of bad teeth, and married a dentist.) Because she was so methodical, everything of hers had to be in its proper place —her frocks neatly arranged in her drawer, her comb

placed in the center of her hairbrush, her picture books
arranged by size. If Nirmila moved even the cap on
Promila's doll, Promila would call her over and patiently give her a lesson in tidiness—in how the cap had
to be just so, and where the doll had to sit on the chest
of drawers to be shown to best advantage. Nirmila
would giggle uncontrollably behind her hand, but Promila, the tolerant older sister, would ignore the giggling and pat her on the head for being a good little
girl.

In contrast, Nirmila, who was nine, was carefree
and lackadaisical. She liked to play outside and to stay
up late. She had a whole scruffy menagerie of animals
and a collection of odds and ends—a chipped clay pi-
geon, a discolored woollen cheetah, a cracked wooden
horse, half of a brass bangle, a bent Egyptian puzzle
ring. Nirmila liked to eat anything, and she laughed at
everything. She was a soft touch—giving a toy to anybody who asked for one, offering half of her mango to
the bearer who served it to her.

Urmila, who was seven, was the sauciest of the
children. She sometimes called Mamaji "Sister-in-Law,"
and said with great pride that she had only Mehta
blood. She felt she owned Daddyji's lap. She always
had a lot to say and could talk circles around people
twice her age. She assumed that she should have first
claim on everything, and she usually got her way. She
was very fond of spicy food, and would lick her fingers
clean. She knew, as if by instinct, the caste and subcaste
of all her little friends, and of Mamaji's and Daddyji's
friends as well.

Om, who was six, had the large nose of the Mehtas

but the retiring manner of Mamaji's side of the family. Since he was the first son, he got a lot of special attention from Mamaji, but the girls never let him forget that he was only the fourth child. Urmila used to tease him by saying that he was more a Mehra than a Mehta, and, indeed, he felt more at home with Mataji than with Bhabiji. Everyone wanted Om to grow up to be good at sports and games, like Daddyji, but although he did play around outside with a hockey stick and a ball, what he liked to do most was to put a record of a film song on the gramophone and sing along with it, clapping his hands and shaking his head like an actor he had seen at the cinema. He said he wanted to be a film star when he grew up. If he saw a picture of an actor in a newspaper or a magazine, he would cut it out and walk around with it, showing it to everyone. When Mamaji was getting him ready to go to Bishop Cotton School, in Simla—one of the best boarding schools in the country—he cried and cried and cried, but stopped when Promila told him that the school had "Kindergarten Dramatics."

Ved, who was three, was fair, like Daddyji. He had been an active baby and had cut his teeth, walked, and talked earlier than the other children. (It is an odd experience to talk about myself in the third person, but, after all, this is Mamaji's story, not mine, and must be told as much as possible from her point of view.)

In July, 1937, while Daddyji was away in England on four months' leave, Mamaji gave birth to their sixth child. The baby, a daughter, was born in Babuji's back cottage, which the family had rented. (The Temple Road house was occupied by tenants, and its annex by

Bibi Parmeshwari Devi and her family. She didn't want to vacate it until her children had finished their examinations, because she considered it a lucky house.) The daughter was named Vipla, because the name, like Promila, Nirmila, and Urmila, had the "la" ending, which Daddyji and Mamaji found musical. But as soon as Vipla learned to talk she refused to answer to Vipla and insisted that her name was Usha, which means "Dawn." And that is what she ended up being called.

Mamaji and Daddyji had two more children: Anand, a son, who was born in 1939 and died the same year, and Ashok Kumar, another son, who was born in 1944.

DADDYJI returned from England in August, before Mamaji had completed the forty-day lying-in period following the birth of Usha. He rejoined his department in the Punjab, and later that month he was posted to the unfamiliar town of Gujrat, some seventy miles to the north of Lahore. He took Mamaji, the baby, and Ved with him; Om was in his boarding school in Simla, and the girls, so that their schooling would not be interrupted by transfers, had been temporarily entered as boarders in a convent school in Lahore. Daddyji went on his first long tour of inspection the following January, and—since he was taking his car—Mamaji, the baby, and Ved, who was then a couple of months short of his fourth birthday, went along for the fun of it; they took an ayah, Ajmero, with them.

The first stop on the tour of inspection was a dak bungalow, little more than a postal address for touring government officers. It was by a canal and was six miles from the closest town, Dinga, which was at the foot of the Himalayas. After a leisurely lunch, Daddyji drove by himself toward Dinga to inspect some villages.

Mamaji expected him to return in a couple of hours, but he didn't. It looked like a nice day, and she thought that it would be good to go out and take a little walk. They had spent the morning travelling in the car, and the dak bungalow was a forlorn place. She left the baby in the care of Ajmero and set out with Ved to meet Daddyji. They walked toward Dinga along the bank of the canal on the open dirt road that she had seen Daddyji take. It began to grow dark, and a cold Himalayan wind suddenly rushed down, catching them up in its sweep. It slapped against their faces, whipped their clothes against their bodies, and swirled around their feet, making walking difficult. Mamaji caught Ved firmly by the hand and quickened her pace. Realizing that she had walked farther than she had intended, in the hope of seeing the headlights of Daddyji's car at any moment, she decided to turn back. She saw a little footbridge leading to a parallel road along the other side of the canal, and, because the other road had leafy shisham trees and looked more sheltered, she crossed over.

When she and Ved reached the bungalow, after a tiring, cold walk in the dark (by later reckoning, they had walked three miles altogether), Daddyji was there, watching for them from the veranda. He hastened to meet them. When he heard Mamaji's story, he said that he must have driven past the footbridge around the time she and Ved crossed it, and just missed them.

Mamaji, as was her habit, got up in the middle of the night to check on Ved and the baby. She woke Daddyji. "Ved feels hot—he's got a high fever," she said. She took Ved's temperature. It was a hundred and five. On the theory that whatever medicine helped her would help her child, she got down a bottle of medicine that she had been taking for bronchitis and that had proved effective for the fevers of her children. She dissolved a pill in a glass of water and gave it to Ved. (Later, she chastised herself for giving him the pill, because she was told that it might have masked the symptoms of the illness and delayed the diagnosis.) The fever didn't go down, and around noon Daddyji interrupted his tour and drove Ved, with Mamaji and the baby, to Gujrat. After a day or two, finding that the doctors there were unable to agree on a diagnosis, he went on to the best hospital in Lahore, where the disease was finally diagnosed as cerebrospinal meningitis —or, in Hindi, "neck-breaking fever."

Mamaji sat by Ved's cot in the hospital room. In a corner, Daddyji stood with some other doctors, discussing Ved's illness. The doctors kept shaking their heads. She looked at Ved's face and thought she saw his soul slipping away from him. She remembered how, just a few days before, he had come running up to her holding an egg. He had put the egg to his ear and listened to faint clicking sounds coming from within, and then had watched, fascinated, as the shell cracked and the little wet head of the chick emerged.

❧

AROUND THE TIME of Ved's illness, Bhabiji had taken to her bed on account of her son Romesh. Romesh, a leading architect in Lahore, was much sought after by matchmakers, and Bhabiji had high expectations of arranging a good marriage for him. Family legend has much changed and embellished the following story, so that the facts are impossible to determine, but Mamaji remembers that one day Romesh, returning from a quick trip to Bombay, arrived at Mehta Gulli with a woman on his arm; he took her to Bhabiji's "room"—as her little flat in Mehta Gulli was called— and presented her to Bhabiji as his wife. She was darker than any Punjabi whom Bhabiji had ever seen, and her dark color was accentuated by a black coat she was wearing. She had garlands of cheap flowers around her neck, and she looked frightened. "I've brought you a daughter-in-law, Bhabiji," Romesh said sheepishly. "There was no time to invite anybody. Ours was a love marriage."

Bhabiji, who was sitting on her bed, stood up, blessed the couple, and fainted. She developed a fever. She started talking in her sleep about the black-coated witch in the house of the Mehtas. Everyone feared that Bhabiji might die. Romesh was inconsolable. He would sit by Bhabiji's bed for a few minutes and then run upstairs to his wife for a few minutes.

Bhabiji, in her moments of lucidity, would cry out, "Who is she?"

"Her name is Savitri, Bhabiji. She is my wife," Romesh would say.

"Who *is* she?" Bhabiji would wail.

"She is a Maharashtrian."

"You mean she's not even a Punjabi? What is her caste? Her subcaste?"

"She has none, Bhabiji. She's not a Hindu. She's an Indian Christian."

Bhabiji, in her semiconscious state, had only one comment, which she repeated whenever she thought Romesh was near: "Son, you've put a garland of razors around your neck. Whichever way you turn, it will cut you."

Gradually, Bhabiji rallied, and, gradually, she began to accept the fact of Savitri.

Mamaji remembers going back and forth between Bhabiji's bedside and Ved's. Bhabiji was sick for only a few days, and then was able to walk around, but Ved was sick for weeks and could scarcely move his head. When Bhabiji recovered, Mamaji feared all the more for her child's life, because it was said that if a very old person gets sick and then gets well, the weight of the old person's illness will settle on the shoulders of a small child. She felt resentful, although she often told herself, "As many tongues, so many sayings."

Mamaji remembers that she visited Bhabiji one day and saw her sitting up and spinning, and then went to the hospital and heard Ved ask, "Is it night or day?"

Mamaji couldn't find her voice to answer.

DADDYJI AND MAMAJI brought Ved home to Babuji's house after he had spent a month in the hospital

—they nursed him at home for another few weeks. Daddyji told Mamaji that the final word from the doctors was that the meningitis had permanently damaged Ved's optic nerves, and as a result he would never be able to see again.

Mamaji didn't understand about the optic nerves. She pictured blindness as a filmlike curtain descending in front of the eyes and shutting out the light. At the beginning of Ved's illness, his eyes had become red, but toward the end they had regained their normal appearance. No one looking into his eyes would have imagined that he couldn't see. In the last few days of his illness, she had often folded back his eyelids and looked into his eyes. They looked nearly clear. She didn't see much of a shadow in them.

She couldn't accept his blindness. Blindness was a fate reserved for beggars—certainly not something that the child of a well-to-do family would suffer. She persuaded herself that he could see some. To prove it, she would approach his bed from one side and hand him a glass of milk; then, while he was drinking the milk, she would stealthily tiptoe to the other side, watching him carefully. He would invariably follow her with his eyes, his head perfectly synchronized with her movements, like the needle of a compass, and hand her the empty glass.

Ved's legs had become so thin that they looked almost brittle. Mamaji was afraid that he might fall, and she didn't like him to walk much. But Daddyji insisted that the girls take him out every day and make him practice walking. Promila would choose a spot beside the back boundary wall and direct Nirmila to

stand there holding one end of a long rope while Urmila took the other end and walked to the grape arbor
in the garden. Then Promila would stand Ved near
Nirmila with his hand on the rope and start him walking. Sometimes she would hold him by the shoulders,
and sometimes she would crawl along with her hands
on his feet, guiding one foot in front of the other, while
Urmila called out "Walk toward me! That's good!
Straight ahead!" and Nirmila called out "Left, right,
left, right!" Each day, the girls would encourage him
to walk a few feet farther. Each day, the girls would
use a longer rope, and Urmila would walk farther
away from the grape arbor, toward the house. As the
"rope walk" continued, Ved gradually gained confidence. Then he started walking without the rope, but
he had trouble going in a straight line. Daddyji, however, had told the girls to keep on telling him how well
he was doing, and they did. Before long, Ved was running about by himself.

🌳

ONE DAY, Bhabiji took the children to a fair that
Romesh had organized on the Lahore exhibition
grounds. At the gate, she bought Ved a balloon filled
with hydrogen gas. She put the string in his hand and
told him to hold on tight or the balloon would fly
away. "Let me see how it flies," Ved said, and he
loosened his grip. The balloon took off. He jumped up
and tried to catch it, but it flew away. He started to cry.
Afterward, when people would ask Ved what had happened to his eyes, he would say cheerfully, "I lost them,
like my balloon."

A little way inside the gate, a barker was shouting, "Come to this booth and see a woman who has been on fire for years! As you watch, she will leap into the Well of Death. As you watch, the water will rise over her head. But when she emerges, she will still be on fire." The barker took Ved's hand and said, "Here, you want to touch the glass of the booth and see how hot it is?" Ved closed his eyes reflexively and shrank back, pulling his hand away.

They walked on and came to a booth called the Witch's Head. In front of the booth was a man dressed in black, who was shouting, "See this head behind the glass? It is the severed head of a wicked queen. It has no neck. It has no body. I brought it back from Bombay, and I keep it as my pet."

The children couldn't believe it. In the booth was a head with dark, long, straggly hair, floating in space. The girls looked under the booth to see if there were feet sticking out. But no, there was just the head, floating in space.

The man called out, "Witch's Head, what do you drink?"

The Witch's Head said, in a chilly monotone, "One teaspoon of Ovaltine in the morning and one teaspoon of cocoa at night."

"Don't look!" Promila called out.

Ved shielded his eyes, just as the other children did.

"What do you eat?"

"One chapatti in the morning and one little child at night."

Ved jumped back and gasped and held his breath, just as the other children did.

"Come here, you little children. Come closer!" the Witch's Head shouted.

"Look! She's moving! Run! Run!" the children cried, and they ran away.

Later, when Urmila was describing the Witch's Head to Mamaji, Bhabiji said under her breath, "These days, you don't have to go to the exhibition grounds to see witches."

❧

VED LIKED TO PLAY with a cocker-spaniel puppy that belonged to Kalu, the boy next door. Ved called the puppy Kalu, after the boy, who wouldn't play with Ved anymore, because he was blind. When Daddyji saw the puppy in Ved's arms, he took the animal from him and told Mamaji, "Don't let Ved go near the wretched puppy. He'll get rabies, like Ishwar Das."

"The puppy has had his rabies vaccination."

"That's no protection if the dog is bitten by a rabid animal."

Ved would wait until Daddyji had gone to the office and the girls were at school, and then he would ask Mamaji to bring Kalu to him. Mamaji could refuse him nothing, and would go and fetch the puppy. The secret of the puppy became the basis of a pact between mother and son. Just as Mamaji didn't tell Daddyji about Kalu, Ved didn't tell Daddyji what Mamaji was doing to get his eyes back.

When Shambu Pandit, the family astrologer, came to the house, Mamaji showed Ved to him. A big, powerful-looking man, Shambu Pandit sat on the veranda, looked at Ved's eyes, and pored over Ved's horoscope. Then he asked for a glass of ice-cold buttermilk. After he had drunk it, he sighed with satisfaction and said, "There is no shadow in the boy's horoscope. His blindness is only temporary."

Ved said, "Panditji, if my eyes get better I will give you our Temple Road house."

"Son, the house is as good as mine," Shambu Pandit said.

Mamaji waited, but the invisible curtain over Ved's eyes didn't lift. She consulted an elderly Muslim seer who lived just inside the Shahalmi Gate.

"Allah made your son blind because he urinated on the holy grave of Ahmed, in Gujrat," the seer said. "Go, daughter, and donate to charity two gold eyeballs as close to the size of the child's eyeballs as may be."

She took her gold bracelets to the family jeweller and asked him to melt them down and make the two eyeballs. She dropped the gold offerings in the tin cup of a half-blind, leprous beggar who was always to be seen camped outside Nedou's Hotel.

She watched Ved and she waited, but still the curtain didn't lift. She turned to the family *hakim* (practitioner of the Unani system of medicine). Daddyji had forbidden her to have the *hakim* care for any of their children, saying that he was a quack and a charlatan, who would give rock salt for appendicitis. But the *hakim* had been coming to Babuji's house for many years—ever since he cured Mataji of irregular periods. Babuji himself had frequently consulted the *hakim* for his digestive problems; he had his father's faith in indigenous systems of medicine. One morning after Daddyji had left for the office, the *hakim,* a thin, elegant Muslim, arrived at the house, carrying, as always, a bulging black cloth satchel, which rattled and crunched as he walked. He lifted Ved up and looked long at the pupils of his eyes and then at the back of his neck. He put Ved down and did some calculations, his fingers and lips moving rapidly. He clicked his tongue—"tch, tch, tch"—and sighed. "It is a very difficult case and will require many kinds of treatment," he said. He took two spice bottles and a newspaper packet out of his satchel. Handing them to Mamaji, he said, "Give him four pinches of salt from this packet of Sulemani Salt with breakfast every morning. Give him one of these yellow pills every night at bedtime. The pill is *terminalia chebula*—the pill of life. Apply this antimony solution to his eyes every morning, afternoon, and evening. Always make sure that he keeps his eyes tightly closed for three minutes after the solution has been applied. Then wash out his eyes with warm water and massage the eyeballs with your finger for a minute or two." Mamaji gave the *hakim* twenty rupees. He folded the notes carefully, pocketed them, and said, "I'm not finished. To exorcise the evil eye, you must gently flog him every day with freshly gathered birch twigs. For a whole week, before the sun is up, you must take two raw eggs and touch them to his eyes and place the eggs on a crossroads. For another whole week, you must put a piece of raw meat under his pillow overnight and, before the sun is up, leave the meat on the crossroads. The eggs will serve as a warning to the evil eye that you are on its trail, and the meat will put the vultures on the evil eye's trail with you."

Mamaji followed the instructions down to the minutest detail. Every day, she gave Ved the Sulemani Salt and the "pill of life." Every day, she faithfully applied the antimony. The solution stung Ved's eyes. No sooner would she approach him than he would start to scream, as if he saw the bottle in her hand. Every day, she flogged him lightly. For two weeks, she got up surreptitiously before dawn, went to Mozang Chowk, and deposited first the eggs and then the meat. Every day, she looked for signs that Ved's sight was returning. Every night, she turned on the light and asked him what he saw. "The light is on," he would say.

After a while, she began to suspect that he was only trying to please her by pretending to see, and that perhaps the click of the switch told him that the light was on. She started testing him by moving the switch back and forth so rapidly that she herself lost count, all the while breathing hard and coughing from the onrush of an asthmatic attack. And yet when she asked him "Is the light on or off?" he was almost always right in his reply.

One day, Mamaji heard that a priestess of Goddess Durga was holding a session in a little *gulli* called Tiliandi-Khui (Small Well of Small Sticks), and she took Ved there. The *gulli* was a cul-de-sac, and its entrance was almost blocked by a broken-down bullock cart. From inside came the hypnotic beat of a drum, and men, women, and children were moving toward it. Mamaji joined the crowd and was swept into the choked, sun-baked *gulli*. Somehow, by expert elbow and knee work, by pushing and nudging, she managed to sit down cross-legged on the bare ground with the rest. Ved, exhausted from the heat, sat almost inert in her lap.

Near the drum sat the hunched figure of a woman, which seemed to be shrinking even as Mamaji watched. Behind the hunched figure stood a young man, perspiring heavily and gesticulating. "Speak Mother, speak!" he called.

Mamaji began swaying to the rhythm of the drum, like everyone around her.

The woman suddenly sprang to her feet. She towered over the crowd, looking wild, as if at any moment she might trample the people.

The drummer stepped up his frenetic beat.

"Speak, Mother, speak!" he exhorted her.

The woman now stood perfectly still and said in a hollow voice, using rustic Punjabi, "There is a sister here whose heart is troubled because her little son's eyes have gone bad."

Mamaji bent forward and listened. The oracle was talking about her.

"Why have they gone bad? Because, the night before her son's illness, she took him on a walk on a road and they passed under a fateful tree. I see the tree. It's a shisham tree. Its shadow has fallen over the child's destiny. Sister, go and find the tree of the shadow, and light four mud lamps at its foot, and keep them burning until the next full moon. Then the shadow will lift."

The Grand Trunk Road, running from Calcutta

to Peshawar, was lined for its hundreds and hundreds of miles with shisham trees. The people considered them a blessing. Thornless, with ample branches and leaves, the trees provided villagers living along the road and wayfarers travelling on it with shade during the hot summer months. The wood was used for the doors of huts, for the hulls of ships, for railway sleepers. As children, Daddyji and Daulat Ram used to do their homework sitting in the shade of a shisham tree.

The woman continued, "On the Grand Trunk Road, on the bank of the canal, by the footbridge, there is the tree of the shadow. Go, sister. Do penance to it."

Although Mamaji was afraid to tell Daddyji about the woman, there was no way she could obey the instructions without his help, so she confided in him.

"She must have found out about the walk from Ajmero or one of her friends," Daddyji said, patting Mamaji's hand. "Such people stay in business by having informers in big houses."

But Mamaji cried and pleaded, and at last he gave in and drove her back to the bungalow, the footbridge, and the shisham tree. They walked around the tree and placed the four mud lamps at its foot and lit them. They had picked up the watchman of the dak bungalow, and they arranged for him to keep the lamps burning until the full moon. Then Mamaji and Daddyji got in the car and sat for a moment looking at the flames.

It was dusk. The air was very still. The crackling, powerful flames at the foot of the tree seemed to draw the color from the orange sky. As the flames grew brighter, the sky grew darker.

They drove back to Lahore.

Mamaji started having asthmatic attacks more
often. Her chest would get tight. Her throat would fill
up with phlegm. Her breathing would become ragged
and short.

Ved, sensitive to all other sounds, was beginning
to be deaf to the sounds of Mamaji's asthmatic attacks.
He associated them with the pain of the many treatments. Whenever he needed to be taken to the bathroom, washed, or dressed, he would no longer call for
her but would shout for one of his aunties. If Mamaji
tried to lift him, he would push her away.

SOME SEVENTEEN YEARS *after that walk near Dinga,
looking for Daddyji's car, and that attack of cerebrospinal meningitis, which left me permanently and
totally blind, I was in America, sitting behind the
wheel of an old, 1948 Chevrolet. Gripped momentarily
by a fantasy that I could see, I was driving the car along
the eleven-mile stretch of freeway between Pasadena and
Los Angeles, which Californians boasted was the best
stretch of highway in the world. Next to me was a dare-
devil girl from the college I was attending. She was
keeping an eye on the road. At first, she was giggling.
Then, suddenly, she lunged and seized the steering
wheel, at the same time climbing over me to get at the
pedals. "We'll both be killed!" she cried.*

*After she had taken over the controls, panting from
the exertion of gaining the driver's seat, she fumbled in
her handbag for a cigarette and then fumbled with the*

cigarette lighter on the dashboard. She pressed the ciga-rette lighter repeatedly, trying to get it to work. There seemed something desperate in her efforts.

It was only at that moment that I remembered, for the first time—and then very fleetingly and without understanding exactly why—the faint clicks of the light switch coming through the sounds of my mother's asthma. It was only years after this drive that I was stirred to find out everything about my mother—her history and my history, and how they came to their crossroads. It was many years later yet before I could bring myself to set it down.

GLOSSARY

ANNA: monetary unit—one-sixteenth of a rupee

AYAH: nursemaid

BABU: respected elder; Hindu gentleman

BARAT: bridegroom's party

BARSATI: rain shelter, usually at top of house

BEGUM: princess or queen (Muslim)

BHAJAN: hymn

BHOOT: demon

BUNJAHI: Kshatriya subcaste

CHAMAR: leather worker; Untouchable

CHAPATTI: unleavened pancake-shaped bread

CHARPOY: light bed-frame strung with tape or light rope

CHAUBARA: women's room or sanctuary

CHELA: spiritual disciple; pupil

CHOWK: square or intersection

DAK BUNGALOW: house for travellers at a postal station

DAL: lentils

DAORI: entrance hall

DARVAZA: gate

DAS: servant of God (Hindu)

DEODAR: East Indian cedar

DEVI: goddess; female servant of God (Hindu)

DHA-EE-GHAR: Kshatriya subcaste

DHARMA: moral duty (Hindu)

DHOBI: washerman

DOHAJU: widower who has remarried

GLOSSARY

DOLI: bridegroom's ceremonial taking away of the bride

GATHRIWALLAH: bundleman

GHI: clarified butter

GHORA-GARI: horse-drawn carriage

GHORI: bridegroom's ceremonial ride on horseback to bride's house

GULLI: narrow street or alleyway

GURU: spiritual leader; master

GUZARA: pittance

HAKIM: practitioner of Unani system of medicine (Muslim)

HALWAH: a confection

HAUWA: fear of a demon

HAVAN: sacred Vedic fire ceremony

JELLABIE: kind of sweetmeat

-JI: suffix denoting affection and respect

KOTHI: bungalow

KURTA: loose shirt

LAKKAR: wood

LALA: caste title

LAVAN: ceremonial lap around the wedding canopy

LINGAM: phallus

LOO: hot wind

MAHARAJA: king (Hindu)

MAHARANI: queen, ranking above *rani* (Hindu)

MAHATMA: great soul

MALTA: orange

MANDI: market

MANDIR: temple (Hindu)

MANTRA: Vedic hymn or prayer

MATA: mother

MILNI: ceremonial meeting of groom's family and bride's family during wedding festivities

GLOSSARY

MOCHI: cobbler

MUNDAN: head-shaving ceremony.

MUNSHI: clerk

MUNSHI KHANNA: clerk's room

NAMASTE: ceremonial greeting (Hindu)

NAUTCH: professional dancing

NAWAB: honorific title for an important or wealthy man (Muslim)

OM: sacred syllable (Hindu)

PANDIT: learned teacher

PAINDU: villager

PAN: betel-leaf masticatory

PARKASH: light

PATRI: horoscope

PHOOS KOTHI: hay house

PICE: monetary unit—one sixty-fourth of a rupee

PICHHCHHA: backing

PUKKA: lasting

PURDAH: curtain; system of secluding women of rank (Muslim)

RAI BAHADUR: title conferred on Indians by the English

RANI: queen (Hindu)

RAORIS: crystallized-sugar sweets

RAZAI: quilt

RUPEE: basic monetary unit

SALMA: gold-thread needlework

SARI: woman's draped garment

SHAGAN: formal betrothal ceremony; also, betrothal offering from bride's family

SHEHRAN: city woman

SHEHRI: city dweller

SHISHAM: large tropical tree

SHRIMATI: Miss or Mrs.

GLOSSARY

SITAR: plucked stringed instrument

SMUGARY: frankincense and myrrh

SUJI: form of wheat flour, a little grittier than white flour

SWADESHI: homespun cloth

SWAMI: holy man (Hindu)

SYCE: groom

UPDESH: short sermon

VAKIL: pleader

VEDI: wedding canopy

WALLAH: person or thing employed about or concerned with
something